D1588798

HOW TO WIN AT CRIBBAGE

HOW TO WIN AT CRIBBAGE

Joseph Petrus Wergin

Winchester Press
Tulsa, Oklahoma

Published by Winchester Press
1421 South Sheridan
Tulsa, Oklahoma 74114

Library of Congress Cataloging in Publication Data

Wergin, Joseph P
   How to win at cribbage.

   Includes index.
   1. Cribbage. I. Title.
GV1295.C9W47   795.4   79-17045
ISBN 0-87691-304-4

Printed in the United States of America
1 2 3 4 5   84 83 82 81 80

Dedicated to Marguerite,
a lovely Cribbage companion
and the inspiration of this work.

Acknowledgments

I want to acknowledge the kind assistance and guidance the following individuals rendered in the preparation of this book: Craig Hessel, Marguerite P. Dukes, Ted Blackney, Peter A. Dukes, Morris Pendleton, John B. Becker, and Donald Itkin for technical and editorial help.

I would also like to thank the following for permission to reprint copyrighted material: Leo A. Blom, author of *The New Cribbage Games*; the Gamblers Book Club, publishers of *Key to Cribbage*; David Parlett, *Games & Puzzles* magazine; and Allen J. Jarvis and publisher Branden Press of *Cribbage as I Think it Should be Played.*

Introduction
by David Parlett

The great thing about a deck of cards is its tremendous versatility.

Once upon a time there were five cardplayers marooned on a desert island. They were getting along fine with their Poker sessions, but a poisonous snake bit the four-flusher and then there were just enough left for Contract Bridge. One night a coconut landed square on dummy's skull and then there were three. So they stripped out all ranks lower than seven and got cracking on Skat. Soon after, the timidest member of the trio got away with a grand solo against four and promptly died of heart failure. Several months later, when we rescued the Solitaire player, the first thing he said was, "It's a good thing we didn't throw those low-spotters away."

"What do you mean?" we asked him.

"Hell, have you ever tried playing Cribbage without the fives?"

Well, if you've never played this great two-hander the unorthodox way then I suggest you turn to the story about fooling the old chemistry teacher (p. 29). And if you've never played it at all—now's the time to get started.

Next to Shakespeare, Cribbage has always struck me as perhaps England's greatest contribution to western civilization, which makes me particularly pleased to have been invited to introduce this latest study of the skills (and fun) involved.

Cribbage is essentially a battle of wits with figures, and I can think of no one more qualified than Joe Wergin to take the back off and show you how it ticks. I daresay more people play Cribbage than Skat (especially in England, where the latter is virtually unknown), but I can tell you that *Wergin on Skat and Sheepshead* has been my favorite and most profitable reading for as long as I can remember. Not for nothing is he known as the Old Fox at the card table. Few people earn a twin reputation as champion player and eminently readable writer. But Joe Wergin is one of them, and once you start dipping into *How to Win at Cribbage* you'll see I'm not exaggerating. Especially when you sit down at your next session and knock the spots off your opponent.

Good cribbing!

David Parlett of Surrey, England, is on the staff of the *Games & Puzzles* magazine, published quarterly in London. He specializes in articles dealing with card games.

About the Game

What needs to be said about a card game invented by a seventeenth-century British poet and played by 2 or 3 million Americans each night?

Sir John Suckling—best known for his "Song" which begins "Why so pale and wan, fond lover?"—built upon the elements of an older game, Noddy, and created "Cribbidge" sometime between 1632 and 1639. Today, Cribbage is immensely popular on both sides of the Atlantic. Combining the intellectual challenge of a game of strategy with the excitement and surprise of a game of chance, Cribbage is known by its millions of enthusiasts as the greatest two-handed game in the world of cards.

In this book, an internationally known expert shares his winning secrets with the reader. *How to Win at Cribbage* has been designed as a complete, step-by-step course. It should prove equally valuable to the beginner and to the experienced player who seeks mastery of the game. Read it, study it—and win!

Contents

I.   FUNDAMENTALS
    How to Learn Cribbage   3
    Mechanics of Cribbage   6

II.   THE PLAY
    Scoring for Go   11
    Scoring for Count of 15   13
    Scoring for Matches and Sequences   13

III.   THE SHOWING
    How to Count for the Showing   21
    Your Memory Bank   28
    A Chemistry Teacher Learns a Lesson   29
    Flushes   30
    High-Scoring Hands   31
    Unusual Hands   36

IV.   ELEMENTARY STRATEGY
    Basics of Discarding   45
    Laws of Probability   49
    Defensive Strategy   55
    Wergin's Pegging Strategy   60
    The Cribbage Board   64

V.   ADVANCED STRATEGY
    Cribbing Along with the Masters   71
    Hot and Cold Decks   74
    Common Sense   75
    Old Irons   79
    A Study in Averages   80
    Muggins   82

VI.   FIVE-CARD CRIBBAGE
       Original Game   85
       Winning Odds for the Dealer   87

VII. OTHER VARIATIONS
       Three-Handed Cribbage   93
       Partnership Play   94
       Crazee Cribbage: Variations on the
           Standard Game   99

VIII. LEAGUE AND TOURNAMENT COMPETITION
       How to Conduct a League   109
       Wergin System of Match-Point Scoring   110
       How to Conduct an Elimination
           Tournament   111

IX.   ALL POSSIBLE COMBINATIONS   123

X.   RULES   207

XI.   BIBLIOGRAPHY AND SOME
       CRIBBOLOGICAL NOTES   215

       INDEX   221

I

Fundamentals

♠ ♡ ♣ ◇

How to Learn Cribbage

When you are ready to learn Cribbage, I suggest you purchase a piece of furniture, a Cribbage board. It is used to keep the running score.

Before securing a teacher for yourself, I recommend that you prepare by reading the following pages. Cribbage, a game of English origin, may be placed in the category of games and combinations, which includes Poker, Old Maid, and the various forms of Rummy. You undoubtedly know how to shuffle the cards and how to play several other card games, but a knowledge of those games will be of little help because Cribbage is unusual.

Standard Deck

Before you start, take a regular fifty-two-card deck and lay the cards face up on the table for study, because most people are eye-minded. Actually see the card combinations instead of trying to visualize them in your mind.

Cribbage has some special terms which you must become familiar with. Let's take a look at a few of them.

Vocabulary

Box	crib
Crib	four cards laid out to the side for the dealer
Cribbage board	board with holes, used to keep score
Deuce	two-spotter
Fifteen-two	when the value of the cards totals 15, 2 holes are awarded on the board

3

15/2	symbol for fifteen-two
Game	121 points in the six-card game; 61 points in the five-card game
Game hole	hole no. 121 (no. 61 in five-card)
Go	last card played under 31 or card that reaches 31 in pegging process
His heels	jack, when it is turned up after the cut as starter card
His nobs	jack in hand, of same suit as starter card
Knave	jack
Peg	little brass, wooden, or plastic piece which fits into the holes of the Cribbage board; to place this piece in a hole
Starter card	card turned up after pack is cut
Trey	three-spotter

Deal Out Hands

After you have read the first two parts, play some practice games by yourself. Deal six cards to each of two hands, one card at a time. Figure out the point combinations and discard two cards into the dealer's crib.

Peg the Points

Peg on the Cribbage board the points each hand scores for you and an imaginary opponent. Then count the points of the crib cards and peg the crib points on the dealer's part of the board. Repeat this over and over until you can count the points of hands quickly. (On the first deal, you may omit the play of the hand, which occurs after the starter card is determined by the cutting of the pack. See part II.)

The Cribbage Board

The scoring board for Cribbage was patterned after the Noddy board (Noddy is thought to be the forerunner of Cribbage).

A Cribbage board has two rows of 30 holes plus a game hole for each player, making a total of 61 holes for each player. Each line of 30 holes is divided into six groups of 5 holes for easier scoring. The board was designed for the original five-card game in which 61 points won, and the first player to arrive at the game hole with his scoring peg was the winner.

In the modern six-card game, the players must make two trips around the board with their pegs, plus the game hole, scoring 121 points to win.

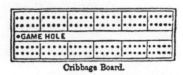

Cribbage Board.

Use Your Spare Time

Spend your daily free time on this learning project, dealing out the cards and analyzing them. Then advance to playing out the hands and pegging as you go along.

Next, find an experienced player or teacher so that you can play your first game.

Refer Back to Book

Play as much Cribbage as possible and be sure to read and reread the material in this book. Also, discuss hands and methods of play selection with veteran players.

Continue dealing out hands to yourself and memorize combinations so that you can quickly announce the points your hand scores. This will make you a welcome opponent.

Play, play, play, and be sure to refer back to the book frequently.

Object

To score points by forming combinations of cards and win the six-card game by totaling 121 points before an opponent can do so.

Mechanics of Cribbage

Number of Players

The basic game for two players is the most popular; however, Cribbage is also played three- and four-handed—the latter being a partnership affair, two against two.

Cards Used

The standard deck of fifty-two cards is used. Each player receives six cards on the deal.

Distributing the Cards

The dealer is chosen by cutting the cards; the player with the lower card deals. (The ace is the lowest card of all.) If there is a tie, cut again.

Shuffling and Cutting

Nondealer may shuffle the cards, but the dealer has the right to make the last shuffle. The pack must be cut once by the nondealer, leaving at least four cards in each packet.

The Las Vegas shuffle or riffle is best for mixing the cards.

Rank of the Cards—Point Count

The four suits are of equal rank and the cards rank from king down to ace (represented by 1):

K— Q— J—10—9—8—7—6—5—4—3—2—1
points: 10 10 10 10 9 8 7 6 5 4 3 2 1

The Crib

Each participant discards two cards into the crib or box, reducing his hand to four cards. The crib is the property of the dealer; it may not be examined or disturbed until after the play.

Starter Card

After both players have discarded, the pone (nondealer) cuts the pack and the dealer turns over the top card of the lower packet onto the table. The top packet is replaced on the lower packet and the turned-over card is placed face up on top. It is the starter card.

Additional Vocabulary

Cradle	crib
Double run	two three-card straights including one pair
Pair	two cards of the same denomination, such as two queens
Pair royal	three of a kind (triplets)
Sequence	straight of at least three cards, such as nine, ten, jack
Showing	exposing the hand and counting the values
Tenth cards	kings, queens, jacks, and tens (they all count 10 points)

His Heels

If the starter is a jack (called the knave in England), the dealer scores 2 points. He must take (peg) them before he plays a card, or he forfeits the 2 points. The starter is not used in the play (part II) but is used in the showing (part III).

II

The Play

An outstanding characteristic of Cribbage is its two-step procedure: first the play, then the showing. The only scoring before the play is his heels (just discussed).

The pone begins his play by selecting a card from his or her hand, and playing it face up on the table on his side of the board, and announcing its count value.

Example: The nondealer plays a trey and says, "Three."

Then the dealer lays down a card, stating the *total* of the two cards.

Example: The dealer plays an eight and says, "Eleven" (not "Eight").

Now the pone places a second card on his stack, stating the total of all three cards played.

Note that each player keeps his cards separate and does not assemble them in tricks. He sets his cards down so as not to cover each other; all the cards played in the series must be visible.

Scoring for Go

Hit 31 and Peg 2 Points . . .

One object of the play is to reach a total of exactly 31 on one of your laydowns and score 2 points. You may not run the count over 31.

If a player cannot lay down a card that will not exceed the 31 count, he says, "Go," which means "Go ahead! I cannot play."

If his adversary can play one or more cards that will not exceed the 31 mark, he must play them, announcing the new total or totals as he plays. If he has no eligible card, he says, "Go" (or "Pass"). Some players knock on the table to signify their inability to make a legal play.

. . . or Peg Only 1 Point for Last Card Played

If no one reaches exactly 31, the person laying down the last card possible under 31 pegs 1 point.

Example 1:

COUNT	A HOLDS	B HOLDS
26	K–6	4–2

It is A's turn to play. The king would bring the total to $26 + 10 = 36$, and the six to $26 + 6 = 32$. As he may not play either card, A says, "Go."

Player B plays the four, making the count 30, and then passes because the deuce would surpass 31. He pegs 1 point for playing the last card.

Example 2:

COUNT	A HOLDS	B HOLDS
24	6–1	9–8

A lays down the six saying, "30." As B does not have an ace to play, he says, "Go," and A continues by laying down his ace, hitting 31. He pegs 2 points.

When the series is completed by the first go, both players may turn the cards already played face down to avoid confusion during the next series.

A new count working from 0 toward the goal of 31 is begun by the player whose turn it is. In Example 2, player A having made the last play with an ace, B opens the second series with his eight or his nine.

Play is continued until both competitors have used up all four cards.

Scoring for Count of 15

Fifteen is a magic number for Cribbage players. By making the playing count 15 a player pegs 2 points immediately. It is an important tactic to prevent your opponent from hitting the 15 mark.

Example: You hold Q–J–3–2.

If you lead off with the queen or jack for a count of 10, your opponent may play a five, totaling 15 and pegging 2 points. The logical lead is to play the three; opponent will stay under 15 no matter what card he plays.

Opponent probably has at least one of the 16 ten-counting cards in the deck (kings, queens, jacks, and tens). If he brings the count up to 13, you can play your deuce for 15.

It is possible to peg 3 points by playing the last card of the two hands and hitting the magic count of 15 at the same time: 2 points for the 15, and 1 for the last card.

Scoring for Matches and Sequences

	POINTS
Pair	2
Triplet	6
Quadruplet	12
Sequence of three cards	3
Sequence of four cards	4
Sequence of five cards	5 (etc.)

Pair

By immediately matching the card played by your opponent, you peg 2 points, which must be racked up at once. You must pair rank as well as count: two kings are a pair, but a king and a queen are not, although they are both tenth cards.

Triplet

Three of a kind played in sequence score 6 points for the player who lays down the third card. Our English cousins, as well as early Americans, call the triplet a pair royal. However, it all means one thing . . . 6 points for the fortunate competitor, and humiliation for the opponent who played the second card, making only 2 points for a pair.

Example: Player A plays a six; B lays down a second six and pegs 2 points for a pair; A retaliates with a third six for 6 big points.

Four of a Kind (Double Pair Royal)

Continuing the example, if B has the fourth six, he comes roaring back to form a quadruplet and peg 12 points, for a very grand total of $2 + 12 = 14$ points, far outscoring A's points.

Four of a kind is very rare and its high score of 12 obeys a law of frequency: the less often a hand occurs, the more it is likely to score.

Sequence

All Poker addicts appreciate the value of sequences (also called straights or runs) in their battle of wits. There are straights in Cribbage too, including three-card straights, four-card straights, and Pokerlike straights. You get 1 point credit for each card in a run of three cards or more: 3 points for three cards, 4 for four cards, and so on.

A sequence can be played in a juggled order such as 4–2–3, which is a legal sequence.

Eleven Three-Card Runs

The basic three-card sequences are the following.

1–2–3	5–6–7	9–10–J
2–3–4	6–7–8	10–J–Q
3–4–5	7–8–9	J–Q–K
4–5–6	8–9–10	

Each basic sequence has six forms: for example, 4–5–6, 4–6–5, 5–4–6, 5–6–4, 6–4–5, and 6–5–4.

Kings and aces are never included in the same run; there is no such run as Q–K–A or K–A–2.

Six Four-Card Straights

The basic four-card straights, each of which can be juggled in 24 orders of play, are:

1–2–3–4	4–5–6–7
2–3–4–5	5–6–7–8
3–4–5–6	6–7–8–9

The 6–7–8–9 sequence makes a count of 30 in the pegging process. It is impossible to use 7–8–9–10 or higher four-card combinations in the play, since they add up to more than 31 points.

A Sequence with a Go

If a straight is formed, and the count of 31 is reached at the same time, the player receives 2 points for making 31 as well as the points for ending the run.

Example: This four-card run ends at 31.

card played	count	pegging
7	7	—
J	17	—
3	20	—
2	22	—
5	27	—
4	31	6

The player who reaches 31 gets 2 pegging points for go and 4 more points for the run of four cards 3–2–5–4, or in its basic form, 2–3–4–5.

Go with a Seven-Card Sequence

Straights may include as many as seven cards. Suppose the first six cards are juggled: 7–5–2–4–3–6. There is no run until the fifth card, when the trey player scores 4 points for 5–2–4–3. When his opponent counters with the six-spotter, a six-card run is formed for 6 points. An ace after the six will make a seven-card run for 7 holes.

As shown below, a seven-card run can mean 7 points plus.

cards played	count	pegging	
3	3	—	
7	10	—	
5	15	2	(15/2)
2	17	—	
3	20	—	
4	24	4	(run of four)
1	25	5	(run of five)
6	31	9	(run of seven & go of 31)

An eight-card straight is unplayable because the lowest such straight has a count of 36 (which is over 31).

(Note that the second trey played did not score 2 points for a pair, because it was not played *immediately* after the first trey.)

Simultaneous Pegging

When you play a card that brings the count on the table to 31, you also get credit for other, simultaneous scoring plays.

Example 1: A pair is formed. If the count is 23 and play of a four makes 27, the play of a second four hits 31 and makes a pair, so the player scores 4 holes—2 for the 31 and 2 for the pair.

Example 2: Three of a kind with a go.

	count	pegging
A lays down a jack	10	—
B pairs him with another jack	20	2
A counters with a third jack	30 & go	7

Neither player holds an ace, so 30 ends the series. A scores 1 point for the go and 6 points for the triplets, a total of 7 holes.

Note: Pairs, triplets, and sequences end with the go. Suppose the count stands at 13, A lays down a nine bringing the count to 22, and B makes 31 with his nine, scoring 4 points—2 for the 31 and 2 for the pair.

The next series starts, and A has another nine-spotter and leads off with it. He cannot claim a score of 6 for triplets, even though three nines were played in succession. He gets no points for the nine.

Example 3: Pegging with quadruplets.

Someday it will happen to you—pegging 12 by lining up four sevens in a row. With 2 holes for the pair and 1 for a go, you can score 15 points in one series of play, while your opponent scores 6 for triplets.

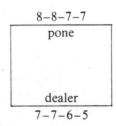

8–8–7–7

pone

dealer

7–7–6–5

Pone plays a seven, dealer pairs, scoring 2 holes, and pone retaliates with a third seven making the count 21 and scoring 6 holes for triplets.

Dealer counters with the fourth seven scoring 12 for four of a kind and takes another point for the go.

III

The Showing

The dealer now has in effect five cards: the four he has just used in the play, plus the starter card. Likewise the nondealer (pone) has in effect five cards, including the same starter card.

The crib, the third hand which scores for the dealer, has in effect five cards: the same starter card, the two cards discarded before the play by the dealer, and the two cards discarded before the play by the pone.

Note that (1) the crib took no part in the play; (2) the dealer and nondealer no longer play out cards against each other, but simply score their own hands: first, the pone's hand; second, the dealer's own hand; and third, the dealer's second (crib) hand.

How to Count for the Showing

Scoring Procedure

The order of scoring is important and the pattern to follow is:
1. The starter card if it is a jack (his heels).
2. The play for various combinations—pegging process.
3. The "go" at the end of pegging.
4. Pone shows his cards and computes scores and records same.
5. The dealer shows and counts his hand.
6. Crib is exposed and dealer counts and records its value.

The showing does not include the 31 count or the go; the only important count that remains is the magic number 15.

	POINT COUNT
King, queen, jack, or ten	10
Nine	9
Eight	8
Seven	7
Six	6
Five	5
Four	4
Three	3
Two	2
Ace	1

This point count is only used to determine the number of combinations totaling 15.

Scoring for the Showing

		POINTS
His nobs	Jack of the same suit as the starter card	1
Fifteen	Each combination of 15	2
Pairs		2
Triplets	Three of a kind	6
Four of a kind		12
Sequence	Three-card	3
	Four-card	4
	Five-card	5
Flush	Four cards in same suit	
(dealer and pone)	(excluding starter)	4
	Four cards plus starter in same suit	5
Flush (crib)	Four cards in same suit (excluding starter)	0
	Four cards plus starter card in same suit	5

1. The dealer may not interchange cards from the crib with cards from his hand. The crib and the dealer's hand are separate units.

2. The cards of the crib may not be counted as a flush unless the starter card is also of the same suit.

3. His nobs is the jack of the starter's suit when the starter card is not a jack. It is scored during the showing (1 point). His heels is a

jack cut as the starter card. It is scored before the play (2 points for the dealer).

4. Each combination adding to 15 is awarded 2 points. Any combinations that differ by one or more cards are considered different.

5. The symbol 15/2 indicates that one 15 combination is formed for 2 points; 15/4, two combinations for 4 points; 15/6, for 6 points; and so on to the maximum of 15/16, for 16 points.

6. A card may be included in more than one type of scoring combination; for example, a queen may be included in a run as well as in a 15/2 group.

The 15 Count

We begin with a holding, with a king as the starter card, which contains two combinations of 15.

Hand no. 1:   9–9–6–Q

first	$9 + 6 = 15/2$
second	$9 + 6 = 15/2$
pair	$9 - 9 = \quad 2$
	6 points

Helpful Hints for Counting

You horse-racing fans know what it means to box a group of horses for betting purposes. It is a common way to wager on the perfecta or the trifecta at the track. For example, the two most favored horses can be boxed by betting on horses no. 1–2–3, 1–2–4, 1–2–5, 1–2–6, and so on.

Here is how to box a Cribbage hand made up of the four fives and a nine-spotter.

  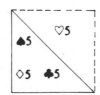

Starting at each corner of the rectangle, we combine the corner five with the five "to the left" and the five "to the right" for a combination of 15 points. Each of the four combinations is shown in a triangle of solid lines. (Note that the nine cannot be used in any combination.)

Announcing the scoring computation for this hand, a player says: "15/2, 15/4, 15/6, 15/8, plus 12 points for holding four of a kind"—four fives—"making 20 points to be pegged."

Here is a similar 20-pointer:

$$\heartsuit 8$$
$$\clubsuit 8$$
$$\spadesuit 8 \qquad\qquad \heartsuit 7 = 15$$
$$\diamondsuit 8$$

We state it as follows: "15/2, 15/4, 15/6, 15/8, and four eights, 12 points, making a total of 20 points."

Study this hand of three eights, a king, and a seven-spotter:

$$\heartsuit 8$$
$$\spadesuit K \qquad \spadesuit 8 \qquad \clubsuit 7 = 15$$
$$\diamondsuit 8$$

There are three 15s made up by combining the seven with the eight-spotters. There are also the 6 points for the eights themselves. (The king is useless in this hand.) So we say, "15/2, 15/4, 15/6, and triplets, making a total of 12."

Note: In figuring the score of a hand, it is easiest to compute the 15s first and then add on any pairs, triplets, runs, and flushes.

Next we have three sevens, any two of which can be combined with an ace to make up a 15 combination:

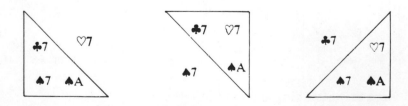

(We have left out a useless queen.) There are three ways to get 15, shown by the three triangles. The scoring is: "15/2, 15/4, 15/6, and 6 points for three of a kind, making 12 holes to be pegged."

Why Pairs, Triplets, and Quadruplets Are Scored as They Are

At this point the reader understands that any *pair* is worth 2 points. Two pairs, such as K–K–2–2, score 4 points.

There are really three distinct sets of pairs in a triplet, which justifies your counting 6 points. Think of a triangle with an ace at each vertex:

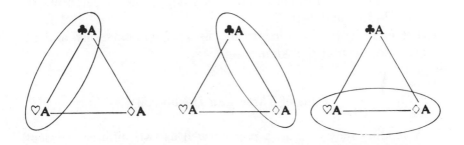

A person is happy to hold *four of a kind* in Poker, and the same is true in Cribbage. The odds are stacked against this holding, and the rewards are correspondingly great.

Those skilled in the laws of probability know that there are six ways to choose a pair from four cards. This is why four of a kind scores 12 points, equal to six pairs.

Instead of boxing the fours, you can view them in a table reading from left to right:

pairs	clubs	spades	hearts	diamonds
1	K———————K			
2	K———————————————K			
3	K———————————————————————K			
4		K———————K		
5		K———————————————K		
6			K———————K	

Note that each king appears in three combinations.

A Lesson in Geometry

The student may visualize the 15/2 combinations of four sevens and an ace from the figure:

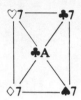

There are four small triangles that form 15/2 combinations. Two more 15/2s can be formed by drawing straight lines from corner to corner: 7–A–7 and 7–A–7.

The hand scores 12 holes for the six 15/2 combinations, and 12 more holes for four of a kind.

Runs of Three Can Double Up

A holding may contain a pair as well as two different runs of three cards:

$$\heartsuit K-\clubsuit K-\spadesuit Q-\diamondsuit J-\diamondsuit 9$$

Analyzing the hand (and ignoring the useless nine), we find:

		POINTS
Run	$\heartsuit$K–$\spadesuit$Q–$\diamondsuit$J	3
Run	$\clubsuit$K–$\spadesuit$Q–$\diamondsuit$J	3
Pair	$\heartsuit$K–$\clubsuit$K	2
		8

A "double run of three" always scores 8 points. When you are counting such a hand you merely state: 'I have a double run for 8,' instead of explaining that you have a sequence of three, and another sequence of three, and a pair.

You must learn to count your hand efficiently.

Double Run of Four Scores 10 Points

Take a four-card straight and pair any card:

♠4–♡4–♣3–♠2–♠A

The player cannot form a 15/2, since the five cards only add up to 14 points. Further analysis shows two sequences, each four cards in length, and a pair of fours:

		POINTS
Run	♡4–♣3–♠2–♣A	4
Run	♠4–♣3–♠2–♣A	4
Pair	♡4–♠4	2
		10

You say: "Double run of four—10 points." Then record it on the board.

Triple Run Counts 15 Points

This includes a triplet and an overlapping three-card run, e.g.:

♢K–♠K–♡K–♣Q–♡J

Let's line up the cards to show the three straights:

	POINTS
♢K–♣Q–♡J	3
♠K–♣Q–♡J	3
♡K–♣Q–♡J	3
Triplet kings	6
	15

Familiarize yourself with the triple run: if there are no 15/2s and no his nobs, the hand always scores 15.

A Straight That Is Quadrupled

Sequences can really get complicated. You will appreciate the next hand because it scores 16 points in a neat package. It comes in handy when you want to make a big move around the corner to Fourth Street:

$$♠3-♡2-♢2-♠A-♣A$$

There are two sets of pairs, the aces and the deuces, making $2 \times 2 = 4$ three-card runs:

	POINTS
♠3–♡2–♣A	3
♠3–♢2–♣A	3
♠3–♡2–♠A	3
♠3–♢2–♠A	3
Two pair	4
	16

First search for the 15/2 possibilities of the hand. (It has none.) Then shock your opponent by saying: "I have 16 points."

Your Memory Bank

Learn to associate cards in groups, to help you count a hand quickly.

File these away in your memory bank:

GROUP	READ AS
1–4	5
2–3	5
1–5	6
2–4	6
1–6	7
2–5	7
3–4	7

6-Point Hands

GROUP	READ AS
2–2–3–Q	5–5–10
2–3–3–K	5–5–10
1–1–6–8	7–7–8
2–2–4–9	6–6–9
2–4–4–9	6–6–9

For each of these, the count is 15/4 plus a pair, for a score of 6.

Memorizing Some 8-Counters

HAND	COUNT
1–2–3–3	8
1–1–2–3	8
1–2–2–3	8
6–7–8–9	8 (15/4 and a run of four)
10–J–Q–Q	8
10–10–J–Q	8

Count similar combinations of four tenth cards as 8 points.

Try making tables of combinations that yield 10, 12, and 16 points.

You will always be welcome as a player if you can compute combinations rapidly.

A Chemistry Teacher Learns a Lesson

If you are thinking of putting a bragging Cribbage player to the test and deflating his ego, here is how I did it once.

"Joe, come up to the house sometime and I'll show you how to play Cribbage," remarked the chemistry teacher at a Wisconsin high school where I was the head football coach some years ago.

"That's my game," continued the test-tube expert. "I know all the hands at a glance, and I know all the tricks of the trade, especially in pegging," my friend with the superiority complex continued.

I thought to myself, "I know how I'll fix him. I'll put him to my special test; and I do hope it works."

So one night when I had no special plans, I casually dropped in on him and he immediately pulled out the board and the deck of cards, saying: "Joe, you'll never forget this night."

I retorted: "I probably won't, and I think that you'll always remember it too."

There was nothing at stake except honor. We split the first two games and he said: "What will you have to drink?" I answered that any kind of soft drink would do, and while he was at the refrigerator I took the four fives out of the deck and placed them neatly under the Cribbage board.

Believe it or not, we played five more games and he never missed the five-spotters. I beat him four of those five games and his balloon was apparently punctured.

I thanked him for the enjoyable evening and lifted the Cribbage board to show him the fives, remarking: "You certainly know your Cribbage. You played five games without missing the fives."

I have used this treatment on other braggarts, and fortunately, no one has popped me on the jaw. So be careful, and keep your distance with your chin up if you try this stunt.

Flushes

Don't count your cards carelessly and miss a flush! Flushes are as important in Cribbage as in Poker. A four-card flush counts 4 points (except for the crib hand), and another point is added if the starter card is of the same suit.

Here is a favorite of mine—a "straight flush" combining a five-card flush and a five-card straight, plus a pair of 15/2s:

8–7–6–5–4 (same suit)

Counting the score:

	POINTS
8–7, combination of 15	2
6–5–4, combination of 15	2
Five-card straight	5
Five-card flush	5
	14

Here are some even higher-scoring hands in which a flush is coupled with other scoring combinations. (The starter card is in another suit in each example.)

FLUSH	STARTER	POINTS
Q–J–10–5	5	21
K–Q–J–5	5	21
8–7–6–1	8	20
7–6–5–4	4	20
6–5–4–3	6	20
Q–3–2–1	2	18
9–8–7–1	7	18
6–5–4–2	4	18
8–7–6–2	6	18
6–5–4–3	3	18
8–7–6–1	1	17

Other starter cards exist that help the hands listed above.

Discarding Problem

The following common type of hand involves the choice of a straight over a flush with the sacrifice of 1 point.

hearts:	Q–J–6–4
clubs:	10–2

It is before the play, and you do not know the starter card yet. Should you keep the heart flush for 4 points, or should you sacrifice a point and try for a double run by keeping the Q–J–10–2 combination?

Study your position on the board. If 1 point looks very important, hold the flush. A pair, for example, will increase the hand value by a moderate 2 points. But if you are in the mood and position to speculate, hold the run of three.

(Discarding will be discussed at length in part IV.)

High-Scoring Hands

Beginning players may have difficulty in computing the correct values of high-scoring hands. Therefore, it is a good idea to memorize the combinations listed below.

The 29-Point Perfect Holding

If you live in Madison, Wisconsin, and are dealt a 29 hand, you will get your name (along with that of your opponent) in a daily newspaper if you report the happening:

5–5–HN–5–5

The "HN" represents his nobs: the starter card is a five of the same suit as the jack you hold. We compute the scoring carefully:

	POINTS
Jack plus first five	2
Jack plus other three fives (2 each)	6
First, second, third five (sum: 15)	2
First, second, fourth five	2
First, third, fourth five	2
Second, third, fourth five	2
Four of a kind	12
His nobs	1
	29

The 28-Pointer

"Closeness only counts in Horseshoes!"

Millions of players have held four fives, and any one of the 16 tenth cards (kings, queens, jacks, and tens) was cut, making a hand with a value of 28. That's the 29-pointer without the 1 point for his nobs—which you can't get because you don't hold a jack.

Impossible Scores

One may hear the remark from veteran players: "I have a 19 hand." This is an indication that there isn't a single point in their hand. Other impossible counts are 25, 26, and 27.

Here are 24-Pointers

People turned from five-card Cribbage to the modern six-card variety because the latter has higher-scoring hands. We all enjoy scoring 16, 17, 18, 20, 21, 22, 23, or even 24—especially when we need a fistful of points to overtake our opponents.

Memorize the following combinations so that when you count your hand you can say, "I have 24 points," without stopping to go through all the calculations.

1–7–7–7–7	4–4–5–6–6
3–3–3–3–9	4–5–5–6–6
3–6–6–6–6	6–7–7–8–8
4–4–4–4–7	7–7–8–8–9
4–4–5–5–6	

Hitting the 23 Mark

This is an unusual score, because there are only two types of combinations which score 23 points:

4–5–5–5–6	5–5–5–HN–J

The 22-Pointer

There are four hands in this classification, made up of three fives and a pair of tenth cards:

5–5–5–K–K	5–5–5–J–J
5–5–5–Q–Q	5–5–5–10–10

Producing 21

Ten of the combinations score 21:

3–3–3–4–5	5–HN–J–J–J
4–4–4–5–6	6–7–7–7–8
4–5–6–6–6	6–7–8–8–8
5–5–5–10–HN	7–7–7–8–9
5–5–HN–J–J	7–8–8–8–9

The Roaring 20s

There are plenty of 20-pointers, especially when you consider that each type can be multiplied by choosing cards from different suits. This list of pleasing 20-pointers will give the reader an idea of the possibilities:

1–1–7–7–7	6–6–6–6–9
2–2–2–2–9	6–6–9–9–9
3–3–3–3–6	6–6–7–7–8
3–3–3–9–9	6–6–7–8–8
3–3–4–4–5	6–6–6–9–9
3–3–4–5–5	6–9–9–9–9
3–3–6–6–6	7–7–7–7–8
3–4–4–4–4	7–7–7–8–8
4–4–4–7–7	7–7–8–8–8
5–5–5–5–	7–7–8–9–9
5–5–10–10–10	7–8–8–8–8
5–10–10–10–10	7–8–8–9–9

The combinations with four fives range from ace to nine.

The 18-Pointers

These are the four 18-counters (not including ones built on his nobs or flushes):

3–3–3–6–6	5–5–10–HN–Q
3–6–6–6–9	5–5–HN–Q–K

Some Lucky 17s

2–3–4–4–4	5–5–10–J–Q
3–4–4–4–5	5–5–HN–Q–Q
3–4–5–5–5	6–6–6–7–8
5–5–5–6–7	7–8–9–9–9

Typical "Sweet 16" Hands

Here is a sampling of the relatively common 16-point hands. Mathematicians tell us that there are 160 possible ways to form them. (X indicates a tenth card—ten, jack, queen, or king—that does not pair a card already listed.)

1–6–7–7–8	5–10–10–J–Q
1–6–7–8–8	6–7–7–8–9
2–2–3–3–4	6–7–8–8–9
2–3–3–4–4	8–8–9–9–10
3–3–3–6–9	9–9–10–J–J
3–4–4–5–5	9–10–10–J–J
4–5–5–6–X	10–10–J–J–Q
5–5–6–6–7	10–10–J–Q–Q
5–5–10–10–X	10–J–J–Q–Q
5–5–J–J–X	J–J–Q–Q–K
5–5–Q–Q–X	J–J–Q–K–K
5–5–K–K–X	J–Q–Q–K–K
5–6–6–7–7	

A Few of the 15s

There are 77 possible 15-point combinations, including:

1–1–1–2–3	9–10–J–J–J
1–2–3–3–3	10–10–10–J–Q
5–6–6–6–7	10–J–J–J–Q
8–8–8–9–10	10–J–Q–Q–Q
9–9–9–10–J	J–Q–Q–Q–K
9–10–10–10–J	J–Q–K–K–K

And here are some 14-pointers that turn into 15-point holdings because they include the jack, his nobs, of the turn-up suit:

4–5–5–5–HN	5–9–10–HN–J
5–5–5–6–HN	5–10–10–10–HN
5–5–5–8–HN	5–HN–J–J–Q
5–5–5–9–HN	5–HN–J–J–K
5–5–10–HN–K	

Lucky 13

I've skipped the plain 14s, but my staff of advisers insisted that special mention be made of one 13-point holding, because the average devotee consistently misses 2 points in counting the hand:

8–7–6–1–1

	POINTS
8–7 makes a 15/2	2
8–6–1 makes it 15/4	2
8–6–1 makes it 15/6	2
7–6–1–1 makes it 15/8	2
Pair of aces makes it 10	2
Run of three makes it 13	3
	13

The combination 7–6–1–1 is the group that is frequently missed. By all means watch for it, and place this hand in your memory bank. It may save a game for you!

Unusual Hands

Every sportsman and cardplayer is interested in the unusual or improbable happening. So it is with Cribbage fanatics.

I have presented the following hands to add something to the annals of Cribbage and to your accumulated knowledge. Maybe someday, sometime, somewhere, you will experience a hand similar to one of these. Then you will have a conversation piece that will serve you forever.

What is the largest number of points a player can get on one deal of six-card Cribbage? He can include his own (the dealer's) hand, his crib, and all the points he can possibly peg. Of course, the opponent's hand must be set up to fit the dealer's, and opponent's cards must be played in the manner most favorable to the dealer.

Old 73

We should be able to work toward the maximum without the aid of a computer. The average player fails to create a really high score when he does not place the perfect 29-point hand in the crib, with three fives and the jack of the same suit as the starter card (the fourth five, shown in the center of the box).

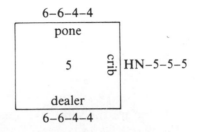

With the 29 crib ("HN" means his nobs, for 1 point) and the 24 points of his own hand, the dealer will get 53 points from the showing. But first, dealer's hand will pick up as many points as possible from the play.

Pone opens with a four; dealer pairs him for 2 points. Pone responds with the third four and dealer counters with the last four for 12 holes.

With the running count at 16, opponent plays a six. Dealer pairs him for 2 holes and takes 1 point for the first go, bringing the count to 28.

Dealer pairs pone's last six and takes another go. He has scored 2, 12, 2, 1, 2, and 1, for a total of 20 holes.

Recapitulation:

	POINTS
Crib	29
Hand	24
Pegging	20
	73

Pone, by the way, pegged 6 for playing the third four and because he also holds a 24 hand, he gets 30 points; so dealer's net gain is 43 points.

The 74-Pointer

This high-scoring dream hand is even more interesting because fewer players would find the solution, and because it makes the best point spread favoring dealer over pone.

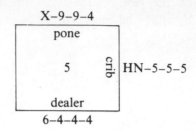

The crib and starter are the same, but dealer modestly settles for a 21-point hand instead of a 24-counter.

But by sacrificing 3 points on the showing, dealer gains 4 points on the play. Pone leads a nine and dealer places his six on the table for 15/2. Pone retaliates with his four, making the running count 19.

Now dealer takes over, leaving pone playless. First he pairs the four, then he plays the third four for triplets, and finally he hits 31 on the last four-spotter.

Pone finishes the play with his two remaining cards and pegs 1 point for the second go.

Dealer pegs 15/2, 2 points for the pair, 6 for triplets, 12 for quadruplets, and 2 for the first go . . . a total of 24.

Recapitulation:

	POINTS
Crib	29
Hand	21
Pegging	24
	74

Adversary gets only 5 points in this hand: 1 point for a go, a 15/2 with the starter card, and a pair of nines.

Deducting the 5 points from dealer's grand total of 74, the point spread is 69 in the dealer's favor.

The 75-Pointer

```
              7–7–6–6
          ┌─────────────┐
          │    pone     │
          │             │ c
          │      5      │ r  HN–5–5–5
          │             │ i
          │    dealer   │ b
          └─────────────┘
              7–7–6–6
```

Dealer has a "mere" 16-point hand this time. Play starts with pone leading a seven. Dealer counters with another seven, scoring 2 points for the pair. Pone makes it triplets and dealer scores 12 on four of a kind and 1 for the go . . . thus piling up 15 holes.

In the second series four sixes go down and dealer again scores 2, 12, and 1 for 15 points.

Recapitulation:

	POINTS
Crib	29
Hand	16
Pegging	30
	75

Pone scores 16 for his hand and pegs triplets twice (6 + 6), for a total of 28 points. Dealer's net gain is 47 holes.

Record 78 Points

In the championship hand, dealer holds 15/4 (he can use either four) with two pairs and four short straights for a 20-pointer. As before, the crib is the 29-pointer.

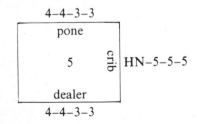

```
              4–4–3–3
          ┌─────────────┐
          │    pone     │
          │             │ c
          │      5      │ r  HN–5–5–5
          │             │ i
          │    dealer   │ b
          └─────────────┘
              4–4–3–3
```

The play is like the 75-pointer: the players put down all the threes, then all the fours. Dealer scores 14 points on each (for a pair, then a quad); he only gets 1 point for go this time because there is only one go. So he pegs 29 points instead of the record 30 on the 75-pointer.

Recapitulation:

	POINTS
Crib	29
Hand	20
Pegging	29
	78

Dealer's point spread over pone is also not a record. Pone scores 32 points (triplets twice and a 20-point hand), for a spread of 46 (compared to the record 69 on the 74-pointer).

A Personal High in Pegging

Your writer has never scored 30 points in the play as in the 75-point superhand above, but he did have the good fortune of holding a seven and three aces in 1977 when opponent held three tenth cards and the fourth ace:

K–Q–J–1

pone
dealer

7–1–1–1

Pone opened his queen for a count of 10. The dealer responded with his seven and pone retaliated with his king; now the count stood at 27.

Dealer continued with an ace, making the total 28, and pone's ace made it 29 and 2 points for the pair.

Dealer pegged six points for triplets with the third ace, making the count 30. Pone passed, and dealer played the fourth ace, scoring 12 for four of a kind. In addition, he finished on 31, so the go was worth 2 points.

Dealer scored:

	POINTS
Triplet	6
Quadruplet	12
Go	2
	20

IV

Elementary Strategy

Basics of Discarding

You will recall that before the starter card is turned, each player discards two of his six cards. The four discards form the crib, are scored on the dealer's side in the showing.

In general the dealer hopes for a strong crib—but is not eager to make discards that will make him score poorly in the play. The nondealer also would like to hold on to good cards, and hopes he can make the crib weak and unproductive in the showing.

We will discuss the sound principles of discarding two cards. The purpose is to get you new players started and bring you to the point where you really enjoy the game.

Fundamentals

1. Players are guided in the discarding process by the dealer's possession of the crib. You might make one kind of discard when dealer and another when pone. Dealer tends to lay out cards favorable to his crib; opponent, to get rid of cards that have little relationship to each other.

2. Keep in mind that games are won or lost with the discard; hence you must make the best discard possible. Your decision about the layaway should be based on the laws of probability.

3. Whether you lead or trail on the Cribbage board is of great importance; your decisions on throwaways must be sound.

4. Consider also the stage of the game. Being ahead a few pegs on First Street and on Fourth Street are two different things.

You may decide to stay even with your opponent on the first three streets and then "play the board" by being conservative—or speculative—as board position dictates near the end of the game.

45

Pone's Discards: Balking the Crib

Our Cribbage forefathers called contributing two cards with intent to destroy the scoring power of the box "balking the crib."

Today you may call it balking or busting the crib, but it is still a matter of keeping dealer from scoring.

Give up two cards that on the average will help least in setting up sequences, pairs, triplets, or 15/2s.

Listed below are methods of control that have been effective for years and that are in the repertory of every Cribbage master. Allen J. Jarvis, in a 1948 pamphlet, states that the average crib hand is worth 4.6 points in the showing. In the records he kept, two experts were competing head to head. For average players, however, who do not balk as expertly, 5.0 points is more like it, and authorities have generally accepted the latter figure.

1. The best balking card is a king because dealer can only make a sequence in one direction: downward through the queen and jack. The king is a more effective stopper than the queen.

2. Next to the king, the most effective crib buster is probably an ace, which only makes a sequence upward through the deuce and trey. The drawback is that an ace can be a valuable asset for pegging (in the play).

3. The favorite pairs of busting cards are K–9, K–8, K–7, K–6, and K–1. A queen may be substituted for the king.

4. Avoid contributing a knave to the dealer's cradle; his "jack-in-the-box" has one chance in four of scoring a point (his nobs), depending on the turn of the starter card.

5. It may not be educationally sound to say it this way, but here are some don'ts:

Don't give an opponent touching cards for his box, and that means K–Q, Q–J, J–10, 10–9, 9–8, 8–7, 7–6, 6–5, 5–4, 4–3, 3–2, or 2–1.

Almost as bad are cards with one space between them: K–J, Q–10, J–9, 10–8, 9–7, 8–6, 7–5, 6–4, 5–3, 4–2, and 3–1. It only takes one card from dealer to form a three-card sequence, and the possibility of a double run is increased.

6. Fear the five-card flush, although the odds against it are high. Other things being equal, pass cards of two different suits to the crib.

7. Try to keep a five-spotter rather than pass it along to your opponent's crib. In general, refrain from discarding an eight or a seven.

8. It may be better to reduce your hand by 2 points rather than make a rich contribution to the box.

9. There are times when you must take a chance of loading up the crib:

8–8–7–7–5–5

Trust to fate, throw caution to the wind, and discard the two fives. You must score in order to win, and in this instance you must hold on to the 12 points in your hand.

10. To end with a do: Place these wide couplets in the crib without hesitation:

K–10   Q–9   10–3   9–2   8–2

There is no guarantee that you will kill the crib, but at least you should limit it to 4, 5, or 6 points.

Dealer's Discards: The Offensive Standpoint

The crib is your treasure box when you are the dealer. Adjust your tactics accordingly.

1. Throw favorable cards to the box. Fives are best, then sevens and eights, then sixes and nines.

2. Placing a pair in the box will often pay large dividends, since the possibility of triplets and double runs is increased.

3. Remember there are sixteen tenth cards, almost one-third of the deck.

Cards such as 3–3–2–9 or 4–4–1–7 are excellent to hold on to because of the good probability of cutting a face card or a ten-spotter for the starter, good for a 15/4 with either hand.

For the same reason, a discard of 4–1 or 3–2 is good if it agrees with the balance of the hand. (See no. 6 below.)

4. Fives are good discards if you don't have picture cards in your hand:

$$7-5-5-4-1-1$$

Throw the two fives into your crib.

5. From a hand composed of high, medium, and low cards, discard the middle cards. This is a common fundamental type of hand:

$$Q-J-9-7-2-1$$

Lay out the nine and seven. After the discard your hand looks like this:

$$Q-J-2-1$$

The high and low groups you keep present good possibilities of being combined into 15s. A starter four or three would be wonderful. Then too, the 9–7 is a good foundation for the crib.

6. Cards that add up to 5 are good to keep. Take this hand:

$$K-K-8-4-4-1$$

Discard a king and the eight. This does not help the crib much, but the 4–4–1 must be kept intact because of the tenth card that may be cut. The chance of turning one of the remaining fourteen tenth cards (you have two kings) is 14 in 46, or 30%.

7. Baiting the crib is sound offensive strategy. Best cards for setting up chances of 15/2s in the crib are:

3–2	5–5	8–7
4–1	6–5	9–6
4–5	5–X	

And don't forget the pairs.

8. Hold on to a run of three cards unless you can score more

with another combination. If the starter card builds a double run, the hand goes up by 5 points—from 3 to 8.

9. With a weak hand containing a couple of points or none at all, set your sights on the pegging process. The middle-ranking and low cards are best for the play, so keep them and lay away the tenth cards. This is especially true if you have 5 or 6 points to go to win the game or escape a possible lurch (where pone gets 121 points and you have less than 91 and lose double stakes):

K–J–8–6–4–2

Discard the king and jack.

10. Take the long chance, trying to turn your holding into a juicy winner when you are dangerously behind:

Q–Q–10–10–4–1   discard the 4–1 and hope for a jack starter
10–9–6–6–4–4   discard the 10–9 and hope for a five starter

11. Consider keeping an ace or a deuce in a problem hand such as:

K–Q–J–10–9–1

As every Cribbage enthusiast knows, an ace—which is a poor card for the crib—is very helpful in pegging. Discard the king and queen, because pone may also throw a king to balk the crib. Using your remaining tenth cards, you may be able to bring the count to 31 with your ace.

Laws of Probability

In Cribbage a player is dealt six cards. The other forty-six are unknown—the six in opponent's hand, and the forty left in the deck. One of the unknown cards, the one that is cut for a starter, is of great concern to both players. How can you increase the probability that you will benefit from the as yet unknown starter card?

You can do it by wise discards, based on a sound understanding of the percentages, or odds, in Cribbage. Other things being equal, you want to retain the four cards which benefit from the greatest number of possible starters. If there is only one card that can help the hand you have selected, your chances are only 1 in 46, or 2.2%; but if there are twenty-four such cards, your chances improve to 24 in 46, or 52.2% (see the Expectancy Table, p. 51).

There are, of course, other factors that will influence your discarding decision: What will the effect of your discard be on the crib? What is your position on the board? Are you ahead or behind your adversary, and by how much? Do you need to take chances, or should you make conservative and balking discards? But always remember that in games involving an element of chance, the successful players are those who have a system—those who play the percentages.

Let's look at a simple example. If you hold 9–9–7–7, how many favorable starters are there? Assume that you have discarded a six and a king.

This hand is already good for 4 holes—the two pairs. With a cut of an eight, the hand explodes into a 20-pointer! Among the forty-six unknown cards there are four eights. What are the odds of drawing one of them? *Answer:* 4 in 46, or 8.7%, or 10.50 to 1 odds against.

But there are several other cards which will also garner points:

	CHANCES
Ace adds 2 points	4
Six adds 4 points	3
Seven adds 4 points	2
Nine adds 4 points	2

(There are only three sixes left—you discarded one.) Altogether there are 15 chances to improve the hand with the starter card: four eights, four aces, three sixes, two sevens, and two nines. What are the odds of drawing one of these cards? *Answer:* 15 in 46, or 32.6%, or 2.07 to 1 against.

To help you answer such questions I have prepared the following table. The table is as simple and understandable as possible, so that you can refer to it during a game or even memorize a few key lines with little effort.

Wergin's Expectancy Table

FAVORABLE CARDS	UNFAVORABLE CARDS	ODDS AGAINST YOU	PERCENTAGE IN YOUR FAVOR
24	22	0.92/1	52.2
23	23	1.00/1	50.0
22	24	1.09/1	47.8
21	25	1.19/1	45.7
20	26	1.30/1	43.5
19	27	1.42/1	41.3
18	28	1.56/1	39.1
17	29	1.71/1	37.0
16	30	1.88/1	34.8
15	31	2.07/1	32.6
14	32	2.29/1	30.4
13	33	2.54/1	28.3
12	34	2.83/1	26.1
11	35	3.18/1	23.9
10	36	3.60/1	21.7
9	37	4.11/1	19.6
8	38	4.75/1	17.4
7	39	5.57/1	15.2
6	40	6.67/1	13.0
5	41	8.20/1	10.9
4	42	10.50/1	8.7
3	43	14.33/1	6.5
2	44	22.00/1	4.3
1	45	45.00/1	2.2

Check the two answers given above with the table.

The lower the odds are against you, and the higher the percentage of events in your favor, the better your chances are of drawing a helpful card.

Apply Logic

The answer to many discarding problems can be found right in front of you—on the Cribbage board. You must play the board!

Are you ahead, or are you trailing, and by how much? Is it your last chance to speculate and try for the big score? Note that some players always "shoot the works" rather than take the sensible approach. They are losing players in the long run.

Let's discuss a riskier discard from our sample hand. We began with 9–9–7–7–6–K and discarded 6–K. Now, what if we retained 9–9–7–6 and discarded the king and a seven, still a good balking throwaway?

The new hand is already good for 6 points, a 2-point improvement over 9–9–7–7. And it has a bright future, since possible starting cards are:

	POINT INCREASE	TOTAL POINTS
Two nines	6	12
Four eights	10	16
Three sixes	6	12

There are nine desirable cards which will at least double the original count from 6 to 12 holes. The odds of hitting one of them is 19.6%; of cutting an eight-spotter, only 8.7%.

Here are several more sample hands, where you must decide which card to discard. Practice using the Expectancy Table, and you will develop a scientific approach to Cribbage.

Hand no. 1: Devotees are continually faced with the choice of discarding a pair and holding a three-card straight, or breaking up the straight by laying away two cards from it:

Q–Q–10–9–8–5

Three of the sixteen tenth cards in the deck are in your hand, leaving thirteen among the unknowns. There are also three fives to add to your list of desirables.

I recommend that the 9–8 be discarded, leaving:

Q–Q–10–5

This hand—already an 8-pointer—has a good percentage opportunity to go places. There are sixteen helping cards:

	POINT INCREASE	TOTAL POINTS
Four kings	2	10
Two queens	6	14
Four jacks	8	16
Three tens	4	12
Three fives	8	16

The Expectancy Table shows that the odds are less than 2 to 1 against, namely 34.8%, that one of the sixteen cards will be turned by the dealer for the starter. Not bad!

Hand no. 2: Shooting for a double run is not always the best policy, because the 15/2 combinations may bring the best results.

Q–J–10–7–3–2

A discard of 2–7 or 3–7 doesn't offer the greatest potential for the hand; a cut for a double run of the tenth cards produces a final count of 8 or 9 holes 34.8% of the time.

Look a little farther, because the 15/2s can bring juicier scores. Here's how the hand will look if you lay out the Q–7, a balking combination:

J–10–3–2

Here are the chances of improvement—all thirty-five of them!

	POINT INCREASE	TOTAL POINTS
Four kings	2	6
Three queens	5	9
Three jacks	4	8
Three tens	4	8
Four nines	3	7
Four fives	4	8
Four fours	3	7
Three treys	6	10
Three deuces	6	10
Four aces	3	7

Now we have 8, 9, or 10 holes 41.3% of the time; the lesser improvements are also more probable, and even without any improvements the hand is a point better.

Hand no. 3: This illustration is particularly interesting: it involves the apparent sacrifice of 4 holes. The sacrifice will pay off in the long run, however, by almost 1 hole:

$$6–6–3–3–2–2$$

If you discard the 6–6 and retain 3–3–2–2, you have 4 points already, and the starter card will improve the average scoring of the hand to 10.26 (every cut except six helps). But if you discard the deuces and hold 6–6–3–3, the hand, which gives you 8 points to begin with instead of 4, will average 9.48 holes, and only a three, six, or nine will be a useful starter card.

A complete analysis shows how 3–3–2–2 is better:

	POINT INCREASE	TOTAL POINTS
Four kings	8	12
Four queens	8	12
Four jacks	8	12
Four tens	8	12
Four nines	2	6
Four eights	4	8
Four sevens	4	8
Two sixes	0	4
Four fives	2	6
Four fours	12	16
Two treys	4	8
Two deuces	4	8
Four aces	12	16

Of every forty-six hands based on 3–3–2–2, on the average, two will score 4 points; eight, 6 points; twelve, 8 points; sixteen, 12 points; and eight, 16 points. Total score for forty-six hands is 472 points, or 10.26 per hand. (You began with 4 points and added an average of 6.26 points.)

But if you keep 6–6–3–3, beginning with 8 points, you will improve by an average of only 1.48 points, leaving you with only 9.48. Of forty-six hands, thirty-eight will still have only 8 points;

four (nines) will have 14 points; two (sixes) will have 20 points; and two (treys) will have 18 points. Total, 436 points for forty-six hands.

It should be added that with the better choice you give a pair of sixes to the crib; with the inferior choice, the crib gets a pair of deuces. Whether you are dealer or pone, there is not much difference what the pair is, either in your play or the crib's showing.

The purpose of this discussion on percentages is to make you a thinking player with a system to follow in making your decisions.

In the future you will be applying logic in selecting discards based upon board position as well as the favorable and unfavorable percentages. Good luck!

Defensive Strategy

Defensive Vocabulary

Balk	to throw two cards to the dealer's crib which tend not to fit into combinations
Left in the lurch	failure to reach the 91st hole before the end of the game
Playing off	laying cards down that prevent sequences
Skunk	same as to leave in the lurch
Street, First	the outside row of 30 holes
Street, Second	inside row of 30 holes
Street, Third	repeats the trail over First Street
Street, Fourth	covers inside row again, ending with 120th hole (game hole is the 121st hole)
Wide cards	cards that avoid the possibility of runs
X	symbol indicating a tenth card (king, queen, jack, or ten)

Defensive strategy refers to the player who has fewer points on the board—not to the pone defending against the dealer.

Athletic coaches say, "Defense you always have with you. A

team may have an off night and have trouble scoring, but the defense will keep it in the game."

The same is true of Cribbage. If the opposition is drawing excellent cards and is blessed with lucky starter cards, you must do your utmost to control the pegging and the crib to eliminate the possibility of being skunked or left in the lurch (the word "lurch" originated in Cribbage).

Some sound defensive tactics are presented so that you may advance in knowledge and eventually receive a master's degree in Cribbage.

When play begins, your first objective is to get some 15/2s. If you can't do it, you must try to prevent your opponent from making a 15/2—which is the same gain in score for you, really, as making one yourself.

Your second objective is to run the count to 31 for 2 points, or at least get a 1-point go. If luck doesn't favor you, why not gain a point by getting opponent to fall short of 31 so he gets a 1-point go instead of a 2-point go?

In the defensive maneuvers presented below, you will note some overlapping of offense and defense, because your countermoves, with luck, may not only keep your opponent from pegging but result in your pegging instead.

1. Playing Off

This action is the opposite of playing on (where you encourage opponent to begin a sequence). Leave enough of a gap between the first card played by pone and your card to eliminate the possibility of a sequence.

Pone leads a nine and you counter with a queen (rather than a jack), making the count 19. The gap of two cards between nine and queen is too large for him to fill in a straight. Keep aware of playing wide, thus defending against runs.

2. Beware of Pairs

When your adversary leads in a two-handed game, defensive play avoids or is wary of pairing his card, which may be his bait for making a triplet.

If opponent has played a card making 15 and scoring 2 points, you are reasonably safe in pairing his card, unless he played a six or an eight. Your six brings the count to the dangerous 21 mark (any tenth card gives him 2 points for go). Your eight sets him up for 8 points if he holds the third eight.

3. Triplets

You often have the choice of making 2 points by pairing pone's leadoff card or by scoring on a 15/2. 'Tis better to make the 15/2 than to allow pone to make triplets and score 6 points!

8–?–?–?

pone
dealer

8–7–6–2

Pone leads his eight. Dealer is safer to play the seven than the eight.

4. Split a Pair of Fives

Don't get into a position where you must lead a five from a pair of these precious cards, thus giving up points.

Holding 9–6–5–5, play a five early, when convenient; otherwise your first five may be the start of the second series of play, after a go.

5. Stay off Thin Ice

Running the count to 21 can get you a cold bath when adversary responds with a roaring "31 for 2 holes."

Tenth cards are plentiful in the deck. There are sixteen of them.

6. The Safest Card to Lead

The reader keeps hearing a monotonous "Don't do this and don't do that. Don't lead this card, and better not lead the other one."

Well, what should you lead?

Solve the problem by leading a four-spotter.

Most writers have indicated that a four is the best defensive lead, because the dealer is unable to make an immediate 15/2. It is better to save the other small, safe cards—the aces, deuces, and treys—for making 15, a go, or even 31.

A tenth card is a relatively safe lead if you have no four-spotter. The high card lets you save low cards for when you may need them.

7. Don't Get Behind the Eight Ball

Take preventive measures with responding cards. As dealer, don't set up the count so that pone can make 4 holes.

After a seven has been led, avoid taking the count to 11 with a four-spotter. Pone may have another four, and by hitting the count at 15, he scores double—2 for the pair and 2 for the 15.

The same is true if the count is 23. Avoid playing a four, upping the total to 27, because there is a possibility of pone scoring 4 holes if he holds another four.

There are other cards that place a person behind the eight ball. Don't make 28 with a trey, 13 with a deuce, 22 with a nine, 26 with a five, 24 with a seven, 23 with an eight, or 21 with a tenth card. If pone matches your last card, he will score double.

8. The Equalizer

With a nine and a three in the hand, an equalizer play will delay the decision of the game. You are pone:

```
           9–3–?–?
        ┌───────────┐
        │   pone    │
        │           │
        │   dealer  │
        └───────────┘
           3–?–?–?
```

Start with the three, and if dealer goes for the pair, counter with the nine, evening the score with a 15/2.

The same principle applies if you hold a four and a seven. Open with the four, and if dealer racks up 2 points for a pair, equalize by playing the seven.

9. The World's Worst Lead

Of course, there must be an opening lead that is stupid, silly, foolish, and irrational. For obvious reasons, the world's worst opening lead is a five-spotter.

Charity begins at home—not over a Cribbage board.

10. Avoid the 16 Count

It's unsafe to take the running count to 16 unless you are sure you can play another card (holding a five or lower);

Q–J–10–5

pone
dealer

9–8–7–6

Pone led the jack and dealer countered with the six, saying, "16." Pone moved the count to 26 with his ten-spotter.

Dealer had to pass, and pone played his five for 31 and 2 points.

Correct play: J–8–10 for 28; pone's play of the five for 31 is prevented.

11. Don't Throw a Boomerang

Leads of sevens and eights are dangerous; they often come back to haunt you, or knock you out. Take this hand:

8–8–7–7

pone
dealer

8–7–7–1
or
8–8–7–7

There is only one sensible lead to avoid getting hit with the Australian flying object: an eight, because four eights are an unplayable 32, while four sevens are 28 and net dealer 12 points for quadruplets and an extra point for go.

If the dealer holds 8–8–7–7, 8–7–7–1, or a similar combination, a seven starts a fateful series. Dealer scores on a pair, pone cashes the third seven for triplets and 6 points, and dealer comes roaring down the stretch with the fourth seven for 12 points—and the go makes it 13.

Yes, these hands do happen and they always seem to occur down on Fourth Street.

Wergin's Pegging Strategy

Games are usually won or lost in the pegging process! Many basketball coaches maintain that a good offense is the best defense. The same is true of the play in Cribbage. Approach the game aggressively, positively, and be prepared to attack with the four cards of your hand and the two cards laid away in the crib.

Because the circle of opponents is limited, active players usually have a daily one-on-one confrontation with a member of the family or someone down at the club or pub. Always be ready to make an illogical play and upset the routine. Put a little spice into the contest. Vary your plays and surprise the opponent.

Pone has opportunities to maneuver pegging points. Here are some tricks of the trade.

1. The Sucker Play

If you hold a deuce and a trey, start the attack by leading the three; often dealer will take the bait and respond with a tenth card, making the count 13. The deuce hits 15 and you peg 2 points immediately.

By the same token, holding a 4–1, open with the four and if pone pushes the count up to 14, the ace brings home 2 points.

The above procedure also tends to prevent the establishment of sequences.

2. Bait the Hook!

To lead from a pair is a standard opening play. If the dealer makes a pair, then counter, lining up three of a kind for 6 holes.

Rarely will the dealer spoil your day by playing the fourth card for 12 points.

But don't lead from a pair of fives: a tenth card makes 15/2.

If you have a pair, avoid starting the attack with one of them; opponent has been tricked before and will shy away from making a pair. Select a higher card for the first play; later, play from the pair. It has a better chance to net you triples after the 15 count has been reached:

10–9–2–2

pone
dealer

8–7–6–2

Pone opens the nine and if dealer brings the count to 15, slips a deuce out, making the count 17. Now, if dealer holds a two, he feels safe in pairing. Pone retaliates with the third deuce for 6 points.

3. An Ounce of Prevention Is Worth a Pound of Cure

If you hold a 9–6 couplet, there is an excellent reason for playing the six rather than the nine.

Lead the six, and if dealer responds with a nine for 15/2, counter with your nine, scoring 2 for a pair and bringing the running score to 24. Now dealer cannot make triplets without going over 31.

If you had opened the nine, and dealer hit 15/2 with a six, your pairing the six would move the running score to 21, to the advantage of the dealer—who slams the door at 31 with a tenth card or takes 6 holes with a six, scoring 4 or 9 holes against 2 for you.

4. Hit the Bull's-eye of 31

J–5–3–3

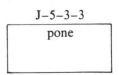

If you open the play with a three, dealer's most common play is to jump the count to 13 with a tenth card. If it is a jack, pair it. Otherwise, move the count to 16 with your remaining three-spotter.

Another tenth card from dealer will advance the count to the 26 mark you've been waiting for, and your five hits 31 for 2 pegging points.

5. Lead the Middle Card

When you have to lead from a sequence of three cards, start with the middle card:

J–10–9–5

pone

Play the ten and you can go up or down to form a sequence.

From 8–7–6 lead the seven; if dealer goes for the 15/2, counter with the six for a three-card sequence, and rack up 3 points.

6. Picture Cards

What should be led from the following?

K–Q–J–5

pone

The queen. Assume, for example, that dealer holds four tenth cards. By leading the queen you have him hooked for 3 points for a sequence of three tenth cards and a 1-point go at 30 for you. If you lead the king dealer can play off with a ten-spotter, conceding you the 1-point go but depriving you of the 3-point straight.

Either way, dealer must start a new series, and your counter of a five nets a 15/2.

7. Use Your Ace

Holding this hand:

Q–J–10–1

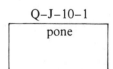

pone

Lead the ten, luring dealer on with the opportunity of avoiding a sequence by playing his king. Counter with the queen or jack to bring the count to 30, and if he lacks an ace, score 2 with your ace.

8. Risky Business

Yes, going into business is risky, but we mean that a player must be aware of the risks when sevens and eights are being played.

It can pay dividends, all the same, to lead out one of them, if you have something to back up your play:

$$8-7-7-1$$

The aggressive play is to lead a seven, and if dealer replies 15/2 with an eight, counter with your eight for a pair, making the count 23. If dealer responds with a seven instead of an eight, you can drill 6 holes with triplets.

In opening with a seven, you are "thinking positive" in that you don't expect him to hold a pair of sevens. If he does . . . well, it's a risky business!

The next illustrations demonstrate countermoves that dealer can use in combating the plays of pone.

9. Jackpot!

On occasion, dealer may encourage pone to form a sequence which will pay dividends on either the sixth or seventh card:

$$Q-7-6-3$$

pone
dealer

$$5-4-2-1$$

On pone's opening play of a seven, respond with a five, allowing adversary to complete a three-card sequence with his six-spotter. Then retaliate with your four, scoring on a four-card straight.

Now if pone extends the run to five cards with a three, stretch the straight to six cards with your deuce and, of course, put the frosting on the cake with your ace, making the running count 25. Take 8 holes—1 for the go and 7 for the run. Net result of this series is pone 8, dealer 18.

10. Playing On

This means playing a card that encourages the formation of a straight. If adversary leads a four, play a deuce, encouraging him to construct a three-card straight.

Of course, you must be able to back up your play with an ace or a five if adversary plays a trey.

11. Setting a Trap

One reliable stunt in a veteran's bag of tricks is playing a seven on pone's eight-spotter for a 15/2. Pone retaliates with a six or a nine for a three-point sequence. But you come out ahead either way:

If pone plays a six, advancing the count to 21, your face card scores 2 holes on a 31 total.

If pone plays a nine, you are ready with a six for the four-card straight and a probable 1 point for go.

12. On the Spot

Always put your opponent on the spot where if he plays a tenth card you can hit 31:

```
        K–?–?–?
      ┌─────────┐
      │  pone   │
      │         │
      │  dealer │
      └─────────┘
        8–7–6–5
```

Pone opens with the king. As dealer, you play the six, bringing the count to 16, so that if pone plays another tenth card, advancing the count to 26, you score 2 points with your five-spotter.

The Cribbage Board

For centuries man has been trying to make a better mousetrap, and many contraptions have been invented. But we still have mice.

Man has also invented many Cribbage boards. In the 1630s, when Cribbage originated and the scoring was registered on a Noddy board (used in a similar game), holes were drilled and lined up on flat pieces of wood and pegs were carved to be placed in the holes.

As time went on, people arranged these holes in different patterns on various-shaped slabs. In all my researching to trace the development of Cribbage, a picture of a Noddy board could not be found. Sketched below is an artist's conception of what a Noddy board may have been like.

Mr. Pond

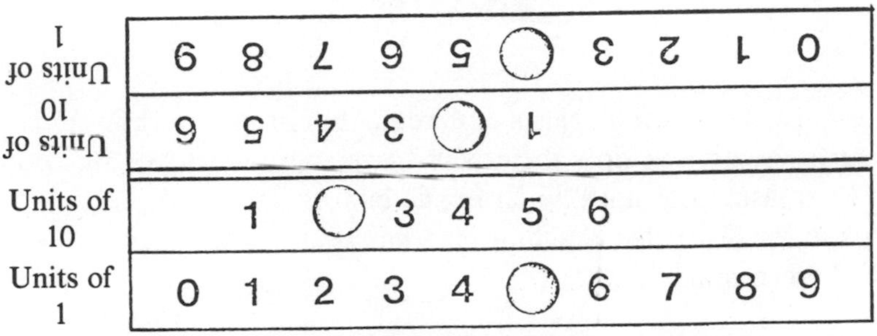
Units of 1
0 1 2 3 5 6 7 8 9
Units of 10
1 3 4 5 6
Units of 10
1 3 4 5 6
Units of 1
0 1 2 3 4 6 7 8 9

Mr. Blackney

Mr. Pond, who is recording his score on the upper half, has a score of 24, while Mr. Blackney's total is 25 points.

If a regular Cribbage board is not available, this design may be drawn on cardboard or paper. Double or triple size.

Number each section as shown, and as the points are scored, move buttons or coins instead of using pegs. Each player should have two disks or objects, one for each line. Because the original Cribbage game ended at 61 points, a third line of 100s was not drawn in.

How would you like to get skunked on a very special board?

A thrifty and imaginative fanatic has found a use for a discarded wooden toilet seat; with holes drilled, it makes a functional Cribbage board, as illustrated on page 66.

In 1976 a Junior Achievement Group had as its project the conversion of oak and maple seats into useful furniture. Hundreds of such discards were retrieved by the young people for their special project. They received training in refinishing, using power tools, advertising, and merchandising their creations.

Perhaps, after these pages are read, hundreds of thousands of discarded seats will find their way to recreation and living rooms and be treasured as antique Cribbage boards.

A use for discarded bowling pins has been found: split a pin and drill the necessary holes.

The 29-point hand is the highest-scoring of all at Cribbage. Several years ago one of our enthusiasts created a unique 29 board. Several Canadian and American plastic manufacturers are producing 29-shaped and toilet boards.

A folding board has been manufactured—for the flying player.

A special three-track board has been developed for three players.

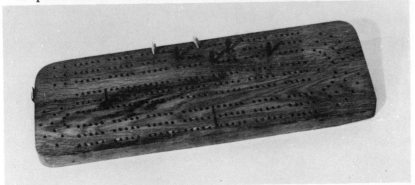

It can also be used by two players. It is especially useful in helping to eliminate the confusion of traveling around the conventional board twice and wondering if you are on Second Street or Fourth Street. With three lanes, there can be no such problem.

In addition to these a zigzag board is also available for variety.

Of course, some board designs are easier to use (more practical or convenient) than others. The "Long Board," shown below, has been developed by officials of The Masters Cribbage Classic for use in major tournaments. This design reduces errors of jumping lanes, reaching over or touching an opponent's pegs, and being uncertain about street identities. It is expected that all major leagues will adopt this new board.

"THE LONG BOARD"·Official for THE MASTERS CLASSICS

V

Advanced Strategy

Cribbing Along with the Masters

Aim for the Last Hole

Maneuvers which facilitate your getting a go:
Holding two low cards and two high cards, lead from the former.

Example: K–Q–3–2. Lead the deuce or trey.

Holding one low card and three high cards, lead from the latter (other things being equal).

Suppose as dealer you hold a ten and a five to start the second series of pegging, and you need two holes to win the game. Lead the ten in the hope that your adversary makes a 15/2; then you can retaliate by pairing his five.

Play the Averages

Situation 1: As dealer you need 3 to 5 points to win the game, while pone needs 7 to 8, or even 6 points. You know that you must peg out during the play to win.

Break up your medium or high pairs and hold pegging cards, thus retaining four cards in your hand that may pair your opponent, keeping a better chance of making a 15/2 or 31:

dealer
Q–9–9–7–5–2

Discard the Q–9 to the crib, because the game will be over before the crib is counted. Retain the 9–7–5–2. If any of the following cards is led by pone, you can peg 2 holes: K–Q–J–10–9–8–7–6–5–2.

If you discard the 2–7 and keep 4 points in your hand (Q–5–9–9) you may never have the chance to count them.

You can peg 2 holes on seven of pone's possible ranks (K–Q–J–10–9–6–5), compared to ten ranks listed above.

Situation 2: With the same score, you hold two pairs:

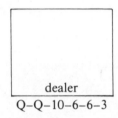

dealer

Q–Q–10–6–6–3

Throw the Q–6 couplet to the crib, and you can peg on leads of Q–10–9–6–5–3.

If you discard the 10–3, keeping Q–Q–6–6 with its 4 points, you won't have time to show and score; the possibilities for pegging are reduced by two denominations, to Q–9–6–5.

Choosing the Dealer of the Second Game

In our travels we have observed players using three methods to determine who deals first in the second and following games of 121 points.

1. Contestants alternate. If B deals the last hand of that first game, A starts the second game as dealer, whether or not he was first dealer in the first game.

2. Loser of one game starts dealing the next game.

3. If A starts dealing Game 1, B starts dealing game 2.

The National Open as well as most other major tournaments follow the second procedure in order to make the events more competitive.

Favor the Crib

Some dealers tend to favor the crib over their own hand when deciding on a discard, because there are more chances to improve the crib after dealer's discard, with the two cards thrown by the pone and the starter card.

This practice is more valid for the five-card contest than for the six-card game. Think about it!

Why Lead a Four-Spotter?

Because you can prevent dealer from making a 15/2. If he plays an ace, you can score the 15/2 with any tenth card.

If he does not play an ace, you can make a 15/2 or pass safely over the 15 count with a tenth card.

Note that if you lead an ace, deuce, or trey, dealer can get to a 4 count himself by playing a low card.

Play Position

Situation: You are using the conventional deal—always—alternates method. You are the dealer and have a comfortable lead. The cards you are holding, along with the pegging, will end the game.

To have the advantage of dealing the first hand of the next game, *do not go out.* Make sure to be short a few holes, by splitting your hand or by passing up opportunities for pegging.

With first count of the pone's succeeding deal, you win the game, and the first deal of the next game is yours.

Have a Game Plan

As dealer, you and pone are equal at the starting gate, both being at home. At first, plan to be cautious, to take only fair risks, and to avoid speculation.

With the start of the second deal, note the relative scores on the board and play on or off accordingly.

You may have to change strategy radically if you go way ahead or fall far behind.

If you trail and you pick up some interesting cards that may help you catch up, play for a lucky cut, which may really put you back in the ball game:

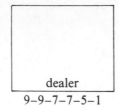

dealer

9–9–7–7–5–1

Discard the 5–1 and hope for a lucky eight starter, rather than discarding the sevens.

If your cards are bad and there is little prospect of improving your position, try to keep your opponent from scoring. Stall until the next hand.

Hot and Cold Decks

Every cardplayer has encountered the superstitious individual who keeps wanting to change decks because the cards are "cold." There is some wisdom in his superstition.

It has been noted that a deck becomes cold because of artificial patterns formed from playing and (often none too thorough) shuffling. Some people naturally deal out low-scoring hands because of the type of shuffle that they employ. This theory is subscribed to by a number of expert Cribbage players.

Other Cribbage fanatics deal high-scoring hands consistently, because with the method of shuffling and perhaps play of the cards, patterns are formed and continuously repeated, shuffle after shuffle. Experts agree with this statement too.

If the cards were dealt in a truly random manner, no such patterns could be predicted, although hot and cold streaks would still appear.

Freak Hands Are Interesting

The most exciting hands are the freak high-scoring combinations, or those with abnormal distribution. It has been noticed that when one player's holding is unusual, the adversary probably has an odd hand too.

In a three-handed game, also, with the usual nonrandom shuffling, when one player holds only 2 points in his hand, the two competitors tend to score a couple of points or so.

The Hot Deck

A "hot" deck is one in which 12-point hands are common and 20-pointers are far from rare. The deck may stay hot for four or five games, but, alas, the lucky cards may favor only your opponent.

Change Decks

If the cards are cold for you, by all means try another deck for the next game. It is your prerogative. However, the change is not permitted during a game.

If your scoring doesn't change with a second deck, then try a third one, and if there is still no improvement, terminate play and reread this book. There must be something else wrong.

Common Sense

Webster offers the following definition for the word "psychology":

   a. the science dealing with the mind and with mental and
      emotional processes.
   b. the science of human behavior.
   c. the sum of the actions, traits, attitudes, thoughts, and mental
      states of a person.

I prefer a simpler definition: the application of pure common sense to a given situation.

There is a lot more to the science of Cribbage than just discarding two cards, turning a starter card, and going through the routine of counting 15/2 and a run of three. You must be aware of your opponent's mental processes, behavior, attitudes, and reactions.

Then, too, you must be in control of your own emotions, habits, mental processes, and actions as well as your physical condition. You must discipline yourself so that you do not give an opponent a psychological advantage.

Rating Your Opponent

Let's discuss, first, your study of an opponent's playing habits in order to take every possible advantage.

Does your adversary revert to "table talk" when playing a card that may start a run? Is he or she baiting you on when he knows that he will gain in the long run?

Does your opponent favor making the opening lead from a pair so that he may score on triplets? Or does he delay the lead until the second series?

Does his play follow any definite routine or pattern?

Does he pair your lead at every opportunity—or does he avoid pairing you with sevens and lower cards only when holding two of a kind, thus setting the trap for quadruplets and 12 holes?

Does your adversary always lead a deuce when he has a trey in his hand, or a four-spotter when holding an ace, to set you up for his 15/2? Your countermove is to play something besides a tenth card when the deuce or four is led, so he can't score with the trey or ace, as the case may be. Furthermore, you have the advantage of knowing one of his unplayed cards.

Does your competitor use playing strategies as used by knowledgeable contestants?

Do you credit him as a very skillful player? If so, you are in a battle of wits.

Has your opponent read this book? If not, you have a great advantage over him.

Conversely, remember that an opponent also observes your habits and patterns of play; so keep out of a rut, and vary your plays. Occasionally make an unorthodox play such as opening the series with an ace, to surprise the opposition.

I have heard of a tournament player who keeps records of the style of play utilized by competitors for reference in the next year's tournament. Such knowledge may be the determining factor in winning a championship.

Conversation

Talk is cheap, but it takes money to buy whiskey!

You must carefully sift the words and remarks that an opponent throws at you during a game as a technique to upset your thinking and play. Such remarks may be in reverse ... complaining with good cards and bragging with poor cards.

False words about the starter card are used by many people. Some players misleadingly delay discarding, trying to convey the impression that they have a problem in selecting a discard.

What should you learn from this discussion? Be poker-faced and keep your mouth shut! Listen and learn!

Worth Two Finesses

There is a saying among Skat and Sheepshead players that "one peek is worth two finesses."

In Cribbage too, a peek can give an opponent a slight advantage and cost you the game.

I refer to the opponent who, while cutting the pack for the starter card, sneaks a peek at the card on the bottom of the packet. The rules provide a 2-point penalty for this offense, but pone may steal a glimpse of the bottom card while you are busy deciding on your discard.

So be alert and note if your opponent tips the packet for an unfair advantage.

Memory

Writers have indicated that Cribbage is a different card game in that you don't have to remember the cards played. But this is not entirely true.

It is a good idea to remember the two cards you have discarded to the crib: the information can guide you in the pegging process. Also, remember the styles of play used by your adversaries.

Beware of the Sharpies

Many sharp players will watch the position from which you draw your cards in order to guess the rank of your remaining cards.

Most cardplayers arrange their cards from left to right by suits, with high cards to the left of each suit. In Cribbage, where suits are relatively unimportant, high cards are still placed on the left and lower cards to the right:

Q–J–10–2 or 9–8–7–6

If your adversary notes the position from which you draw the jack in the first example, he knows you have one higher card, a king or a queen. If you play the seven from the second example, he knows you have two cards higher than the seven and one card lower.

For self-preservation, watch your opponent's eyes to ascertain whether he is taking advantage of you. And be sure to mix up the cards in your hand—or simply leave them the way they are when you pick them up.

Of course, you too can note how your opponent holds his pasteboards and attempt to read his hand.

Mental Attitudes

Your mental condition has a definite effect on your caliber of play. Many of us retreat to the card table to forget our personal problems, at least for a short time.

However, it takes great effort for a person to play normally when under mental stress.

Here are some don'ts:

1. Don't get frustrated or angry when things are breaking badly for you.
2. Don't gamble on uncalled-for long chances.
3. Don't complain about your bad luck or opponent's good fortune.
4. Don't argue with opponent.

Positive Thinking

Assume that you are superior to your opponent and be confident that you are going to win. Then you will compete with a relaxed attitude.

If you are nervous and feel tight, take time out. Take a short walk and get a soft drink or a snack.

Here are some dos:

1. Maintain a happy-go-lucky attitude as it rains one minute and the sun shines the next minute.
2. Forget the games that have been lost and concentrate on the present contest.
3. Stick with the percentages. Over the long pull your skill and the percentages will win for you.

Physical Condition

In major tournaments which require two or three days of intense play, some competitors can be observed spending all their spare time playing cards.

They would be better off if they went out for a walk and got some exercise. If tired, you should take a nap and relax. Be sure to get enough sleep at night.

The worst thing to do is to drink alcoholic beverages to excess. Perhaps one drink will help you relax but cut it off there, as alcohol influences one's judgment, usually causing one to take unnecessary chances. Remember that alcohol may seem at first a stimulant but is really a depressant: you may get tired during the last games of the evening and make foolish mistakes.

Old Irons

A system of side bets or stakes called old irons has been in vogue in England, especially in the London area.

Old irons is a set of bonuses awarded a player for accomplishing something special at Cribbage.

In the pubs or taverns where daily Cribbage games are a way of life, records are kept with chalk lines when a player scores an old iron such as:

1. Turning his heels.
2. Finding 12 points in the crib.
3. Counting 20 points in the hand.
4. Totaling 24 or 28 points in the showing (two irons).
5. Discovering a flush in the crib.
6. Finding nothing in the crib.

The chalk marks are made on the bar and at the end of the game, especially in a four-handed contest, the player with the fewest irons buys a round of drinks, or the player with the most irons collects stakes previously agreed on.

A Study in Averages

In a 1948 booklet Allen J. Jarvis reported a study of 250 deals between two expert players indicating that Cribbage hands average 8 holes each while the cribs average 4.6 holes,

	HOLES	AVERAGE HOLES
500 hands	4,001	8.0
250 cribs	1,150	4.6

The 500 hands, of course, are 250 dealer's hands and 250 pone's hands. Note that the pegging in the play was not reported.

In the home stretch when dealer must decide whether to try to peg out in the play or depend on his hand plus the crib in the showing, he should bear in mind that the crib can be expected to contain 4 or 5 points. (As stated above, with average rather than expert players competing, the crib is not balked by pone quite as well and is thought to average 5.0 holes. Larger samples of experts and of average players are needed.)

Consider the Average

I believe that the average player leaves a stronger crib than the expert (5.0 holes instead of 4.6), and he leaves his hand a little weaker than the expert (7 to 8 holes instead of 8.0 holes). Furthermore, in the play he pegs an average of 4 to 5 holes. Adding:

	HOLES
Hand	7.5
Crib	5.0
Play	4.5
	17.0

Thus dealer can expect to score 17 holes on a deal (hand, crib, and play). Pone, without the crib, averages 12 holes. (Experts will average slightly higher, since their play is better.)

VI

Five-Card Cribbage

Original Game

Cribbage was originally played two-handed in Great Britain, with each player receiving five cards. The old form, which has several notable differences from the six-card game, is considered more scientific but has fewer followers.

In the five-card format, each player discards two cards into the crib and has only three to use in the play.

Game Is 61 Points

A player must score 61 holes to win, instead of the 121 holes for game in the six-card affair. Because of the advantage the first dealer gets from the shorter game, the nondealer receives 3 points as a handicap or spot, points that are usually recorded immediately after the initial dealer has been determined.

The Go Is Very Important

There is only one go in each deal. After a player gets a 2-point go (31 points) or a 1-point go (last playable card, but under 31 points), the cards are *not* played.

Average Scores

The crib can still be expected to yield 5 points, but the average dealer's or pone's hand (with one card less) is worth less than 5 points. In the shorter playing process, dealer can expect to peg 2 points; pone, 1 point plus.

Every point is of great value, because the scoring level is so low. Master players stress playing for the go, which wins or loses 1 or 2 points.

Balking Is Favored

Pone must try even harder to discard two cards that tend to balk or contain the dealer's crib, if it is necessary to sacrifice the scoring potential of the cards retained, because the crib consists of five cards including the starter card, while the hand of each player, again including the starter card, includes only four cards.

In the showing, dealer or pone will very rarely get more than 12 points; but the five-card crib, as in the six-card game, readily scores from 12 to 29 holes.

Watching the Score

Masters of the science of Cribbage are constantly watching the positions on the board with a view toward the objective of 61 points and victory.

A player can expect about 4.5 (hand) + 5 (crib) + 2 (play) = 11.5 points as dealer, and 4.5 (hand) + 1 (play) = 5.5 points as pone. Thus after two deals, the average score is about 17 points for each player (compared to 29 points in the six-card game).

As the game progresses, on the average, first dealer goes ahead by 6 points each time he deals, only to lose this advantage when he is pone. Although this averages out to the 3-point handicap second dealer received at the beginning of the game, in fact dealer has an advantage, as he is likely to reach 61 while dealing before opponent has time to deal and catch up.

By watching the score, player can tell not only if he's ahead but if he's ahead (or behind) as much as can be expected from his current position as dealer or pone. He can adjust his strategy accordingly, either by pushing and speculating or by balking the crib and taking a conservative approach.

Special Regulations

There are a few more regulations that are different in five-card Cribbage. Three cards of a suit in dealer's or pone's hand constitute a flush in the showing: player scores 3 holes, one for each card. If the turned-up card is of the same suit, a fourth point is added. A flush in the crib is counted, as usual, only when all four cards and the turned-up card are of the same suit; such a crib flush counts 5 holes. During the play, flushes are disregarded.

Discarding and Other Tips

You as pone should balk, balk, balk the crib. Use the methods discussed at the beginning of part IV under "Basics of Discarding." The crib in five-card Cribbage is the same as in the usual game, so the same principles apply.

Play Cribbage for Fun, for Health, and for Love

If you as dealer have no pair to discard, put down the cards that are as close in rank as possible, hoping that the two cards discarded by pone and the starter card will build a sequence.

Other things being equal, lay out two cards of the same suit for your crib, in order not to eliminate the possibility of a flush.

It is good strategy to avoid breaking up a sequence in dealer's hand; it's especially good when such a sequence is a flush.

Otherwise, tend to favor the crib even at the expense of your hand. Crib hands are larger and higher-scoring. In fact, your only chance of a big catch-up score is in the crib.

Old Cribbage players do not die. They merely fail to count all their points.

Winning Odds for the Dealer

One trip around the Cribbage board, 61 points, is all that is required for victory in five-card Cribbage. Remember, an initial spot of 3 points is awarded to the nondealer at the start of the game.

Odds of the Five-Card Game

Here is an interesting table that was included in 1886 by Dick and Fitzgerald in their rulebook of cards, *Hoyle's Games*. First, situations that favor the dealer are listed; then, even-money situations; and finally, situations that favor the pone.

TIE SCORE (HOLES)	DEALER'S WINNING ODDS
5	6–4
10	12–11
15	7–4
20	6–4
25	11–10
30	9–5
35	7–6
40	10–9
45	12–8
50	5–2
55	21–20
60	2–1

	DEALER'S WINNING ODDS
Dealer needs 3, pone needs 4	5–1
15 points of the end	3–1
Same, when 15 of the end	8–1
Dealer needs 6, pone 11	10–1
Dealer is 10 ahead	4½–1
10 ahead and near the end of game	12–1
Dealer needs 16, pone 11	21–20

	ODDS
Players even at 59 holes	even
Nondealer is 3 ahead—not within 20 of the end	even
Dealer needs 14, pone 9	even
Dealer needs 11, pone 7	even

	PONE'S WINNING ODDS
Players even at 56 holes	7–5
Even at 57	7–4
Even at 58	3–2
Dealer needs 20, pone 17	5–4
Dealer is 5 points behind, before turning last corner	6–5
Dealer is 31, pone 36	6–4
Dealer is 36, pone 41	7–4

To fully enjoy Cribbage, the author recommends that you play both the five-card and six-card versions. Our correspondents in England report that in many areas five-card Cribbage remains the favorite.

Oddity in the Five-Card Game

For players who are interested in the unusual and the possibility of freak happenings, here is a situation to analyze.

It is possible for a player who hasn't pegged a single hole and who is 56 points behind his adversary, to win the game 61 to 60 within two deals.

One-Card Discard

An American variant begins like five-card Cribbage in that five cards are dealt to each player—and two cards into the crib.

Each contestant discards only one card to the crib, retaining four cards in his hand. Except for the discard, this variant is played and scored like six-card Cribbage.

VII

Other Variations

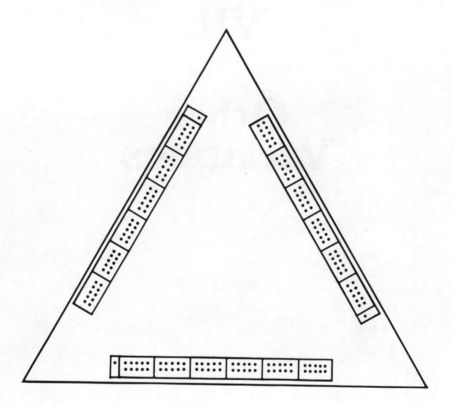

Three-Handed Cribbage

When a trio of Cribbage buffs assemble around a perforated wooden slab there is plenty of action, and the pegs can really fly.

Strategy is complicated by the addition of a third player. In play it is a good idea to favor a trailing adversary at the expense of a leading one.

Early Cribbage freaks constructed a board for threesomes with three separate sets of 61 holes. This evolved into the modern rectangular or oval board with three parallel lanes—a refinement which has contributed greatly to the excitement of the match by displaying the players' relative positions in their struggle to reach the game hole.

Two popular forms of three-handed play are in vogue: (1) each contestant competes on an individual basis, and (2) two join in a partnership against the third person.

Except as noted, the standard two-handed rules guide the play.

Play as Competing Individuals

1. The first dealer is chosen by the cut of the pack with the low card awarded the deal. In case of a tie the old adage "Two tie, all tie" applies, and all three players cut again until the low person is decided.

2. Number of cards: Each participant is dealt five cards, one at a time, and a sixteenth card is dealt into the crib. (A variation is to deal five cards to each player except the dealer, who receives six cards by taking the sixteenth card into his hand. Then dealer discards two cards instead of one as below.)

3. Each player discards one card to the crib.

4. The eldest or senior hand—that is, the player to the dealer's left—makes the initial lead in the pegging series. Pone, who sits on

the dealer's right, plays the second card, and the dealer, the third card.

5. The first player reaching the 121st hole is the winner. (A variation: After a player reaches the win hole, the two remaining participants continue to the finish, thus determining the runner-up.)

6. To keep score, use two regular Cribbage boards; or better, purchase or construct a board with three lanes of holes.

7. When a contestant cannot make a play, he says, "Go," and the next player to the left must make a play if able to do so. The turn then moves to the third player until the series is completed. The go is scored by the last person to make the play.

8. The eldest position shows first and records his holes. Then pone shows, followed by the dealer. Finally, the crib is counted.

9. The deal passes to the left.

Partnership Play

Four-Handed Competition

A very competitive but sociable form of Cribbage is played with partners sitting opposite as in Bridge. During discards to the crib and during the play partners must be cooperative in order to garner the most points from their combined cards.

Game is 121 points, twice around the board, and a side is lurched if it does not get 91 points.

Partners may be decided by a challenge, by mutual agreement, or by cutting the cards, the two low cards competing against the two highs.

The Deal

Decide which two adversaries are to record the score, for only one board is used. These two parties cut the pack; the low card wins the initial deal.

After the cards are properly shuffled, pone, the player on the dealer's right, must cut the pack. This is important, because one of the players usually sees the bottom card as the shuffle is completed. The advantage of knowing one card that is out of play may decide the contest.

Dealer distributes the cards one at a time, clockwise around the table beginning with the senior hand, the player who sits to the left of the dealer.

The Crib

The crib is the property of the dealer. Each player pitches in one card; players and crib then have four cards each.

The left-hand adversary must discard first, and so around the table, the dealer laying out last. Before you discard, always know which side owns the crib.

Deciding on just one card to be discarded is seldom difficult. Fives are the best cards to lay out to your own or your partner's crib, but *not* to an opponent's crib.

In general, low cards from the deuce up help the crib, while kings and aces are balkers or killers. Sevens and eights also help the crib.

If you are confident that the game will be decided during the pegging and that you will not need to show your hand, discarding a helping card to an adversary's crib will not affect the outcome. Split your medium and high pairs and keep the low pegging cards.

The Starter

When the players have discarded to the crib, the pack is cut to select the starter card.

The person to the dealer's left must cut the cards, leaving at least four in each packet. (Note that the right-hand adversary cut before the deal.)

Dealer lifts up the top card of the lower packet, and the top section is returned to the original position. Dealer then places the card face up on top of the deck.

If a jack becomes the starting card, the dealer's side immediately scores 2 points for his heels.

Scoring

The partnership scores are pooled and recorded on the board by one member of each side. The other two players are not allowed to touch the board or the pegs; however, each may prompt his partner and point out any omissions or irregularities he discovers in the computation.

The person who marks scores has a troublesome task: he must maintain constant vigilance in order not to omit scoring points made by his partner (he is less likely to fail to record his own points). Nonmarking partner must acquire the habit of seeing that marking partner marks the full number gained.

Partners may assist each other in counting their cribs and hands, since their interests are mutual. They should also watch and check all scores that the adversaries claim and record.

To avoid confusion about which cards have been played, turn over all cards in a series after each go.

In four-handed Cribbage, a situation may arise in which neither of the dealer's opponents holds a single point in hand. The dealer and his partner, with the assistance of a knave turned up, can make 61 points in one deal, while the adversaries only get 24 points. Such a situation may occur only once in many years.

Pegging and Strategy for Leadoff Player

The senior hand, in choosing the initial lead of the first series, should exercise great care not only at the start but after every 1- or 2-point go.

A five is a bad lead because the chances of a tenth card succeeding it are so high; and an ace is seldom a good lead, since a good play for the next player is a tenth card, bringing the count to 11. Your partner cannot pair him without making 21—a bad count, since the next player can probably hit 31 for 2 points.

The lead of a nine is not recommended because your left-hand adversary may bring the count to 15/2 with a six, and your partner does not dare to pair him since the count would then become 21. It is better to open with a six; if opponent makes a 15/2 with a nine, partner can safely pair the nine without fear of the opponent scoring triplets (another nine would take the count over 31).

Keep this advice in mind: Never make the number 21 yourself, or compel your partner to do so.

Deuces, treys, and fours are safe leads, which force opponent to set up a possible 15/2 combination for your partner.

Pegging and Strategy for Second Player

The second player must observe caution in pairing a card, in case of triplets. He is safer if he sees one of the two missing cards as the starter card or in his hand, or if he has seen one already played.

Second hand should not play closely on, unless compelled by the card. If your right-hand adversary leads a three, and you reply with a two or a four, you present your left-hand antagonist with the opportunity of forming a sequence. Playing off with a six or higher card would be safer.

On the other hand, you may play on intentionally, to tempt adversary to form a sequence when you feel your partner can cash in on a longer sequence. Or the board may tell you that a few holes are of paramount value and should be pegged at any risk.

As second player, you are safer hitting 15/2 than pairing the preceding card.

If the score indicates it is crucial to prevent opponents from scoring, second or other player should retain cards that are all wide apart.

Pegging and Strategy for Third Player

The third player should keep the count under 21 so his partner, rather than dealer, has the best chance to get a go of 31 or under.

Pegging and Strategy for Dealer

As last discarder, don't give an ace, deuce, or trey to the crib.

Playing the Board

Life is based on averages. In sports, key figures can be batting and earned run averages, yards gained per pass received, or percent of free throws hooped; elsewhere in life, the average lifespan, average amount a family spends on food, and so on, are very important. As time passes we see statistics and statistics, and more statistics.

Cribbage players fell into that same obsession many years ago. They studied and compared scores of hands, the pegging, and the crib for four-handed play and came up with figures for the average player that are close to those for two-handed play: 7 for the hand, 5 for the crib, and 4.5 for the play. (Experts may average a little more.)

The nondealing partners should each get 11.5 points on a deal. The partnership gets 23 points.

Dealer's partner gets 11.5 points, but dealer gets 16.5 (including 5 for the crib), so the dealing partnership should average 28 points per deal.

Therefore, the following pattern of scoring of progressive totals represents average play, where A and B are first dealer and partner, and Y and Z are first dealer's opponents.

DEAL NO.	A–B HOLES	Y–Z HOLES
1	28	23
2	51	51
3	79	74
4	102	102
5	119	121 and wins

The seating arrangement:

```
┌─────────────┐
│      Y      │
│  A       B  │
│      Z      │
└─────────────┘
```

A, the first dealer, also deals the fifth hand. On the fifth deal, each side pegs the average 9 points, raising the totals from 102 to 111. The showing of hands decides the game. According to the rules, Y (player to left of dealer) shows first, then B, Z, A, and the crib.

Y shows 7 holes and the Y–Z total advances to 118. B shows 7 holes and the A–B total advances to 118.

Z has 7 holes, so he can move his peg 3 holes into the game hole and win for dealer's opponents.

Predicting the Winner

A slight deviation from average, of course, can allow the first dealer's team to show the crucial crib hand and win.

1. The original nondealers have a very slight edge.

2. They should observe moderate caution in the first hand and pay close attention to the medium hands, which are the bread and butter of the average pattern.

3. They should watch the board continuously and compare their position with the opponents', maintaining an average position.

4. There will be fluctuations—highs and lows that upset averages and make the game more exciting, while suggesting modification of the game plan by using an aggressive offense or a conservative defense.

5. If trailing, team members must take every opportunity for pairing and should try to garner all possible points. With a comfortable lead, they should avoid playing on and should beware of the pairs.

6. On the fifth or sixth deal, if pegging appears to be the deciding factor, a team should retain its best pegging cards, no matter what they have to discard.

Crazee Cribbage: Variations on the Standard Game

There are 2 or 3 million Americans playing Cribbage every night, and there is always someone trying to invent a variation.

People get bored with activities or lack of activity when they have a losing streak, so they try to inject some novelty.

Under this heading of "Crazee Cribbage" we present a number of variations which have survived the acid tests of time and worldwide exposure.

Play in Reverse

This variant is just right for the unlucky player who is always on the short end of the score and who believes that his opponents always draw winning cards. The object is to push your opponent to the 121 mark, at which point he loses the game.

As pone, by discarding points to dealer's crib you create favorable pegging situations for him, and you spoil your own hand by retaining as few points as possible. You make all the "wrong" plays on purpose to push opponent to the game hole.

And, of course, he loses two games if you can lurch or skunk yourself by not reaching the 91st hole.

A very interesting hybrid!

Auction Cribbage

Auction Cribbage has been played in England and America for a decade.

The crib is up for grabs, and is awarded to the highest bidder. Bids in points are made alternately by the two adversaries, who are willing to reduce their total on the board for the privilege of purchasing the treasure box.

Included in the purchase price is the right to make the first play of the game, and also the right to show first. Near the end of a game, as scores near 121, possession of the crib as well as the opportunity to count first can be a great advantage, but to get the crib then, you will have to bid high, which serves as an equalizer.

Proponents of this arrangement insist it is the best way to make the game fairer, but we believe the intention really was to add some spice.

Marine Madness

Playing against the averages has been a favorite of the Marine Corps for many years in card games as well as in military tactics. On his turn, dealer is awarded 16 points, no more and no less, and does not count any pegging points in the play.

Pone counts his own hand and the pegging points he accumulates. Game is 121 holes.

This variant is actually a test of averages.

Seven-Card Cribbage

Number of players:	Two.
Deal:	Distribute cards one at a time, giving each player seven cards.

Crib: Each player discards two cards to the box and keeps five cards.

Hands: After discarding, each hand consists of six cards including the starter card. High-scoring combinations are readily formed.

Play and showing: Regular, as in six-card Cribbage.

Game: Player scoring 181 holes first wins.

Eleven-Card Cribbage

Number of players: Three.

Deal: Distribute cards one at a time, giving each player eleven cards.

Crib: Each contestant discards three cards to the crib and keeps eight cards.

Hands: Each player forms two hands of four cards each.

Starter: Eldest hand, player to left, cuts the starting card. Each player selects one of his two hands for the playing-pegging process.

Hand no. 1: The game proceeds from the left of the dealer clockwise.

Showing: Senior hand shows first, then pone, then dealer. Crib is not shown until hand no. 2.

Hand no. 2: Play and show as in hand no. 1. At end, dealer turns the nine-card crib, rejects one card, and then forms two four-card cribs and scores each using the starter card as the fifth card.

Game: Player with high score after each player has dealt once wins.

Eleven-Card Partnership Cribbage

Number of Players:	Four, with partners sitting opposite each other.
Deal:	Eleven cards to each player. Discard is three cards to the crib.
Crib:	Dealer forms three cribs of four cards each.
Play and showing:	As in eleven-card Cribbage.
Game:	Player with high score after each player has dealt once wins.

Thirteen-Card Cribbage

From England comes a variant in which thirteen cards are dealt to each of two players. Each rejects five cards.

The starter card is turned; then each player divides his eight cards into two cribbage hands.

Each player decides which hand to play first and the pegging process starts. Hand no. 1 is played and shown as usual; the crib is not shown yet.

After the combatants play hand no. 2, pegging and counting up, the dealer turns over the ten cards of the crib, throws out two cards, and forms two four-card cribs. Then he scores each crib as a five-card hand with the help of the starter card.

Four deals make up each game. The high score wins.

Solitary Moments

Everyone has some extra time on his hands, while waiting for someone, or just waiting for dinner; this is an opportune time to relax and entertain oneself with a game of Solitaire.

You are not wasting time, because you are practicing the memorizing of combinations. The skills of counting points quickly and recognizing the scoring of unusual hands are sharpened.

Type no. 1: Shuffle and cut the deck. Deal out three cards to your hand, two cards to the crib, and three more to your hand.

Pick up the six cards and decide on a two-card discard. Of

course, make the choice from the dealer's standpoint and don't balk the crib (now of four cards) if you can help it.

Turn up the starter card; since there is no play, simply count the hand and the crib for points (including the starter in both), recording the points on the board.

Place the starter on the bottom of the deck and lay the eight cards which have been played aside. Then deal out the eight cards of the hand and crib for the next hand, score, and repeat the procedure (treating the same card as the starter) until there are only four cards left in the pack. Turn the four cards over and record the points as for a hand without a starter.

Thus, you have dealt out six hands, six cribs, and a seventh hand without a starter. Consider your game won when you score 91 points and have gone through the deck only once.

If a second player is present, you may play Solitaire competitively, each having a deck and scoring on his or her side of the board. Play as above and compare scores, after each player has gone through his deck, to decide the winner.

Keep a Record

It is educational if you keep a record of the points scored in each game of Solitaire.

Here is a suggested form to use.

HAND NO.	HIS HEELS TURNED UP	POINTS IN HAND	POINTS IN CRIB
1			
2			
3			
4			
etc.			

After you accumulate data from several thousand games, you will really have a conversation piece for your Cribbage cronies as you report your results and compare them with the accepted average. From the practice you've accumulated, you may have an edge over these same cronies.

Type no. 2: Form a tableau of sixteen cards, four by four, attempting to arrange the best scoring hands (vertical and horizontal) as in the illustration on the following page.

Draw a card off the top of the deck and place it in square marked with an *X*, face up.

Place the next card you draw next to the first, in one of the eight squares marked with an *O*.

After a card is once played in a square, it must remain there until the end of the game. The third card must be "next to" the second card in the same way.

Toward the end, if no "next to" square is open, you may use squares that are two squares away; if none of these are open, you may use squares that are three squares away.

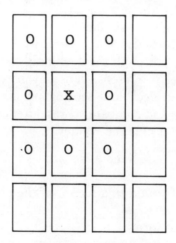

Double Solitaire

Two players decide who is to make the first deal. Dealer shuffles and pone cuts the pack.

Dealer turns the top four cards, one at a time, and places them in a row horizontally on the table. The fifth card is dealt face down to the side to begin the construction of the crib.

The sixth card is turned and may be placed under any of the exposed cards, keeping in mind the goal of creating the best scoring hands possible. After a card is placed, it may not be moved. The seventh, eighth, and ninth cards are placed in the second row, and the tenth card is thrown face down to the crib.

Now fill up the third and fourth rows, remembering to deal the fifteenth and the twentieth cards to the crib. There are four *vertical* hands and a four-card crib.

Pone cuts the pack and dealer turns the starter card. There is no play. The vertical hands are shown and scored, then the crib. (For both, include the starter as a fifth card.)

The second player then deals a set of twenty cards. When he is finished, the high score wins.

This variant may also be played by one player. Beginners especially will profit by indulging in this pleasure.

VIII

League
and
Tournament
Competition

How to Conduct a League

The fun of Cribbage is found in enjoying the game with many other people; a league or a tournament promotes good fellowship and affords players the opportunity to demonstrate their Cribbage-playing abilities.

Clubs and recreation centers sponsor leagues that play once a week and then, for a grand finale, stage an elimination tournament.

Round-Robin Series

Here is a schedule for league play for eight players, pairs, or teams.

ROUND 1	ROUND 2	ROUND 3	ROUND 4	ROUND 5	ROUND 6	ROUND 7
1–7	1–6	1–5	1–4	1–3	1–2	1–8
8–6	7–5	6–4	5–3	4–2	3–8	2–7
2–5	8–4	7–3	6–2	5–8	4–7	3–6
3–4	2–3	8–2	7–8	6–7	5–6	4–5

On the scheduled evening, league members draw for position number and follow the above schedule of competition. After everyone has played everyone else, the standings are based on the Wergin match-point system.

If you have more players than can be accommodated by this suggested schedule, you may set up your own round-robin pattern; if you need help, consult a bowling secretary or the athletic director of your local high school.

Wergin System of Match-Point Scoring

Deciding a championship on the basis of games won and lost is not accurate enough, because such a system fails to consider the point spread in the defeat of an adversary. In football we read, every week, the national rankings of the teams. The sportswriters who vote in these pools rate the teams on number and percent of wins and also on the scores they win or lose by.

The following match-point system for rating Cribbage players in league competition was devised for the U.S. Forest Products League at Madison, Wisconsin, and has been used for years by the league in deciding its championships.

Winning player of each game receives 121 match points, plus a bonus of 20 match points, plus the number of points he wins by.

If he limits his opponent to 89 or less points, a "skunk" in this system, he receives a bonus of 5 match points; 10 match points if opponent fails to make 61 points.

The loser receives the number of points he scored in the game.

Example: Dukes defeats Goeden 121-86, skunking the latter and winning by 35 points.

Dukes gets $121 + 20 + 35 + 5 = 181$ match points.

Goeden gets 86 match points.

Typical Standings

With eight players competing, the standings may look like this after the first game.

	GAME	WIN	POINT SPREAD	SKUNK	MATCH POINTS
Dukes	121	20	35	5	181
Hilgers	121	20	18	—	159
White	121	20	7	—	148
Hessel	121	20	1	—	142
Siebert	120	—	—	—	120
Blackney	114	—	—	—	114
Becker	103	—	—	—	103
Goeden	86	—	—	—	86

Personal Record Form

To keep an individual record of the seven games played in an evening, you may employ forms following this pattern:

Name of Player _____ Date _____

	GAME POINTS	WIN	POINT SPREAD	SKUNK	MATCH POINTS
Game 1					
2					
3					
4					
5					
6					
7					
TOTALS					

How to Conduct an Elimination Tournament

Plan Ahead

If you intend to stage a Cribbage Tournament, plan thoroughly to ensure that the event runs smoothly. A little foresight will keep you from getting into difficulties and being the object of criticism. Your objective is to keep the players satisfied so that they will look forward to the next meet; here are some simple but crucial steps to help you reach this objective.

Have some organization sponsor the event so that you will have a place to play without charge. Call a meeting of interested leaders, and select your chairman, whose job is to supervise and direct committees. Then appoint your drawing, publicity, and awards committees.

Set the Date

Before deciding the date, consider all possible problems, such as weather, conflicts with athletic and other events, and holidays. Also decide on the entry fee and the number of sessions to be played.

To keep the players happy, select a tournament site with adequate tables, chairs, lighting, and rest rooms, and with facilities for lunch and refreshments. From your mailing list and past experience you can make quite accurate predictions of how many players will show up, but be prepared to have tables and playing space available for an overflow. Of course, it is easier to have advance registration.

Duties of the Drawing Committee

Set the time and start on time. Permit no delays. Mix together players from different areas or cities so that there is an opportunity to initiate new friendships. Have the drawing tickets and record cards prepared in advance, and have scorecards and new decks of playing cards ready. Require players to bring along their own Cribbage boards, but have a few extra boards on hand.

Publicity Committee

At least two or three weeks in advance announce, with posters and news releases to local media, the date of your tournament, and the names of committee members and prominent players who will be participating. Keep the information before the public; arrange for periodic reminders in newspapers, organizational newsletters, etc. Contact television and radio stations, supplying them with announcements and news items; generally it is good policy to maintain friendly relations with the media, because they can give you lots of help. Find out the name of the PSA (public service announcements) director in each case, and contact him directly.

In your advertising and press releases, use names and pictures, and play up prominent individuals who are expected to participate.

The most effective means of recruiting players is a direct first-class mail campaign launched two or three weeks before the actual event. Your announcement should include a registration form—to be filled out and returned to you by the prospective participant—and a request for advance payment of the entry fee. Your chances of packing a full house are greater when a large number of people have already paid to attend.

A few days before the tournament, release a news article to all papers and stations in the area, giving a list of the names of the probable participants. Intensify your advertising campaign, and make sure your posters are still up, replacing those that have disappeared or been damaged.

To foster good public relations and to score advertising points for your next event, add the final touch to your publicity: announce prize-winners to all the media, providing a follow-up to your earlier stories.

Keep Expenses to a Minimum

Operate efficiently to keep expenses low. Try to avoid paying salaries or expenses to committee members. Usually a tavern, restaurant, or private club will provide facilities in exchange for the patronage it will receive.

Awards Committee

Before the tournament starts, announce how many prizes will be awarded, and the amount of each. If there are many entries, announce the ratio of prizes to players, 1 to 5, 1 to 7, 1 to 10, etc.

Be sure that the players understand under what conditions the tournament is being staged. It will save a lot of grief if you keep an official rulebook on hand and appoint a tournament judge to resolve all problems that may come up.

Double Elimination Tournament

It has been our experience that double elimination competition is superior to single elimination because Cribbage fanatics want to play as much as possible—not to go to the sidelines after one loss.

This format may be used either for an individual championship or a pair tournament. Draw for positions and insert names accordingly.

In double elimination each individual or pair must lose two matches to be eliminated. Winner of match 13 must defeat match 7 winner in two matches to win the championship, while match 7 winner needs only one victory.

The illustration on the following page shows double elimination for eight entries. With sixteen entries, just double the format.

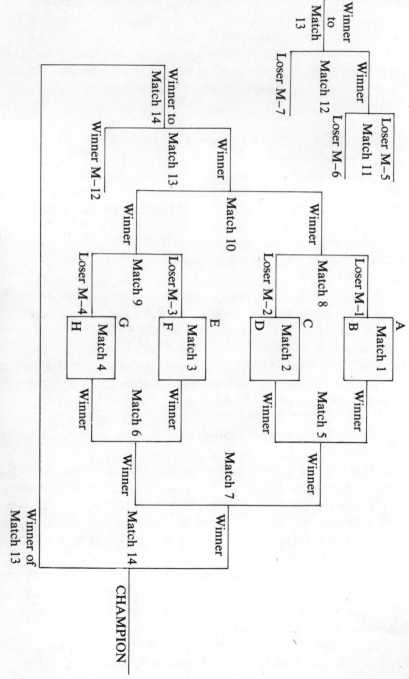

Double Elimination Tournament

What to Do with 150 Entries

You may be besieged by 100 or more entries, so be prepared. Here is a plan for qualifying applicants for a place in the 64-player elimination bracket.

Qualifying rounds will be played on the first three nights; after each night's play, the low-scoring players are eliminated from the tournament.

For each night, draw up schedules for each player so that he will compete against eight other players. You may use the following sample for guidance.

GAME	TABLE
1	1
2	8
3	15
4	22
5	29
6	4
7	11
8	18

In scheduling, place two players at each table.

Rate According to Match Points

Use the Wergin match-point system to determine the standings of the players for the first night. With 150 entries, eliminate the players finishing 129th to 150th from further play.

On the second night set the cutoff at 96; those in 97th through 128th position are eliminated.

The third night, set the cutoff at 64.

The fourth night, players draw for position on the 64-bracket plan and begin a double elimination tournament. The top eight players of the qualifying rounds may be seeded to start the elimination rounds. Play as many matches as possible the first day.

A match should consist of two out of three games and should not use the match-point rating system from here on. The semifinals and the finals will be won by four out of seven games, with a skunk counting as two games.

If you have difficulties in setting up the brackets for 64 players, consult someone experienced in conducting tournaments.

Wisconsin Method of Rating Players: Net Games

A simpler method is used by the Wisconsin Cribbage Association. Players are ranked by games: each winning game receives a rating of 2 game points, with 1 point for skunking an opponent, and another point for double skunking. The Association has taken the position that a skunk does not have the value of a whole game but should receive the equivalent of one-half game. In order to avoid fractions, the 2–3–4 scoring was adopted.

There will be ties, which are determined by net point spread, e.g., a player who wins by 5 points, then loses by 10, then wins by 30 has a net point spread of 25.

Example: Twenty-one preliminary games; the first 28 places in a 100-player tournament are filled by players who have accumulated twenty-seven or more game points. Six players tie (on the game point basis) for the remaining four slots.

Place		Game Points	Sum of Winning Spread	Sum of Losing Spread	Net Spread
29	Green	26	180	73	107
30	Peterson	26	172	69	103
31	Schmitz	26	146	63	83
32	Hessel	26	140	70	70
33	Becker	26	155	90	65
34	O'Connor	26	152	99	53

The net point spreads determine who qualifies. If there is still a tie, the player losing the fewer games qualifies. If still tied, either have a playoff of one game or toss a coin.

The top 32 players are placed in the elimination brackets and the tournament proceeds head-to-head until the winner is determined.

Tournament officials may want to set up a consolation series or partnership tournament for those who failed in the qualification rounds.

Seeding

We close with single elimination charts for seeded players (eight and sixteen entries). The player with the highest qualifying score is seeded no. 1, and so on.

Individual Tournament Record Card

Name_____

ID No._____

WISCONSIN CRIBBAGE ASSOCIATION
Official Scorecard

Game	Game Points	Point Spread +	Point Spread −	Opponent's Signatures	ID No.
1					
2					
3					
4					
5					
6					
7					
8					
9					
10					
11					
12					
13					
14					
15					
16					
17					
18					
19					
20					
21					
TOTAL				Checked by:	

Net Points

Each person plays three games against seven different opponents. Results verified by the opponent who signs the record card and enters his identification number.

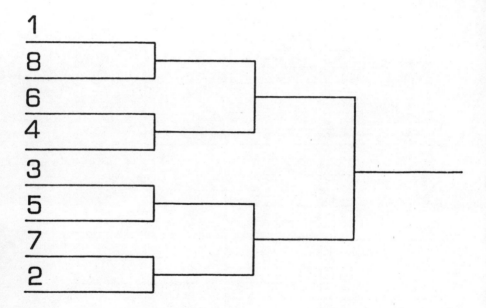

**Single Elimination Tournament Chart for
Eight Players or Fewer**

**Single Elimination Tournament Chart for
Sixteen Players or Fewer**

IX

All
Possible
Combinations

Back in 1882, William H. Green published a booklet in San Diego, California, entitled *Key to Cribbage*, which listed 6,175 hands—every possible numerical combination for the showing of Cribbage hands of four cards plus starter. The booklet was reprinted in 1975 by the Gamblers Book Club of Las Vegas, Nevada.

After each combination, the first column gives the "regular" score. The second column adds 1 point for his nobs if there is a jack in the hand. The third column adds 4 points for a four-card flush if there are four different denominations in the hand. (The crib is not eligible for this bonus.)

The fourth column adds 5 points for a five-card flush (indicating the starter) if there are five different denominations in the hand. And the fifth column adds 6 points if a hand that qualifies for a five-card flush contains a jack (1 more point for his heels if the jack is not the starter card).

You can quickly refer to this list and verify your counting of a hand.

The most common scoring hand is 6 points (2,597 combinations); 1,833 hands score 8 points, often considered an average Cribbage score.

Many of these hands are unlikely to occur in actual play; after discarding two undesirable cards, a player is not usually stuck with a 0-point hand.

How to Use the Key

It does not matter which of the five cards is the one turned up, but in order to find the answer, commence with the lowest card first, including the one turned up. Below are given a few examples:

Hand.				Turn-up.	To be placed thus.				
10	2	3	1	2	1	2	2	3	10
5	5	3	4	5	3	4	5	5	5
8	7	7	6	9	6	7	7	8	9
6	6	3	3	3	3	3	3	6	6
3	3	K	K	8	3	3	8	K	K
6	1	7	8	1	1	1	6	7	8
1	3	2	5	4	1	2	3	4	5
10	10	7	9	J	7	9	10	10	J
5	5	4	4	6	4	4	5	5	6
K	K	K	J	Q	J	Q	K	K	K

ABBREVIATIONS

The following abbreviations are used in this work :

J—Jack.   Fl—Flush.   Q—Queen.

Seq—Sequence. K—King.   . .—Impossible.

Key to Cribbage

CARDS.					Fifteens, Prs & Seq	With J of Turn-up	If Flush in Hand	If Fl with Turn-up	If Fl&J of Turn up	CARDS.					Fifteens, Prs & Seq	With J of Turn-up	If Flush in Hand	If Fl with Turn-up	If Fl&J of Turn up
1	1	1	1	2	12					1	1	1	4	8	8				
1	1	1	1	3	12					1	1	1	4	9	12				
1	1	1	1	4	12					1	1	1	4	10	12				
1	1	1	1	5	12					1	1	1	4	J	12	13			
1	1	1	1	6	12					1	1	1	4	Q	12				
1	1	1	1	7	12					1	1	1	4	K	12				
1	1	1	1	8	12					1	1	1	5	5	8				
1	1	1	1	9	12					1	1	1	5	6	6				
1	1	1	1	10	12					1	1	1	5	7	8				
1	1	1	1	J	12	13				1	1	1	5	8	12				
1	1	1	1	Q	12					1	1	1	5	9	12				
1	1	1	1	K	12					1	1	1	5	10	8				
1	1	1	2	2	8					1	1	1	5	J	8	9			
1	1	1	2	3	15					1	1	1	5	Q	8				
1	1	1	2	4	6					1	1	1	5	K	8				
1	1	1	2	5	6					1	1	1	6	6	10				
1	1	1	2	6	6					1	1	1	6	7	12				
1	1	1	2	7	6					1	1	1	6	8	12				
1	1	1	2	8	6					1	1	1	6	9	8				
1	1	1	2	9	6					1	1	1	6	10	6				
1	1	1	2	10	8					1	1	1	6	J	6	7			
1	1	1	2	J	8	9				1	1	1	6	Q	6				
1	1	1	2	Q	8					1	1	1	6	K	6				
1	1	1	2	K	8					1	1	1	7	7	14				
1	1	1	3	3	8					1	1	1	7	8	8				
1	1	1	3	4	6					1	1	1	7	9	6				
1	1	1	3	5	6					1	1	1	7	10	6				
1	1	1	3	6	6					1	1	1	7	J	6	7			
1	1	1	3	7	6					1	1	1	7	Q	6				
1	1	1	3	8	6					1	1	1	7	K	6				
1	1	1	3	9	8					1	1	1	8	8	8				
1	1	1	3	10	12					1	1	1	8	9	6				
1	1	1	3	J	12	13				1	1	1	8	10	6				
1	1	1	3	Q	12					1	1	1	8	J	6	7			
1	1	1	3	K	12					1	1	1	8	Q	6				
1	1	1	4	4	8					1	1	1	8	K	6				
1	1	1	4	5	6					1	1	1	9	9	8				
1	1	1	4	6	6					1	1	1	9	10	6				
1	1	1	4	7	6					1	1	1	9	J	6	7			

KEY TO CRIBBAGE.

CARDS.					Fifteens, Pairs & Seq..	With Jack of Turn-up..	If Flush in Hand......	If Flush with Turn-up.	If Fl& Jack of Turn-up
1	1	1	9	Q	6				
1	1	1	9	K	6				
1	1	1	10	10	8				
1	1	1	10	J	6	7			
1	1	1	10	Q	6				
1	1	1	10	K	6				
1	1	1	J	J	8	9			
1	1	1	J	Q	6	7	7		
1	1	1	J	K	6	7			
1	1	1	Q	Q	8				
1	1	1	Q	K	6				
1	1	1	K	K	8				
1	1	2	2	2	8				
1	1	2	2	3	16				
1	1	2	2	4	4				
1	1	2	2	5	4				
1	1	2	2	6	4				
1	1	2	2	7	4				
1	1	2	2	8	4				
1	1	2	2	9	6				
1	1	2	2	10	8				
1	1	2	2	J	8	9			
1	1	2	2	Q	8				
1	1	2	2	K	8				
1	1	2	3	3	16				
1	1	2	3	4	10		14		
1	1	2	3	5	8		12		
1	1	2	3	6	8		12		
1	1	2	3	7	8		12		
1	1	2	3	8	10		14		
1	1	2	3	9	12		16		
1	1	2	3	10	12		16		
1	1	2	3	J	12	13	16		
1	1	2	3	Q	12		16		
1	1	2	3	K	12		16		
1	1	2	4	4	4				
1	1	2	4	5	2		6		
1	1	2	4	6	2		6		
1	1	2	4	7	4		8		
1	1	2	4	8	6		10		
1	1	2	4	9	6		10		
1	1	2	4	10	6		10		
1	1	2	4	J	6	7	10		
1	1	2	4	Q	6		10		
1	1	2	4	K	6		10		
1	1	2	5	5	4				
1	1	2	5	6	4		8		
1	1	2	5	7	6		10		
1	1	2	5	8	6		10		
1	1	2	5	9	6		10		
1	1	2	5	10	4		8		
1	1	2	5	J	4	5	8		
1	1	2	5	Q	4		8		
1	1	2	5	K	4		8		
1	1	2	6	6	8				
1	1	2	6	7	6		10		
1	1	2	6	8	6		10		
1	1	2	6	9	4		8		
1	1	2	6	10	2		6	6	
1	1	2	6	J	2	3	6	6	
1	1	2	6	Q	2		6	6	
1	1	2	6	K	2			6	
1	1	2	7	7	8				
1	1	2	7	8	4		8		
1	1	2	7	9	2		6		
1	1	2	7	10	2		6		
1	1	2	7	J	2	3	6		
1	1	2	7	Q	2		6		
1	1	2	7	K	2		6		
1	1	2	8	8	4				
1	1	2	8	9	2		6		
1	1	2	8	10	2		6		
1	1	2	8	J	2	3	6	6	
1	1	2	8	Q	2		6		
1	1	2	8	K	2		6		
1	1	2	9	9	4				
1	1	2	9	10	2		6		
1	1	2	9	J	2	3	6		

KEY TO CRIBBAGE.

Cards					Fifteens, Pairs & Seq.	With Jack of Turn-up.	If Flush in Hand.	If Flush with Turn-up.	If Fl & Jack of Turn-up.
1	1	2	9	Q	2		6		
1	1	2	9	K	2		6		
1	1	2	10	10	4		6		
1	1	2	10	J	2	3	6		
1	1	2	10	Q	2		6		
1	1	2	10	K	2		6		
1	1	2	J	J	4	5			
1	1	2	J	Q	2	3	6		
1	1	2	J	K	2	3	6		
1	1	2	Q	Q	4				
1	1	2	Q	K	2		6		
1	1	2	K	K	8				
1	1	3	3	4	4				
1	1	3	3	5	4				
1	1	3	3	6	4				
1	1	3	3	7	6				
1	1	3	3	8	8				
1	1	3	3	9	6				
1	1	3	3	10	8				
1	1	3	3	J	8	9			
1	1	3	3	Q	8				
1	1	3	3	K	8				
1	1	3	4	4	4				
1	1	3	4	5	5		9		
1	1	3	4	6	4		8		
1	1	3	4	7	6		10		
1	1	3	4	8	4		8		
1	1	3	4	9	4		8		
1	1	3	4	10	8		12		
1	1	3	4	J	8	9	12		
1	1	3	4	Q	8		12		
1	1	3	4	K	8		12		
1	1	3	5	5	6				
1	1	3	5	6	6		10		
1	1	3	5	7	4		8		
1	1	3	5	8	4		8		
1	1	3	5	9	6		10		
1	1	3	5	10	6		10		
1	1	3	5	J	8	7	10		
1	1	3	5	Q	6		10		
1	1	3	5	K	6		10		
1	1	3	6	6	6				
1	1	3	6	7	4		8		
1	1	3	6	8	6		10		
1	1	3	6	9	4		8		
1	1	3	6	10	4		8		
1	1	3	6	J	4	5	8		
1	1	3	6	Q	4		8		
1	1	3	6	K	4		8		
1	1	3	7	7	8				
1	1	3	7	8	4		8		
1	1	3	7	9	2		6		
1	1	3	7	10	4		8		
1	1	3	7	J	4	5	8		
1	1	3	7	Q	4		8		
1	1	3	7	K	4		8		
1	1	3	8	9	2		6		
1	1	3	8	10	4		8		
1	1	3	8	J	4	5	8		
1	1	3	8	Q	4		8		
1	1	3	8	K	4		8		
1	1	3	9	9	4				
1	1	3	9	10	4		8		
1	1	3	9	J	4	5	8		
1	1	3	9	Q	4		8		
1	1	3	9	K	4		8		
1	1	3	10	10	8				
1	1	3	10	J	6	7	10		
1	1	3	10	Q	6		10		
1	1	3	10	K	6		10		
1	1	3	J	J	8	9			
1	1	3	J	Q	6	7	10		
1	1	3	J	K	6	7	10		
1	1	3	Q	Q	8				
1	1	3	Q	K	6		10		
1	1	3	K	K	8				

KEY TO CRIBBAGE.

Cards					Fifteens, Pairs & Seq.	With Jack of Turn-up	If Flush in Hand	If Flush with Turn-up	If Fl & Jack of Turn-up
1	1	4	4	4	8				
1	1	4	4	5	6				
1	1	4	4	6	8				
1	1	4	4	7	6				
1	1	4	4	8	4				
1	1	4	4	9	8				
1	1	4	4	10	12				
1	1	4	4	J	12	13			
1	1	4	4	Q	12				
1	1	4	4	K	12				
1	1	4	5	5	8				
1	1	4	5	6	7		11		
1	1	4	5	7	2		6		
1	1	4	5	8	4		8		
1	1	4	5	9	8		12		
1	1	4	5	10	8		12		
1	1	4	5	J	8	9	12		
1	1	4	5	Q	8		12		
1	1	4	5	K	8		12		
1	1	4	6	6	4				
1	1	4	6	7	4		8		
1	1	4	6	8	6		10		
1	1	4	6	9	6		10		
1	1	4	6	10	6		10		
1	1	4	6	J	6	7	10		
1	1	4	6	Q	6		10		
1	1	4	6	K	6		10		
1	1	4	7	7	8				
1	1	4	7	8	4		8		
1	1	4	7	9	4		8		
1	1	4	7	10	6		10		
1	1	4	7	J	6	7	10		
1	1	4	7	Q	6		10		
1	1	4	7	K	6		10		
1	1	4	8	9	4				
1	1	4	8	10	6		10		
1	1	4	8	J	6	7	10		
1	1	4	8	Q	6		10		

Cards					Fifteens, Pairs & Seq.	With Jack of Turn-up	If Flush in Hand	If Flush with Turn-up	If Fl & Jack of Turn-up
1	1	4	8	K	6		10		
1	1	4	9	9	8		12		
1	1	4	9	10	8		12		
1	1	4	9	J	8	9	12		
1	1	4	9	Q	8		12		
1	1	4	9	K	8		12		
1	1	4	10	10	12				
1	1	4	10	J	10	11	14		
1	1	4	10	Q	10		14		
1	1	4	10	K	10		14		
1	1	4	J	J	12	13			
1	1	4	J	Q	10	11	14		
1	1	4	J	K	10	11	14		
1	1	4	Q	Q	12				
1	1	4	Q	K	10		14		
1	1	4	K	K	12				
1	1	5	5	5	10				
1	1	5	5	6	4				
1	1	5	5	7	4				
1	1	5	5	8	8				
1	1	5	5	9	12				
1	1	5	5	10	8				
1	1	5	5	J	8	9			
1	1	5	5	Q	8				
1	1	5	5	K	8				
1	1	5	6	6	4				
1	1	5	6	7	7		11		
1	1	5	6	8	8		12		
1	1	5	6	9	8		12		
1	1	5	6	10	4		8		
1	1	5	6	J	4	5	8		
1	1	5	6	Q	4		8		
1	1	5	6	K	4		8		
1	1	5	7	7	8				
1	1	5	7	8	6		10		
1	1	5	7	9	6		10		
1	1	5	7	10	4		8		
1	1	5	7	J	4	5	8		
1	1	5	7	Q	4		8		

KEY TO CRIBBAGE.

CARDS					Fifteens, Pairs & Seq.	With Jack of Turn-up	If Flush in Hand	If Flush with Turn-up	If Fl& Jack of Turn-up
1	1	5	7	K	4	..	8	..	..
1	1	5	8	8	8	..	..	..	..
1	1	5	8	9	8	..	12	..	..
1	1	5	8	10	6	..	10	..	..
1	1	5	8	J	6	7	10	..	..
1	1	5	8	Q	6	..	10	..	..
1	1	5	8	K	6	..	10	..	..
1	1	5	9	9	12	..	..	..	..
1	1	5	9	10	8	..	12	..	..
1	1	5	9	J	8	9	12	..	..
1	1	5	9	Q	8	..	12	..	..
1	1	5	9	K	8	..	12	..	..
1	1	5	10	10	8	..	..	..	..
1	1	5	10	J	6	7	10	..	..
1	1	5	10	Q	6	..	10	..	..
1	1	5	10	K	6	..	10	..	..
1	1	5	J	J	8	9	..	..	..
1	1	5	J	Q	6	7	10	..	..
1	1	5	J	K	6	7	10	..	..
1	1	5	Q	Q	8	..	..	..	..
1	1	5	Q	K	6	..	10	..	..
1	1	5	K	K	8	..	..	..	..
1	1	6	6	6	8	..	..	..	..
1	1	6	6	7	8	..	..	..	..
1	1	6	6	8	12	..	..	..	..
1	1	6	6	9	8	..	..	..	..
1	1	6	6	10	4	..	..	..	..
1	1	6	6	J	4	5	..	..	..
1	1	6	6	Q	4	..	..	..	..
1	1	6	6	K	4	..	..	..	..
1	1	6	7	7	12	..	..	..	..
1	1	6	7	8	13	..	17	..	..
1	1	6	7	9	6	..	10	..	..
1	1	6	7	10	4	..	8	..	..
1	1	6	7	J	4	5	8	..	..
1	1	6	7	Q	4	..	8	..	..
1	1	6	7	K	4	..	8	..	..
1	1	6	8	8	12	..	..	..	..
1	1	6	8	9	8	..	12	..	..

CARDS					Fifteens, Pairs & Seq.	With Jack of Turn-up	If Flush in Hand	If Flush with Turn-up	If Fl&Jack of Turn-up
1	1	6	8	10	6	..	10	..	..
1	1	6	8	J	6	7	10	..	..
1	1	6	8	Q	6	..	10	..	..
1	1	6	8	K	6	..	10	..	..
1	1	6	9	9	8	..	..	..	..
1	1	6	9	10	4	..	8	..	..
1	1	6	9	J	4	5	8	..	..
1	1	6	9	Q	4	..	8	..	..
1	1	6	9	K	4	..	8	..	..
1	1	6	10	10	4	..	..	..	..
1	1	6	10	J	2	3	6	..	..
1	1	6	10	Q	2	..	6	..	..
1	1	6	10	K	2	..	6	..	..
1	1	6	J	J	4	5	..	..	..
1	1	6	J	Q	2	3	6	..	..
1	1	6	J	K	2	3	6	..	..
1	1	6	Q	Q	4	..	..	..	..
1	1	6	Q	K	2	..	6	..	..
1	1	6	K	K	4	..	..	..	..
1	1	7	7	7	20	..	..	..	..
1	1	7	7	8	12	..	..	..	..
1	1	7	7	9	8	..	..	..	..
1	1	7	7	10	8	..	..	..	..
1	1	7	7	J	8	9	..	..	..
1	1	7	7	Q	8	..	..	..	..
1	1	7	7	K	8	..	..	..	..
1	1	7	8	8	8	..	..	..	..
1	1	7	8	9	7	..	11	..	..
1	1	7	8	10	4	..	8	..	..
1	1	7	8	J	4	5	8	..	..
1	1	7	8	Q	4	..	8	..	..
1	1	7	8	K	4	..	8	..	..
1	1	7	9	9	4	..	..	..	..
1	1	7	9	10	2	..	6	..	..
1	1	7	9	J	2	3	6	..	..
1	1	7	9	Q	2	..	6	..	..
1	1	7	9	K	2	..	6	..	..
1	1	7	10	10	4	..	..	..	..
1	1	7	10	J	2	3	6	..	..

KEY TO CRIBBAGE.

Cards	Fifteens, Pairs & Seq.	With Jack of Turn-up	If Flush in Hand	If Flush with Turn-up	If Fl. & Jack of Turn-up
1 1 7 10 Q	2		6		
1 1 7 10 K	2		6		
1 1 7 J J	4	5			
1 1 7 J Q	2	3	6		
1 1 7 J K	2	3	6		
1 1 7 Q Q	4				
1 1 7 Q K	2		6		
1 1 7 K K	4				
1 1 8 8 8	8				
1 1 8 8 9	4				
1 1 8 8 10	4				
1 1 8 8 J	4	5			
1 1 8 8 Q	4				
1 1 8 8 K	4				
1 1 8 9 9	4				
1 1 8 9 10	5		9		
1 1 8 9 J	2	3			
1 1 8 9 Q	2		6		
1 1 8 9 K	2		6		
1 1 8 10 10	4				
1 1 8 10 J	2	3	6		
1 1 8 10 Q	2		6		
1 1 8 10 K	2		6		
1 1 8 J J	4	5			
1 1 8 J Q	2	3	6		
1 1 8 J K	2	3	6		
1 1 8 Q Q	4				
1 1 8 Q K	2		6		
1 1 8 K K	4				
1 1 9 9 9	8				
1 1 9 9 10	4				
1 1 9 9 J	4	5			
1 1 9 9 Q	4				
1 1 9 9 K	4				
1 1 9 10 10	4		6		
1 1 9 10 J	5	6	9		
1 1 9 10 Q	2		6		
1 1 9 10 K	2		6		
1 1 9 J J	4	5			
1 1 9 J Q	2	3	6		
1 1 9 J K	2	3	6		
1 1 9 Q Q	4		6		
1 1 9 Q K	2		6		
1 1 9 K K	4				
1 1 10 10 10	8				
1 1 10 10 J	4	5			
1 1 10 10 Q	4				
1 1 10 10 K	4				
1 1 10 J J	4	5			
1 1 10 J Q	5	6	9		
1 1 10 J K	2	3	6		
1 1 10 Q Q	4		6		
1 1 10 Q K	2		6		
1 1 10 K K	4				
1 1 J J J	8	9			
1 1 J J Q	4	5			
1 1 J J K	4	5			
1 1 J Q Q	4	5			
1 1 J Q K	5	6	9		
1 1 J K K	4	5			
1 1 Q Q Q	8				
1 1 Q Q K	4				
1 1 Q K K	4				
1 1 K K K	8				
1 2 2 2 2	12				
1 2 2 2 3	15				
1 2 2 2 4	6				
1 2 2 2 5	6				
1 2 2 2 6	6				
1 2 2 2 7	6				
1 2 2 2 8	6				
1 2 2 2 9	8				
1 2 2 2 10	8				
1 2 2 2 J	12				
1 2 2 2 Q	12	13			
1 2 2 2 K	12				
1 2 2 3 3	16				
1 2 2 3 4	10				14

KEY TO CRIBBAGE.

Cards					Fifteens, Pairs & Seq.	With Jack of Turn-up.	If Flush in Hand.	If Flush with Turn-up.	If Fl. & Jack of Turn-up.
1	2	2	3	5	8		12		
1	2	2	3	6	8		12		
1	2	2	3	7	10		14		
1	2	2	3	8	10		14		
1	2	2	3	9	12		16		
1	2	2	3	10	14		18		
1	2	2	3	J	14	15	18		
1	2	2	3	Q	14		18		
1	2	2	3	K	14		18		
1	2	2	4	4	4				
1	2	2	4	5	2		6		
1	2	2	4	6	4		8		
1	2	2	4	7	4		8		
1	2	2	4	8	6		10		
1	2	2	4	9	6		10		
1	2	2	4	10	6		10		
1	2	2	4	J	6	7	10		
1	2	2	4	Q	6		10		
1	2	2	4	K	6		10		
1	2	2	5	5	6				
1	2	2	5	6	4		8		
1	2	2	5	7	6		10		
1	2	2	5	8	6		10		
1	2	2	5	9	4		8		
1	2	2	5	10	6		10		
1	2	2	5	J	6	7	10		
1	2	2	5	Q	6		10		
1	2	2	5	K	6		10		
1	2	2	6	6	8				
1	2	2	6	7	6		10		
1	2	2	6	8	4		8		
1	2	2	6	9	4		8		
1	2	2	6	10	4		8		
1	2	2	6	J	4	5	8		
1	2	2	6	Q	4		8		
1	2	2	6	K	4		8		
1	2	2	7	7	6				
1	2	2	7	8	4		8		
1	2	2	7	9	2		6		
1	2	2	7	10	4		8		
1	2	2	7	J	4	5	8		
1	2	2	7	Q	4		8		
1	2	2	7	K	4		8		
1	2	2	8	9	4		8		
1	2	2	8	10	2		6		
1	2	2	8	J	4	5	8		
1	2	2	8	Q	4		8		
1	2	2	8	K	4		8		
1	2	2	9	9	4				
1	2	2	9	10	4		8		
1	2	2	9	J	4	5	8		
1	2	2	9	Q	4		8		
1	2	2	9	K	4		8		
1	2	2	10	10	8				
1	2	2	10	J	6	7	10		
1	2	2	10	Q	6		10		
1	2	2	10	K	6		10		
1	2	2	J	J	8	9			
1	2	2	J	Q	6	7	10		
1	2	2	J	K	6	7	10		
1	2	2	Q	Q	8				
1	2	2	Q	K	6		10		
1	2	2	K	K	8				
1	2	3	3	3	15				
1	2	3	3	4	10		14		
1	2	3	3	5	8		12		
1	2	3	3	6	10		14		
1	2	3	3	7	10		14		
1	2	3	3	8	10		14		
1	2	3	3	9	14		18		
1	2	3	3	10	12		16		
1	2	3	3	J	12	13	16		
1	2	3	3	Q	12		16		
1	2	3	3	K	12		16		
1	2	3	4	4	10		14		
1	2	3	4	5	7		11	12	
1	2	3	4	6	6		10	11	

KEY TO CRIBBAGE.

CARDS.					Fifteens, Pairs & Seq..	With Jack of Turn-up.	If Flush in Hand......	If Flush with Turn-up.	If Fl& Jack of Turn-up
1	2	3	4	7	6	..	10	11	..
1	2	3	4	8	8	..	12	13	..
1	2	3	4	9	8	..	12	13	..
1	2	3	4	10	8	..	12	13	..
1	2	3	4	J	8	9	12	13	14
1	2	3	4	Q	8	..	12	13	..
1	2	3	4	K	8	..	12	13	..
1	2	3	5	5	7	..	11	..	..
1	2	3	5	6	5	..	9	10	..
1	2	3	5	7	7	..	11	12	..
1	2	3	5	8	5	..	9	10	..
1	2	3	5	9	7	..	11	12	..
1	2	3	5	10	7	..	11	12	..
1	2	3	5	J	7	8	11	12	13
1	2	3	5	Q	7	..	11	12	..
1	2	3	5	K	7	..	11	12	..
1	2	3	6	6	9	..	13	..	..
1	2	3	6	7	5	..	9	10	..
1	2	3	6	8	5	..	9	10	..
1	2	3	6	9	7	..	11	12	..
1	2	3	6	10	5	..	9	10	..
1	2	3	6	J	5	6	9	10	11
1	2	3	6	Q	5	..	9	10	..
1	2	3	6	K	5	..	9	10	..
1	2	3	7	7	7	..	11	..	..
1	2	3	7	8	5	..	9	10	..
1	2	3	7	9	5	..	9	10	..
1	2	3	7	10	5	..	9	10	..
1	2	3	7	J	5	6	9	10	11
1	2	3	7	Q	5	..	9	10	..
1	2	3	7	K	5	..	9	10	..
1	2	3	8	8	5	..	9	..	..
1	2	3	8	9	5	..	9	10	..
1	2	3	8	10	5	..	9	10	..
1	2	3	8	J	5	6	9	10	11
1	2	3	8	Q	5	..	9	10	..
1	2	3	8	K	5	..	9	10	..
1	2	3	9	9	9	..	13	..	..
1	2	3	9	10	7	..	11	12	..

CARDS.					Fifteens, Pairs & Seq..	With Jack of Turn-up.	If Flush in Hand......	If Flush with Turn-up.	If Fl& Jack of Turn-up
1	2	3	9	J	7	8	11	12	13
1	2	3	9	Q	7	..	11	12	..
1	2	3	9	K	7	..	11	12	..
1	2	3	10	10	9	..	13	..	..
1	2	3	10	J	7	8	11	12	13
1	2	3	10	Q	7	..	11	12	..
1	2	3	10	K	7	..	11	12	..
1	2	3	J	J	9	10	13	..	..
1	2	3	J	Q	7	8	11	12	13
1	2	3	J	K	7	8	11	12	13
1	2	3	Q	Q	9	..	13	..	..
1	2	3	Q	K	7	..	11	12	..
1	2	3	K	K	9	..	13	..	..
1	2	4	4	4	8	..	..	..	..
1	2	4	4	5	4	..	8	..	..
1	2	4	4	6	4	..	8	..	..
1	2	4	4	7	4	..	8	..	..
1	2	4	4	8	6	..	10	..	..
1	2	4	4	9	6	..	10	..	..
1	2	4	4	10	6	..	10	..	..
1	2	4	4	J	6	7	10	..	..
1	2	4	4	Q	6	..	10	..	..
1	2	4	4	K	6	..	10	..	..
1	2	4	5	5	4	..	8	..	..
1	2	4	5	6	5	..	9	10	..
1	2	4	5	7	2	..	6	7	..
1	2	4	5	8	4	..	8	9	..
1	2	4	5	9	4	..	8	9	..
1	2	4	5	10	4	..	8	9	..
1	2	4	5	J	4	5	8	9	10
1	2	4	5	Q	4	..	8	9	..
1	2	4	5	K	4	..	8	9	..
1	2	4	6	6	4	..	8	..	..
1	2	4	6	7	2	..	6	7	..
1	2	4	6	8	4	..	8	9	..
1	2	4	6	9	4	..	8	9	..
1	2	4	6	10	2	..	6	7	..
1	2	4	6	J	2	3	6	7	8
1	2	4	6	Q	2	..	6	7	..

KEY TO CRIBBAGE.

Cards					Fifteens, Pairs & Seq.	With Jack of Turn-up	If Flush in Hand	If Flush with Turn-up	If Fl& Jack of Turn-up
1	2	4	6	K	2	..	6	7	..
1	2	4	7	7	4	..	8	..	..
1	2	4	7	8	4	..	8	9	..
1	2	4	7	9	2	..	6	7	..
1	2	4	7	10	2	..	6	7	..
1	2	4	7	J	2	3	6	7	8
1	2	4	7	Q	2	..	6	7	..
1	2	4	7	K	2	..	6	7	..
1	2	4	8	8	6	..	10	..	..
1	2	4	8	9	4	..	8	9	..
1	2	4	8	10	4	..	8	9	..
1	2	4	8	J	4	5	8	9	10
1	2	4	8	Q	4	..	8	9	..
1	2	4	8	K	4	..	8	9	..
1	2	4	9	9	6	..	10	..	..
1	2	4	9	10	4	..	8	9	..
1	2	4	9	J	4	5	8	9	10
1	2	4	9	Q	4	..	8	9	..
1	2	4	9	K	4	..	8	9	..
1	2	4	10	10	6	..	10	..	..
1	2	4	10	J	4	5	8	9	10
1	2	4	10	Q	4	..	8	9	..
1	2	4	10	K	4	..	8	9	..
1	2	4	J	J	6	7	10	..	..
1	2	4	J	Q	4	5	8	9	10
1	2	4	J	K	4	5	8	9	10
1	2	4	Q	Q	6	..	10	..	..
1	2	4	Q	K	4	..	8	9	..
1	2	4	K	K	6	..	10	..	..
1	2	5	5	5	8	..	..	..	..
1	2	5	5	6	2	..	6	..	..
1	2	5	5	7	6	..	10	..	..
1	2	5	5	8	6	..	10	..	..
1	2	5	5	9	6	..	10	..	..
1	2	5	5	10	6	..	10	..	..
1	2	5	5	J	6	7	10	..	..
1	2	5	5	Q	6	..	10	..	..
1	2	5	5	K	6	..	10	..	..
1	2	5	6	6	4	..	8	..	..
1	2	5	6	7	7	..	11	12	..
1	2	5	6	8	4	..	8	9	..
1	2	5	6	9	4	..	8	9	..
1	2	5	6	10	2	..	6	7	..
1	2	5	6	J	2	3	6	7	8
1	2	5	6	Q	2	..	6	7	..
1	2	5	6	K	2	..	6	7	..
1	2	5	7	7	8	..	12	..	..
1	2	5	7	8	6	..	10	11	..
1	2	5	7	9	4	..	8	9	..
1	2	5	7	10	4	..	8	9	..
1	2	5	7	J	4	5	8	9	10
1	2	5	7	Q	4	..	8	9	..
1	2	5	7	K	4	..	8	9	..
1	2	5	8	8	6	..	10	..	..
1	2	5	8	9	4	..	8	9	..
1	2	5	8	10	4	..	8	9	..
1	2	5	8	J	4	5	8	9	10
1	2	5	8	Q	4	..	8	9	..
1	2	5	8	K	4	..	8	9	..
1	2	5	9	9	6	..	10	..	..
1	2	5	9	10	4	..	8	9	..
1	2	5	9	J	4	5	8	9	10
1	2	5	9	Q	4	..	8	9	..
1	2	5	9	K	4	..	8	9	..
1	2	5	10	10	6	..	10	..	..
1	2	5	10	J	4	5	8	9	10
1	2	5	10	Q	4	..	8	9	..
1	2	5	10	K	4	..	8	9	..
1	2	5	J	J	6	7	10	..	..
1	2	5	J	Q	4	5	8	9	10
1	2	5	J	K	4	5	8	9	10
1	2	5	Q	Q	6	..	10	..	..
1	2	5	Q	K	4	..	8	9	..
1	2	5	K	K	6	..	10	..	..
1	2	6	6	6	12	..	..	..	..
1	2	6	6	7	8	..	12	..	..
1	2	6	6	8	8	..	12	..	..
1	2	6	6	9	8	..	12	..	..

KEY TO CRIBBAGE.

Cards	Fifteens, Pairs & Seq.	With Jack of Turn-up	If Flush in Hand	If Flush with Turn-up	If Fl& Jack of Turn-up
1 2 6 6 10	4		8		
1 2 6 6 J	4	5	8		
1 2 6 6 Q	4		8		
1 2 6 6 K	4		8		
1 2 6 7 7	8		12		
1 2 6 7 8	9		13	14	
1 2 6 7 9	4		8	9	
1 2 6 7 10	2		6	7	
1 2 6 7 J	2	3	6	7	8
1 2 6 7 Q	2		6	7	
1 2 6 7 K	2		6	7	
1 2 6 8 9	6		10		
1 2 6 8 10	4		8	9	
1 2 6 8 J	2		6	7	
1 2 6 8 Q	2	3	6	7	8
1 2 6 8 K	2		6	7	
1 2 6 9 9	6		10		
1 2 6 9 10	2		6	7	
1 2 6 9 J	2	3	6	7	8
1 2 6 9 Q	2		6	7	
1 2 6 9 K	2		6	7	
1 2 6 10 10	2		6		
1 2 6 10 J	0	1	4	5	6
1 2 6 10 Q	0		4	5	
1 2 6 10 K	0		4	5	
1 2 6 J J	2	3	4		
1 2 6 J Q	0	1	4	5	6
1 2 6 J K	0	1	4	5	6
1 2 6 Q Q	2		6		
1 2 6 Q K	0		4	5	
1 2 6 K K	2		6		
1 2 7 7 7	12		12		
1 2 7 7 8	8		12		
1 2 7 7 9	4		8		
1 2 7 7 10	4		8		
1 2 7 7 J	4	5	8		
1 2 7 7 Q	4		8		
1 2 7 7 K	4		8		
1 2 7 8 8	6		10		
1 2 7 8 9	5		9	10	
1 2 7 8 10	2		6	7	
1 2 7 8 J	2	3	6	7	8
1 2 7 8 Q	2		6	7	
1 2 7 8 K	2		6	7	
1 2 7 9 9	2		6		
1 2 7 9 10	0		4	5	
1 2 7 9 J	0	1	4	5	6
1 2 7 9 Q	0		4	5	
1 2 7 9 K	0		4	5	
1 2 7 10 10	2		6		
1 2 7 10 J	0	1	4	5	6
1 2 7 10 Q	0		4	5	
1 2 7 10 K	0		4	5	
1 2 7 J J	2	3	6		
1 2 7 J Q	0	1	4	5	6
1 2 7 J K	0	1	4	5	6
1 2 7 Q Q	2		6		
1 2 7 Q K	0		4	5	
1 2 7 K K	2		6		
1 2 8 8 8	6		6		
1 2 8 8 9	2		6		
1 2 8 8 10	2		6		
1 2 8 8 J	2	3	6		
1 2 8 8 Q	2		6		
1 2 8 8 K	2		6		
1 2 8 9 9	2		6		
1 2 8 9 10	3		7	8	
1 2 8 9 J	0	1	4	5	6
1 2 8 9 Q	0		4	5	
1 2 8 9 K	0		4	5	
1 2 8 10 10	2		6		
1 2 8 10 J	0	1	4	5	6
1 2 8 10 Q	0		4	5	
1 2 8 10 K	0		4	5	
1 2 8 J J	2	3	6		6
1 2 8 J Q	0	1	4	5	6
1 2 8 J K	0	1	4	5	6

KEY TO CRIBBAGE.

CARDS.					Fifteens, Pairs & Seq.	With Jack of Turn-up	If Flush in Hand	If Flush with Turn-up	If Fl& Jack of Turn-up
1	2	8	Q	Q	2		6		
1	2	8	Q	K	0		4	5	
1	2	8	K	K	2		6		
1	2	9	9	9	6				
1	2	9	9	10	2		6		
1	2	9	9	J	2	3	6		
1	2	9	9	Q	2		6		
1	2	9	9	K	2		6		
1	2	9	10	10	2		6		
1	2	9	10	J	3	4	7	8	9
1	2	9	10	Q	0		4	5	
1	2	9	10	K	0		4	5	
1	2	9	J	J	2	3	6		
1	2	9	J	Q	0	1	4	5	6
1	2	9	J	K	0	1	4	5	6
1	2	9	Q	Q	2		6		
1	2	9	Q	K	0		4	5	
1	2	9	K	K	2		6		
1	2	10	10	10	6				
1	2	10	10	J	2	3	6		
1	2	10	10	Q	2		6		
1	2	10	10	K	2		6		
1	2	10	J	J	2	3	6		
1	2	10	J	Q	3	4	7	8	9
1	2	10	J	K	0	1	4	5	6
1	2	10	Q	Q	2		6		
1	2	10	Q	K	0		4	5	
1	2	10	K	K	2		6		
1	2	J	J	J	6	7			
1	2	J	J	Q	2	3	6		
1	2	J	J	K	2	3	6		
1	2	J	Q	Q	2	3	6		
1	2	J	Q	K	3	4	7	8	9
1	2	J	K	K	2	3	6		
1	2	Q	Q	Q	6				
1	2	Q	Q	K	2		6		
1	2	Q	K	K	2		6		
1	2	K	K	K	6				
1	3	3	3	3	12				

CARDS.					Fifteens, Pairs & Seq.	With Jack of Turn-up	If Flush in Hand	If Flush with Turn-up	If Fl& Jack of Turn-up
1	3	3	3	4	6				
1	3	3	3	5	8				
1	3	3	3	6	8				
1	3	3	3	7	6				
1	3	3	3	8	12				
1	3	3	3	9	12				
1	3	3	3	10	6				
1	3	3	3	J	6	7			
1	3	3	3	Q	6				
1	3	3	3	K	6				
1	3	3	4	4	6				
1	3	3	4	5	10		14		
1	3	3	4	6	2		6		
1	3	3	4	7	6		10		
1	3	3	4	8	8		12		
1	3	3	4	9	4		8		
1	3	3	4	10	4		8		
1	3	3	4	J	4	5	8		
1	3	3	4	Q	4		8		
1	3	3	4	K	4		8		
1	3	3	5	5	4				
1	3	3	5	6	6		10		
1	3	3	5	7	6		10		
1	3	3	5	8	4		8		
1	3	3	5	9	6		10		
1	3	3	5	10	4		8		
1	3	3	5	J	4	5	8		
1	3	3	5	Q	4		8		
1	3	3	5	K	4		8		
1	3	3	6	6	8				
1	3	3	6	7	2		6		
1	3	3	6	8	6		10		
1	3	3	6	9	6		10		
1	3	3	6	10	2		6		
1	3	3	6	J	2	3	6		
1	3	3	6	Q	2		6		
1	3	3	6	K	2		6		
1	3	3	7	7	6				
1	3	3	7	8	6		10		

KEY TO CRIBBAGE.

Cards					Fifteens, Pairs & Seq.	With Jack of Turn-up.	If Flush in Hand.	If Flush with Turn-up.	If Fl & Jack of Turn-up.
1	3	3	7	9	4		8		
1	3	3	7	10	2		6		
1	3	3	7	J	2	3	6		
1	3	3	7	Q	2		6		
1	3	3	7	K	2		6		
1	3	3	8	8	8			10	
1	3	3	8	9	6			10	
1	3	3	8	10	4		8		
1	3	3	8	J	4	5	8		
1	3	3	8	Q	4		8		
1	3	3	8	K	4		8		
1	3	3	9	9	8				
1	3	3	9	10	4		8		
1	3	3	9	J	4	5	8		
1	3	3	9	Q	4		8		
1	3	3	9	K	4		8		
1	3	3	10	10	4				
1	3	3	10	J	2	3	6		
1	3	3	10	Q	2		6		
1	3	3	10	K	2		6		
1	3	3	J	J	4	5			
1	3	3	J	Q	2	3	6		
1	3	3	J	K	2	3	6		
1	3	3	Q	Q	4				
1	3	3	Q	K	2		6		
1	3	3	K	K	4				
1	3	4	4	4	8			12	
1	3	4	4	5	8		12		
1	3	4	4	6	4		8		
1	3	4	4	7	8		12		
1	3	4	4	8	6		10		
1	3	4	4	9	2		6		
1	3	4	4	10	6		10		
1	3	4	4	J	6	7	10		
1	3	4	4	Q	6		10		
1	3	4	4	K	6		10		
1	3	4	5	5	10		14		
1	3	4	5	6	8		12	13	
1	3	4	5	7	7		11	12	

Cards					Fifteens, Pairs & Seq.	With Jack of Turn-up.	If Flush in Hand.	If Flush with Turn-up.	If Fl & Jack of Turn-up.
1	3	4	5	8	5		9	10	
1	3	4	5	9	5		9	10	
1	3	4	5	10	7		11	12	
1	3	4	5	J	7	8	11	12	13
1	3	4	5	Q	7		11	12	
1	3	4	5	K	7		11	12	
1	3	4	6	6	4		8		
1	3	4	6	7	2		6	7	
1	3	4	6	8	4		8	9	
1	3	4	6	9	2		6	7	
1	3	4	6	10	2		6	7	
1	3	4	6	J	2	3	6	7	8
1	3	4	6	Q	2		6	7	
1	3	4	6	K	2		6	7	
1	3	4	7	7	8		12		
1	3	4	7	8	6		10	11	
1	3	4	7	9	2		6	7	
1	3	4	7	10	4		8	9	
1	3	4	7	J	4	5	8	9	10
1	3	4	7	Q	4		8	9	
1	3	4	7	K	4		8	9	
1	3	4	8	8	6		10		
1	3	4	8	9	2		6	7	
1	3	4	8	10	4		8	9	
1	3	4	8	J	4	5	8	9	10
1	3	4	8	Q	4		8	9	
1	3	4	8	K	4		8	9	
1	3	4	9	9	2		6	7	
1	3	4	9	10	2		6	7	
1	3	4	9	J	2	3	6	7	8
1	3	4	9	Q	2		6	7	
1	3	4	9	K	2		6	7	
1	3	4	10	10	6		10		
1	3	4	10	J	4	5	8	9	10
1	3	4	10	Q	4		8	9	
1	3	4	10	K	4		8	9	
1	3	4	J	J	6	7	10		
1	3	4	J	Q	4	5	8	9	10
1	3	4	J	K	4	5	8	9	10

KEY TO CRIBBAGE.

CARDS.					Fifteens, Pairs & Seq..	With Jack of Turn-up	If Flush in Hand......	If Flush with Turn-up.	If Fl& Jack of Turn-up
1	3	4	Q	Q	6	..	10	..	..
1	3	4	Q	K	4	..	8	9	..
1	3	4	K	K	6	..	10	..	..
1	3	5	5	5	8	..	..	..	..
1	3	5	5	6	6	..	10	..	..
1	3	5	5	7	6	..	10	..	..
1	3	5	5	8	2	..	6	..	..
1	3	5	5	9	6	..	10	..	..
1	3	5	5	10	6	..	10	..	..
1	3	5	5	J	6	7	10	..	..
1	3	5	5	Q	6	..	10	..	..
1	3	5	5	K	6	..	10	..	..
1	3	5	6	6	8	..	12	..	..
1	3	5	6	7	7	..	11	12	..
1	3	5	6	8	4	..	8	9	..
1	3	5	6	9	6	..	10	11	..
1	3	5	6	10	4	..	8	9	..
1	3	5	6	J	4	5	8	9	10
1	3	5	6	Q	4	..	8	9	..
1	3	5	6	K	4	..	8	9	..
1	3	5	7	7	8	..	12	..	..
1	3	5	7	8	4	..	8	9	..
1	3	5	7	9	4	..	8	9	..
1	3	5	7	10	4	..	8	9	..
1	3	5	7	J	4	5	8	9	10
1	3	5	7	Q	4	..	8	9	..
1	3	5	7	K	4	..	8	9	..
1	3	5	8	8	2	..	6	..	..
1	3	5	8	9	2	..	6	7	..
1	3	5	8	10	2	..	6	7	..
1	3	5	8	J	2	3	6	7	8
1	3	5	8	Q	2	..	6	7	..
1	3	5	8	K	2	..	6	7	..
1	3	5	9	9	6	..	10	..	..
1	3	5	9	10	4	..	8	9	..
1	3	5	9	J	4	5	8	9	10
1	3	5	9	Q	4	..	8	9	..
1	3	5	9	K	4	..	8	9	..
1	3	5	10	10	6	..	10	..	..
1	3	5	10	J	4	5	8	9	10
1	3	5	10	Q	4	..	8	9	..
1	3	5	10	K	4	..	8	9	..
1	3	5	J	J	6	7	10	..	..
1	3	5	J	Q	4	5	8	9	10
1	3	5	J	K	4	5	8	9	10
1	3	5	Q	Q	6	..	10	..	..
1	3	5	Q	K	4	..	8	9	..
1	3	5	K	K	6	..	10	..	..
1	3	6	6	6	12	..	..	..	..
1	3	6	6	7	4	..	8	..	..
1	3	6	6	8	8	..	12	..	..
1	3	6	6	9	8	..	12	..	..
1	3	6	6	10	4	..	8	..	..
1	3	6	6	J	4	5	8	..	..
1	3	6	6	Q	4	..	8	..	..
1	3	6	6	K	4	..	8	..	..
1	3	6	7	7	4	..	8	..	..
1	3	6	7	8	7	..	11	12	..
1	3	6	7	9	2	..	6	7	..
1	3	6	7	10	0	..	4	5	..
1	3	6	7	J	0	1	4	5	6
1	3	6	7	Q	0	..	4	5	..
1	3	6	7	K	0	..	4	5	..
1	3	6	8	8	6	..	10	..	..
1	3	6	8	9	4	..	8	9	..
1	3	6	8	10	2	..	6	7	..
1	3	6	8	J	2	3	6	7	8
1	3	6	8	Q	2	..	6	7	..
1	3	6	8	K	2	..	6	7	..
1	3	6	9	9	6	..	10	..	..
1	3	6	9	10	2	..	6	7	..
1	3	6	9	J	2	3	6	7	8
1	3	6	9	Q	2	..	6	7	..
1	3	6	9	K	2	..	6	7	..
1	3	6	10	10	2	..	6	..	..
1	3	6	10	J	0	1	4	5	6
1	3	6	10	Q	0	..	4	5	..
1	3	6	10	K	0	..	4	5	..

KEY TO CRIBBAGE.

Cards	Fifteens, Pairs & Seq..	With Jack of Turn-up..	If Flush in Hand......	If Flush with Turn-up.	If Fl & Jack of Turn-up
1 3 6 J J	2	3	6	..	..
1 3 6 J Q	0	1	4	5	6
1 3 6 J K	0	1	4	5	6
1 3 6 Q Q	2	..	6	..	..
1 3 6 Q K	0	..	4	5	..
1 3 6 K K	2	..	6	..	..
1 3 7 7 7	12	..	..	..	..
1 3 7 7 8	8	..	12	..	..
1 3 7 7 9	4	..	8	..	..
1 3 7 7 10	4	..	8	..	..
1 3 7 7 J	4	5	8	..	..
1 3 7 7 Q	4	..	8	..	..
1 3 7 7 K	4	..	8	..	..
1 3 7 8 8	6	..	10	..	..
1 3 7 8 9	5	..	9	10	..
1 3 7 8 10	2	..	6	7	..
1 3 7 8 J	2	3	6	7	8
1 3 7 8 Q	2	..	6	7	..
1 3 7 8 K	2	..	6	7	..
1 3 7 9 9	2	..	6	..	..
1 3 7 9 10	0	..	4	5	..
1 3 7 9 J	0	1	4	5	6
1 3 7 9 Q	0	..	4	5	..
1 3 7 9 K	0	..	4	5	..
1 3 7 10 10	2	..	6	..	..
1 3 7 10 J	0	1	4	5	6
1 3 7 10 Q	0	..	4	5	..
1 3 7 10 K	0	..	4	5	..
1 3 7 J J	2	3	6	..	..
1 3 7 J Q	0	1	4	5	6
1 3 7 J K	0	1	4	5	6
1 3 7 Q Q	2	..	6	..	..
1 3 7 Q K	0	..	4	5	..
1 3 7 K K	2	..	6	..	..
1 3 8 8 8	6	..	..	..	..
1 3 8 8 9	2	..	6	..	..
1 3 8 8 10	2	..	6	..	..
1 3 8 8 J	2	3	6	..	..
1 3 8 8 Q	2	..	6	..	..

Cards	Fifteens, Pairs & Seq..	With Jack of Turn-up..	If Flush in Hand......	If Flush with Turn-up.	If Fl & Jack of Turn-up
1 3 8 8 K	2	..	6	..	..
1 3 8 9 9	2	..	6	..	..
1 3 8 9 10	3	..	7	8	..
1 3 8 9 J	0	1	4	5	6
1 3 8 9 Q	0	..	4	5	..
1 3 8 9 K	0	..	4	5	..
1 3 8 10 10	2	..	6	..	..
1 3 8 10 J	0	1	4	5	6
1 3 8 10 Q	0	..	4	5	..
1 3 8 10 K	0	..	4	5	..
1 3 8 J J	2	3	6	..	..
1 3 8 J Q	0	1	4	5	6
1 3 8 J K	0	1	4	5	6
1 3 8 Q Q	2	..	6	..	..
1 3 8 Q K	0	..	4	5	..
1 3 8 K K	2	..	6	..	..
1 3 9 9 9	6	..	..	..	..
1 3 9 9 10	2	..	6	..	..
1 3 9 9 J	2	3	6	..	..
1 3 9 9 Q	2	..	6	..	..
1 3 9 9 K	2	..	6	..	..
1 3 9 10 10	2	..	6	..	..
1 3 9 10 J	3	4	7	8	9
1 3 9 10 Q	0	..	4	5	..
1 3 9 10 K	0	..	4	5	..
1 3 9 J J	2	3	6	..	..
1 3 9 J K	0	1	4	5	6
1 3 9 Q Q	2	..	6	..	..
1 3 9 Q K	0	..	4	5	..
1 3 9 K K	2	..	6	..	..
1 3 10 10 10	6	..	..	..	..
1 3 10 10 J	2	3	6	..	..
1 3 10 10 Q	2	..	6	..	..
1 3 10 10 K	2	..	6	..	..
1 3 10 J J	2	3	6	..	..
1 3 10 J Q	3	4	7	8	9
1 3 10 J K	0	1	4	5	6
1 3 10 Q Q	2	..	6	..	..

KEY TO CRIBBAGE.

CARDS.					Fifteens, Pairs & Seq.	With Jack of Turn-up.	If Flush in Hand.	If Flush with Turn-up.	If Fl & Jack of Turn-up
1	3	10	Q	K	0	..	4	5	..
1	3	10	K	K	2	..	6	..	..
1	3	J	J	J	6	7	..	..	..
1	3	J	J	Q	2	3	6	..	..
1	3	J	J	K	2	3	6	..	..
1	3	J	Q	Q	2	3	6	..	..
1	3	J	Q	K	3	4	7	8	9
1	3	J	K	K	2	3	6	..	..
1	3	Q	Q	Q	6	..	..	..	..
1	3	Q	Q	K	2	..	6	..	..
1	3	Q	K	K	2	..	6	..	..
1	3	K	K	K	6	..	..	..	..
1	4	4	4	4	12	..	..	..	..
1	4	4	4	5	6	..	..	..	..
1	4	4	4	6	12	..	..	..	..
1	4	4	4	7	12	..	..	..	..
1	4	4	4	8	6	..	..	..	..
1	4	4	4	9	6	..	..	..	..
1	4	4	4	10	12	..	..	..	..
1	4	4	4	J	12	13	..	..	..
1	4	4	4	Q	12	..	..	..	..
1	4	4	4	K	12	..	..	..	..
1	4	4	5	5	8	..	..	..	..
1	4	4	5	6	14	..	18	..	..
1	4	4	5	7	4	..	8	..	..
1	4	4	5	8	2	..	6	..	..
1	4	4	5	9	4	..	8	..	..
1	4	4	5	10	8	..	12	..	..
1	4	4	5	J	8	9	12	..	..
1	4	4	5	Q	8	..	12	..	..
1	4	4	5	K	8	..	12	..	..
1	4	4	6	6	8	..	..	..	..
1	4	4	6	7	6	..	10	..	..
1	4	4	6	8	6	..	10	..	..
1	4	4	6	9	6	..	10	..	..
1	4	4	6	10	8	..	12	..	..
1	4	4	6	J	8	9	12	..	..
1	4	4	6	Q	8	..	12	..	..
1	4	4	6	K	8	..	12	..	..

CARDS.					Fifteens, Pairs & Seq.	With Jack of Turn-up.	If Flush in Hand.	If Flush with Turn-up.	If Fl & Jack of Turn-up
1	4	4	7	7	10	..	..	..	..
1	4	4	7	8	6	..	10	..	..
1	4	4	7	9	4	..	8	..	..
1	4	4	7	10	8	..	12	..	..
1	4	4	7	J	8	9	12	..	..
1	4	4	7	Q	8	..	12	..	..
1	4	4	7	K	8	..	12	..	..
1	4	4	8	8	4	..	..	..	..
1	4	4	8	9	2	..	6	..	..
1	4	4	8	10	6	..	10	..	..
1	4	4	8	J	6	7	10	..	..
1	4	4	8	Q	6	..	10	..	..
1	4	4	8	K	6	..	10	..	..
1	4	4	9	9	4	..	..	..	..
1	4	4	9	10	6	..	10	..	..
1	4	4	9	J	6	7	10	..	..
1	4	4	9	Q	6	..	10	..	..
1	4	4	9	K	6	..	10	..	..
1	4	4	10	10	12	..	..	..	..
1	4	4	10	J	10	11	14	..	..
1	4	4	10	Q	10	..	14	..	..
1	4	4	10	K	10	..	14	..	..
1	4	4	J	J	12	13	..	..	..
1	4	4	J	Q	10	11	14	..	..
1	4	4	J	K	10	11	14	..	..
1	4	4	Q	Q	12	..	..	..	..
1	4	4	Q	K	10	..	14	..	..
1	4	4	K	K	12	..	..	..	..
1	4	5	5	5	14	..	..	..	..
1	4	5	5	6	14	..	18	..	..
1	4	5	5	7	4	..	8	..	..
1	4	5	5	8	4	..	8	..	..
1	4	5	5	9	8	..	12	..	..
1	4	5	5	10	10	..	14	..	..
1	4	5	5	J	10	11	14	..	..
1	4	5	5	Q	10	..	14	..	..
1	4	5	5	K	10	..	14	..	..
1	4	5	6	6	12	..	16	..	..
1	4	5	6	7	6	..	10	11	..

KEY TO CRIBBAGE.

CARDS.					Fifteens, Pairs & Seq..	With Jack of Turn-up.	If Flush in Hand......	If Flush with Turn-up.	If Fl& Jack of Turn-up	CARDS.					Fifteens, Pairs & Seq..	With Jack of Turn-up.	If Flush in Hand......	If Flush with Turn-up.	If Fl& Jack of Turn-up
1	4	5	6	8	7	..	11	12	..	1	4	6	6	J	4	5	8	..	..
1	4	5	6	9	9	..	13	14	..	1	4	6	6	Q	4	..	8	..	..
1	4	5	6	10	9	..	13	14	..	1	4	6	6	K	4	..	8	..	..
1	4	5	6	J	9	10	13	14	15	1	4	6	7	7	4	..	8	..	..
1	4	5	6	Q	9	..	13	14	..	1	4	6	7	8	7	..	11	12	..
1	4	5	6	K	9	..	13	14	..	1	4	6	7	9	2	..	6	7	..
1	4	5	7	7	4	..	8	..	..	1	4	6	7	10	2	..	6	7	..
1	4	5	7	8	2	..	6	7	..	1	4	6	7	J	2	3	6	7	8
1	4	5	7	9	2	..	6	7	..	1	4	6	7	Q	2	..	6	7	..
1	4	5	7	10	4	..	8	9	..	1	4	6	7	K	2	..	6	7	..
1	4	5	7	J	4	5	8	9	10	1	4	6	8	8	6	..	10	..	..
1	4	5	7	Q	4	..	8	9	..	1	4	6	8	9	4	..	8	9	..
1	4	5	7	K	4	..	8	9	..	1	4	6	8	10	4	..	8	9	..
1	4	5	8	8	2	..	6	..	..	1	4	6	8	J	4	5	8	9	10
1	4	5	8	9	2	..	6	7	..	1	4	6	8	Q	4	..	8	9	..
1	4	5	8	10	4	..	8	9	..	1	4	6	8	K	4	..	8	9	..
1	4	5	8	J	4	5	8	9	10	1	4	6	9	9	6	..	10	..	..
1	4	5	8	Q	4	..	8	9	..	1	4	6	9	10	4	..	8	9	..
1	4	5	8	K	4	..	8	9	..	1	4	6	9	J	4	5	8	9	10
1	4	5	9	9	6	..	10	..	..	1	4	6	9	Q	4	..	8	9	..
1	4	5	9	10	6	..	10	11	..	1	4	6	9	K	4	..	8	9	..
1	4	5	9	J	6	7	10	11	12	1	4	6	10	10	6	..	10	..	..
1	4	5	9	Q	6	..	10	11	..	1	4	6	10	J	4	5	8	9	10
1	4	5	9	K	6	..	10	11	..	1	4	6	10	Q	4	..	8	9	..
1	4	5	10	10	10	..	14	..	..	1	4	6	10	K	4	..	8	9	..
1	4	5	10	J	8	9	12	13	14	1	4	6	J	J	6	7	10	..	..
1	4	5	10	Q	8	..	12	13	..	1	4	6	J	Q	4	5	8	9	10
1	4	5	10	K	8	..	12	13	..	1	4	6	J	K	4	5	8	9	10
1	4	5	J	J	10	11	14	..	..	1	4	6	Q	Q	6	..	10	..	..
1	4	5	J	Q	8	9	12	13	14	1	4	6	Q	K	4	..	8	9	..
1	4	5	J	K	8	9	12	13	14	1	4	6	K	K	6	..	10	..	..
1	4	5	Q	Q	10	..	14	..	..	1	4	7	7	7	12	..	..	..	..
1	4	5	Q	K	8	..	12	13	..	1	4	7	7	8	8	..	12	..	..
1	4	5	K	K	10	..	14	..	..	1	4	7	7	9	4	..	8	..	..
1	4	6	6	6	6	..	..	..	..	1	4	7	7	10	6	..	10	..	..
1	4	6	6	7	2	..	6	..	..	1	4	7	7	J	6	7	10	..	..
1	4	6	6	8	6	..	10	..	..	1	4	7	7	Q	6	..	10	..	..
1	4	6	6	9	6	..	10	..	..	1	4	7	7	K	6	..	10	..	..
1	4	6	6	10	4	..	8	..	..	1	4	7	8	8	6	..	10	..	..

KEY TO CRIBBAGE.

CARDS					Fifteens, Pairs & Seq.	With Jack of Turn-up	If Flush in Hand	If Flush with Turn-up	If Fl& Jack of Turn-up
1	4	7	8	9	5	..	9	10	..
1	4	7	8	10	4	..	8	9	..
1	4	7	8	J	4	5	8	9	10
1	4	7	8	Q	4	..	8	9	..
1	4	7	8	K	4	..	8	9	..
1	4	7	9	9	2	..	6	..	..
1	4	7	9	10	2	..	6	7	..
1	4	7	9	J	2	3	6	7	8
1	4	7	9	Q	2	..	6	7	..
1	4	7	9	K	2	..	6	7	..
1	4	7	10	10	6	..	10	..	..
1	4	7	10	J	4	5	8	9	10
1	4	7	10	Q	4	..	8	9	..
1	4	7	10	K	4	..	8	9	..
1	4	7	J	J	6	7	10	..	..
1	4	7	J	Q	4	5	8	9	10
1	4	7	J	K	4	5	8	9	10
1	4	7	Q	Q	6	..	10	..	..
1	4	7	Q	K	4	..	8	9	..
1	4	7	K	K	6	..	10	..	..
1	4	8	8	8	6	..	..	..	..
1	4	8	8	9	2	..	6	..	..
1	4	8	8	10	4	..	8	..	..
1	4	8	8	J	4	5	8	..	..
1	4	8	8	Q	4	..	8	..	..
1	4	8	8	K	4	..	8	..	..
1	4	8	9	9	2	..	6	..	..
1	4	8	9	10	5	..	9	10	..
1	4	8	9	J	2	3	6	7	8
1	4	8	9	Q	2	..	6	7	..
1	4	8	9	K	2	..	6	7	..
1	4	8	10	10	6	..	10	..	..
1	4	8	10	J	4	5	8	9	10
1	4	8	10	Q	4	..	8	9	..
1	4	8	10	K	4	..	8	9	..
1	4	8	J	J	6	7	10	..	..
1	4	8	J	Q	4	5	8	9	10
1	4	8	J	K	4	5	8	9	10
1	4	8	Q	Q	6	..	10	..	..

CARDS					Fifteens, Pairs & Seq.	With Jack of Turn-up	If Flush in Hand	If Flush with Turn-up	If Fl& Jack of Turn-up
1	4	8	Q	K	4	..	8	9	..
1	4	8	K	K	6	..	10	..	..
1	4	9	9	9	6	..	..	..	..
1	4	9	9	10	4	..	8	..	..
1	4	9	9	J	4	5	8	..	..
1	4	9	9	Q	4	..	8	..	..
1	4	9	9	K	4	..	8	..	..
1	4	9	10	10	6	..	10	..	..
1	4	9	10	J	7	8	11	12	13
1	4	9	10	Q	4	..	8	9	..
1	4	9	10	K	4	..	8	9	..
1	4	9	J	J	6	7	10	..	..
1	4	9	J	Q	4	5	8	9	10
1	4	9	J	K	4	5	8	9	10
1	4	9	Q	Q	6	..	10	..	..
1	4	9	Q	K	4	..	8	9	..
1	4	9	K	K	6	..	10	..	..
1	4	10	10	10	12	..	..	..	..
1	4	10	10	J	8	9	12	..	..
1	4	10	10	Q	8	..	12	..	..
1	4	10	10	K	8	..	12	..	..
1	4	10	J	J	8	9	12	..	..
1	4	10	J	Q	9	10	13	14	15
1	4	10	J	K	6	7	10	11	12
1	4	10	Q	Q	8	..	12	..	..
1	4	10	Q	K	6	..	10	11	..
1	4	10	K	K	8	..	12	..	..
1	4	J	J	J	12	13	..	..	..
1	4	J	J	Q	8	9	12	..	..
1	4	J	J	K	8	9	12	..	..
1	4	J	Q	Q	8	9	12	..	..
1	4	J	Q	K	9	10	13	14	15
1	4	J	K	K	8	9	12	..	..
1	4	Q	Q	Q	12	..	..	..	..
1	4	Q	Q	K	8	..	12	..	..
1	4	Q	K	K	8	..	12	..	..
1	4	K	K	K	12	..	..	..	..
1	5	5	5	5	20	..	..	..	..
1	5	5	5	6	8	..	..	..	..

21   **KEY TO CRIBBAGE.**

CARDS					Fifteens, Pairs & Seq.	With Jack of Turn-up.	If Flush in Hand......	If Flush with Turn-up.	If Fl& Jack of Turn-up
1	5	5	5	7	8				
1	5	5	5	8	8				
1	5	5	5	9	14				
1	5	5	5	10	14				
1	5	5	5	J	14	15			
1	5	5	5	Q	14				
1	5	5	5	K	14				
1	5	5	6	6	4				
1	5	5	6	7	8		12		
1	5	5	6	8	4		8		
1	5	5	6	9	8		12		
1	5	5	6	10	6		10		
1	5	5	6	J	6	7	10		
1	5	5	6	Q	6		10		
1	5	5	6	K	6		10		
1	5	5	7	7	6				
1	5	5	7	8	4		8		
1	5	5	7	9	6		10		
1	5	5	7	10	6		10		
1	5	5	7	J	6	7	10		
1	5	5	7	Q	6		10		
1	5	5	7	K	6		10		
1	5	5	8	8	4				
1	5	5	8	9	6		10		
1	5	5	8	10	6		10		
1	5	5	8	J	6	7	10		
1	5	5	8	Q	6		10		
1	5	5	8	K	6		10		
1	5	5	9	9	12				
1	5	5	9	10	10		14		
1	5	5	9	J	10	11	14		
1	5	5	9	Q	10		14		
1	5	5	9	K	10		14		
1	5	5	10	10	12				
1	5	5	10	J	10	11	14		
1	5	5	10	Q	10		14		
1	5	5	10	K	10		14		
1	5	5	J	J	12	13	14		
1	5	5	J	Q	10	11	14		
1	5	5	J	K	10	11	14		
1	5	5	Q	Q	12				
1	5	5	Q	K	10		14		
1	5	5	K	K	12				
1	5	6	6	6	6				
1	5	6	6	7	8		12		
1	5	6	6	8	6		10		
1	5	6	6	9	8		12		
1	5	6	6	10	4		8		
1	5	6	6	J	4	5	8		
1	5	6	6	Q	4		8		
1	5	6	6	K	4		8		
1	5	6	7	7	10		14		
1	5	6	7	8	8		12	13	
1	5	6	7	9	7		11	12	
1	5	6	7	10	5		9	10	
1	5	6	7	J	5	6	9	10	11
1	5	6	7	Q	5		9	10	
1	5	6	7	K	5		9	10	
1	5	6	8	8	6		10		
1	5	6	8	9	6		10	11	
1	5	6	8	10	4		8	9	
1	5	6	8	J	4	5	8	9	10
1	5	6	8	Q	4		8	9	
1	5	6	8	K	4		8	9	
1	5	6	9	9	10		14		
1	5	6	9	10	6		10	11	
1	5	6	9	J	6	7	10	11	12
1	5	6	9	Q	6		10	11	
1	5	6	9	K	6		10	11	
1	5	6	10	10	6		10		
1	5	6	10	J	4	5	8	9	10
1	5	6	10	Q	4		8	9	
1	5	6	10	K	4		8	9	
1	5	6	J	J	6	7	10		
1	5	6	J	Q	4	5	8	9	10
1	5	6	J	K	4	5	8	9	10
1	5	6	Q	Q	6		10		
1	5	6	Q	K	4		8	9	

KEY TO CRIBBAGE.

CARDS.					Fifteens, Pairs & Seq.	With Jack of Turn-up	If Flush in Hand	If Flush with Turn-up	If Fl & Jack of Turn-up
1	5	6	K	K	6		10		
1	5	7	7	7	12				
1	5	7	7	8	8		12		
1	5	7	7	9	6		10		
1	5	7	7	10	6		10		
1	5	7	7	J	6	7	10		
1	5	7	7	Q	6		10		
1	5	7	7	K	6		10		
1	5	7	8	8	6		10		
1	5	7	8	9	7		11	12	
1	5	7	8	10	4		8	9	
1	5	7	8	J	4	5	8	9	10
1	5	7	8	Q	4		8	9	
1	5	7	8	K	4		8	9	
1	5	7	9	9	6		10		
1	5	7	9	10	4		8	9	
1	5	7	9	J	4	5	8	9	10
1	5	7	9	Q	4		8	9	
1	5	7	9	K	4		8	9	
1	5	7	10	10	6		10		
1	5	7	10	J	4	5	8	9	10
1	5	7	10	Q	4		8	9	
1	5	7	10	K	4		8	9	
1	5	7	J	J	6	7	10		
1	5	7	J	Q	4	5	8	9	10
1	5	7	J	K	4	5	8	9	10
1	5	7	Q	Q	6		10		
1	5	7	Q	K	4		8	9	
1	5	7	K	K	6		10		
1	5	8	8	8	6				
1	5	8	8	9	4		8		
1	5	8	8	10	4		8		
1	5	8	8	J	4	5	8		
1	5	8	8	Q	4		8		
1	5	8	8	K	4		8		
1	5	8	9	9	6		10		
1	5	8	9	10	7		11	12	
1	5	8	9	J	4	5	8	9	10
1	5	8	9	Q	4		8	9	

CARDS.					Fifteens, Pairs & Seq.	With Jack of Turn-up	If Flush in Hand	If Flush with Turn-up	If Fl & Jack of Turn-up
1	5	8	9	K	4		8	9	
1	5	8	10	10	6		10		
1	5	8	10	J	4	5	8	9	10
1	5	8	10	Q	4		8	9	
1	5	8	10	K	4		8	9	
1	5	8	J	J	6	7	10		
1	5	8	J	Q	4	5	8	9	10
1	5	8	J	K	4	5	8	9	10
1	5	8	Q	Q	6		10		
1	5	8	Q	K	4		8	9	
1	5	8	K	K	6		10		
1	5	9	9	9	12				
1	5	9	9	10	8		12		
1	5	9	9	J	8	9	12		
1	5	9	9	Q	8		12		
1	5	9	9	K	8		12		
1	5	9	10	10	8		12		
1	5	9	10	J	9	10	13	14	15
1	5	9	10	Q	6		10	11	
1	5	9	10	K	6		10	11	
1	5	9	J	J	8	9	12		
1	5	9	J	Q	6	7	10	11	12
1	5	9	J	K	6	7	10	11	12
1	5	9	Q	Q	8		12		
1	5	9	Q	K	6		10	11	
1	5	9	K	K	8		12		
1	5	10	10	10	12				
1	5	10	10	J	8	9	12		
1	5	10	10	Q	8		12		
1	5	10	10	K	8		12		
1	5	10	J	J	8	9	12		
1	5	10	J	Q	9	10	13	14	15
1	5	10	J	K	6	7	10	11	12
1	5	10	Q	Q	8		12		
1	5	10	Q	K	6		10	11	
1	5	10	K	K	8		12		
1	5	J	J	J	12	13			
1	5	J	J	Q	8	9	12		
1	5	J	J	K	8	9	12		

KEY TO CRIBBAGE.

CARDS	Fifteens, Pairs & Seq.	With Jack of Turn-up	If Flush in Hand	If Flush with Turn-up	If Fl & Jack of Turn-up
1 5 J Q Q	8	9	12		
1 5 J Q K	9	10	13	14	15
1 5 J K K	8	9	12		
1 5 Q Q Q	12				
1 5 Q Q K	8		12		
1 5 Q K K	8		12		
1 5 K K K	12				
1 6 6 6 6	12				
1 6 6 6 7	6				
1 6 6 6 8	12				
1 6 6 6 9	12				
1 6 6 6 10	6				
1 6 6 6 J	6	7			
1 6 6 6 Q	6				
1 6 6 6 K	6				
1 6 6 7 7	6				
1 6 6 7 8	14		18		
1 6 6 7 9	6		10		
1 6 6 7 10	2		6		
1 6 6 7 J	2	3	6		
1 6 6 7 Q	2		6		
1 6 6 7 K	2		6		
1 6 6 8 8	12				
1 6 6 8 9	10		14		
1 6 6 8 10	6		10		
1 6 6 8 J	6	7	10		
1 6 6 8 Q	6		10		
1 6 6 8 K	6		10		
1 6 6 9 9	12				
1 6 6 9 10	6		10		
1 6 6 9 J	6	7	10		
1 6 6 9 Q	6		10		
1 6 6 9 K	6		10		
1 6 6 10 10	4				
1 6 6 10 J	2	3	6		
1 6 6 10 Q	2		6		
1 6 6 10 K	2		6		
1 6 6 J J	4	5			
1 6 6 J Q	2	3	6		

CARDS	Fifteens, Pairs & Seq.	With Jack of Turn-up	If Flush in Hand	If Flush with Turn-up	If Fl & Jack of Turn-up
1 6 6 J K	2	3	6		
1 6 6 Q Q	4			6	
1 6 6 Q K	2		6		
1 6 6 K K	4				
1 6 7 7 7	12				
1 6 7 7 8	16		20		
1 6 7 7 9	6		10		
1 6 7 7 10	4		8		
1 6 7 7 J	4	5	8		
1 6 7 7 Q	4		8		
1 6 7 7 K	4		8		
1 6 7 8 9	16		20		
1 6 7 8 10	10		14	15	
1 6 7 8 J	7		11	12	
1 6 7 8 Q	7	8	11	12	13
1 6 7 8 K	7		11	12	
1 6 7 9 9	6		10		
1 6 7 9 10	2		6	7	
1 6 7 9 J	2	3	6	7	8
1 6 7 9 Q	2		6	7	
1 6 7 9 K	2		6	7	
1 6 7 10 10	2		6		
1 6 7 10 J	0	1	4	5	6
1 6 7 10 Q	0		4	5	
1 6 7 10 K	0		4	5	
1 6 7 J J	2	3	6		
1 6 7 J Q	0	1	4	5	6
1 6 7 J K	0	1	4	5	6
1 6 7 Q Q	2		6		
1 6 7 Q K	0		4	5	
1 6 7 K K	2		6		
1 6 8 8 8	12				
1 6 8 8 9	8		12		
1 6 8 8 10	6		10		
1 6 8 8 J	6	7	10		
1 6 8 8 Q	6		10		
1 6 8 8 K	6		10		
1 6 8 9 9	8		12		

KEY TO CRIBBAGE.

Cards					Fifteens, Pairs & Seq..	With Jack of Turn-up	If Flush in Hand......	If Flush with Turn-up	If Fl& Jack of Turn-up
1	6	8	9	10	7	..	11	12	..
1	6	8	9	J	4	5	8	9	10
1	6	8	9	Q	4	..	8	9	..
1	6	8	9	K	4	..	8	9	..
1	6	8	10	10	4	..	8	9	..
1	6	8	10	J	2	3	6	7	8
1	6	8	10	Q	2	..	6	7	..
1	6	8	10	K	2	..	6	7	..
1	6	8	J	J	4	5	8	..	..
1	6	8	J	Q	2	3	6	7	8
1	6	8	J	K	2	3	6	7	8
1	6	8	Q	Q	4	..	8	..	..
1	6	8	Q	K	2	..	6	7	..
1	6	8	K	K	4	..	8	..	..
1	6	9	9	9	12	..	..	..	..
1	6	9	9	10	6	..	10	..	..
1	6	9	9	J	6	7	10	..	..
1	6	9	9	Q	6	..	10	..	..
1	6	9	9	K	6	..	10	..	..
1	6	9	10	10	4	..	8	..	..
1	6	9	10	J	5	6	9	10	11
1	6	9	10	Q	2	..	6	7	..
1	6	9	10	K	2	..	6	7	..
1	6	9	J	J	4	5	8	..	..
1	6	9	J	Q	2	3	6	7	8
1	6	9	J	K	2	3	6	7	8
1	6	9	Q	Q	4	..	8	..	..
1	6	9	Q	K	2	..	6	7	..
1	6	9	K	K	4	..	8	..	..
1	6	10	10	10	6	..	..	..	..
1	6	10	10	J	2	3	6	..	..
1	6	10	10	Q	2	..	6	..	..
1	6	10	10	K	2	..	6	..	..
1	6	10	J	J	2	3	6	..	..
1	6	10	J	Q	3	4	7	8	9
1	6	10	J	K	0	1	4	5	6
1	6	10	Q	Q	0	2	..	4	6
1	6	10	Q	K	0	..	4	5	..
1	6	10	K	K	2	..	4	6	..

Cards					Fifteens, Pairs & Seq..	With Jack of Turn-up	If Flush in Hand......	If Flush with Turn-up	If Fl& Jack of Turn-up
1	6	J	J	J	6	7	..	..	..
1	6	J	J	Q	2	3	6	..	..
1	6	J	J	K	2	3	6	..	..
1	6	J	Q	K	3	4	7	8	9
1	6	J	K	K	2	3	6	..	..
1	6	Q	Q	Q	6	..	..	..	..
1	6	Q	Q	K	2	..	6	..	..
1	6	Q	K	K	2	..	6	..	..
1	6	K	K	K	6	..	..	..	..
1	7	7	7	7	24	..	..	..	..
1	7	7	7	8	18	..	..	..	..
1	7	7	7	9	12	..	..	..	..
1	7	7	7	10	12	..	..	..	..
1	7	7	7	J	12	13	..	..	..
1	7	7	7	Q	12	..	..	..	..
1	7	7	7	K	12	..	..	..	..
1	7	7	8	8	14	..	..	..	..
1	7	7	8	9	14	..	18	..	..
1	7	7	8	10	8	..	12	..	..
1	7	7	8	J	8	9	12	..	..
1	7	7	8	Q	8	..	12	..	..
1	7	7	8	K	8	..	12	..	..
1	7	7	9	9	6	..	..	..	..
1	7	7	9	10	4	..	8	..	..
1	7	7	9	J	4	5	8	..	..
1	7	7	9	Q	4	..	8	..	..
1	7	7	9	K	4	..	8	..	..
1	7	7	10	10	6	..	..	..	..
1	7	7	10	J	4	5	8	..	..
1	7	7	10	Q	4	..	8	..	..
1	7	7	10	K	4	..	8	..	..
1	7	7	J	J	6	7	..	..	..
1	7	7	J	Q	4	5	8	..	..
1	7	7	J	K	4	5	8	..	..
1	7	7	Q	Q	6	..	..	..	..
1	7	7	Q	K	4	..	8	..	..
1	7	7	K	K	6	..	..	..	..
1	7	8	8	8	12	..	..	..	..

KEY TO CRIBBAGE.

Cards	Fifteens, Pairs & Seq.	With Jack of Turn-up	If Flush in Hand	If Flush with Turn-up	If Fl. & Jack of Turn-up
1 7 8 8 9	12		16		
1 7 8 8 10	6		10		
1 7 8 8 J	6	7	10		
1 7 8 8 Q	6		10		
1 7 8 8 K	6		10		
1 7 8 9 9	10		14		
1 7 8 9 10	6		10	11	
1 7 8 9 J	5	6	9	10	11
1 7 8 9 Q	5		9	10	
1 7 8 9 K	5		9	10	
1 7 8 10 10	4		8		
1 7 8 10 J	2	3	6	7	8
1 7 8 10 Q	2		6	7	
1 7 8 10 K	2		6	7	
1 7 8 J J	4	5	8		
1 7 8 J Q	2	3	6	7	8
1 7 8 J K	2	3	6	7	8
1 7 8 Q Q	4		8		
1 7 8 Q K	2		6	7	
1 7 8 K K	4		8		
1 7 9 9 9	6				
1 7 9 9 10	2		6		
1 7 9 9 J	2	3	6		
1 7 9 9 Q	2		6		
1 7 9 9 K	2		6		
1 7 9 10 10	2		6		
1 7 9 10 J	3	4	7	8	9
1 7 9 10 Q	0		4	5	
1 7 9 10 K	0		4	5	
1 7 9 J J	2	3	6		
1 7 9 J Q	0	1	4	5	6
1 7 9 J K	0	1	4	5	6
1 7 9 Q Q	2		6		
1 7 9 Q K	0		4	5	
1 7 9 K K	2		6		
1 7 10 10 10	6				
1 7 10 10 J	2	3	6		
1 7 10 10 Q	2		6		
1 7 10 10 K	2		6		

Cards	Fifteens, Pairs & Seq.	With Jack of Turn-up	If Flush in Hand	If Flush with Turn-up	If Fl. & Jack of Turn-up
1 7 10 J J	2	3	6		
1 7 10 J Q	3	4	7	8	9
1 7 10 J K	0	1	4	5	6
1 7 10 Q Q	2		6		
1 7 10 Q K	0		4	5	
1 7 10 K K	2		6		
1 7 J J J	6	7			
1 7 J J Q	2	3	6		
1 7 J J K	2	3	6		
1 7 J Q Q	2	3	6		
1 7 J Q K	3	4	7	8	9
1 7 J K K	2	3	6		
1 7 Q Q Q	6				
1 7 Q Q K	2		6		
1 7 Q K K	2		6		
1 7 K K K	6				
1 8 8 8 9	12				
1 8 8 8 10	6				
1 8 8 8 J	6	7			
1 8 8 8 Q	6				
1 8 8 8 K	6				
1 8 8 9 9	4				
1 8 8 9 10	8		12		
1 8 8 9 J	2	3	6		
1 8 8 9 Q	2		6		
1 8 8 9 K	2		6		
1 8 8 10 10	4				
1 8 8 10 J	2	3	6		
1 8 8 10 Q	2		6		
1 8 8 10 K	2		6		
1 8 8 J J	4	5	6		
1 8 8 J Q	2	3	6		
1 8 8 J K	2	3	6		
1 8 8 Q Q	4		6		
1 8 8 Q K	2		6		
1 8 8 K K	4				
1 8 9 9 9	6				
1 8 9 9 10	8		12		

KEY TO CRIBBAGE

CARDS	Fifteens, Pairs & Seq.	With Jack of Turn-up	If Flush in Hand	If Flush with Turn-up	If Fl& Jack of Turn-up
1 8 9 9 J	2	3	6		
1 8 9 9 Q	2		6		
1 8 9 9 K	2		6		
1 8 9 10 10	8		12		
1 8 9 10 J	4	5	8	9	10
1 8 9 10 Q	3		7	8	
1 8 9 10 K	3		7	8	
1 8 9 J J	2	3	6		
1 8 9 J Q	0	1	4	5	6
1 8 9 J K	0	1	4	5	6
1 8 9 Q Q	2		6		
1 8 9 Q K	0		4	5	
1 8 9 K K	2		6		
1 8 10 10 10	6				
1 8 10 10 J	2	3	6		
1 8 10 10 Q	2		6		
1 8 10 10 K	2		6		
1 8 10 J J	2	3	6		
1 8 10 J Q	3	4	7	8	9
1 8 10 J K	0	1	4	5	6
1 8 10 Q Q	2		6		
1 8 10 Q K	0		4	5	
1 8 10 K K	2		6		
1 8 J J J	6	7			
1 8 J J Q	2	3	6		
1 8 J J K	2	3	6		
1 8 J Q Q	2	3	6		
1 8 J Q K	3	4	7	8	9
1 8 J K K	2	3	6		
1 8 Q Q Q	6				
1 8 Q Q K	2		6		
1 8 Q K K	2		6		
1 8 K K K	6				
1 9 9 9 9	12				
1 9 9 9 10	6				
1 9 9 9 J	6	7			
1 9 9 9 Q	6				
1 9 9 9 K	6				
1 9 9 10 10	4				
1 9 9 10 J	8	9	12		
1 9 9 10 Q	2		6		
1 9 9 10 K	2		6		
1 9 9 J J	4	5			
1 9 9 J Q	2	3	6		
1 9 9 J K	2	3	6		
1 9 9 Q Q	4				
1 9 9 Q K	2		6		
1 9 9 K K	4				
1 9 10 10 10	6				
1 9 10 10 J	8	9	12		
1 9 10 10 Q	2		6		
1 9 10 10 K	2		6		
1 9 10 J J	8	9	12		
1 9 10 J Q	4	5	8	9	10
1 9 10 J K	3	4	7	8	9
1 9 10 Q Q	2		6		
1 9 10 Q K	0		4	5	
1 9 10 K K	2		6		
1 9 J J J	6	7			
1 9 J J Q	2	3	6		
1 9 J J K	2	3	6		
1 9 J Q Q	2	3	6		
1 9 J Q K	3	4	7	8	9
1 9 J K K	2	3	6		
1 9 Q Q Q	6				
1 9 Q Q K	2		6		
1 9 Q K K	2		6		
1 9 K K K	6				
1 10 10 10 10	12				
1 10 10 10 J	6	7			
1 10 10 10 Q	6				
1 10 10 10 K	6				
1 10 10 J J	4	5			
1 10 10 J Q	8	9	12		
1 10 10 J K	2	3	6		
1 10 10 Q Q	4				
1 10 10 Q K	2		6		
1 10 10 K K	4				

KEY TO CRIBBAGE.

Cards					Fifteens, Pairs & Seq.	With Jack of Turn-up	If Flush in Hand	If Flush with Turn-up	If Fl& Jack of Turn-up
1	10	J	J	J	6	7			
1	10	J	J	Q	8	9	12		
1	10	J	J	K	2	3	6		
1	10	J	Q	Q	8	9	12		
1	10	J	Q	K	4	5	8	9	10
1	10	J	K	K	2	3	6		
1	10	Q	Q	Q	6				
1	10	Q	Q	K	2		6		
1	10	Q	K	K	2		6		
1	10	K	K	K	6				
1	J	J	J	J	12	13			
1	J	J	J	Q	6	7			
1	J	J	J	K	6	7			
1	J	J	Q	Q	4	5			
1	J	J	Q	K	8	9	12		
1	J	J	K	K	4	5			
1	J	Q	Q	Q	6	7			
1	J	Q	Q	K	8	9	12		
1	J	Q	K	K	8	9	12		
1	J	K	K	K	6	7			
1	Q	Q	Q	Q	12				
1	Q	Q	Q	K	6				
1	Q	Q	K	K	4				
1	Q	K	K	K	6				
1	K	K	K	K	12				
2	2	2	2	3	12				
2	2	2	2	4	12				
2	2	2	2	5	12				
2	2	2	2	6	12				
2	2	2	2	7	14				
2	2	2	2	8	12				
2	2	2	2	9	20				
2	2	2	2	10	12				
2	2	2	2	J	12	13			
2	2	2	2	Q	12				
2	2	2	2	K	12				
2	2	2	3	3	8				
2	2	2	3	4	15				
2	2	2	3	5	6				

Cards					Fifteens, Pairs & Seq.	With Jack of Turn-up	If Flush in Hand	If Flush with Turn-up	If Fl& Jack of Turn-up
2	2	2	3	6	8				
2	2	2	3	7	6				
2	2	2	3	8	12				
2	2	2	3	9	8				
2	2	2	3	10	12				
2	2	2	3	J	12	13			
2	2	2	3	Q	12				
2	2	2	3	K	12				
2	2	2	4	4	8				
2	2	2	4	5	8				
2	2	2	4	6	6				
2	2	2	4	7	12				
2	2	2	4	8	6				
2	2	2	4	9	14				
2	2	2	4	10	6				
2	2	2	4	J	6	7			
2	2	2	4	Q	6				
2	2	2	4	K	6				
2	2	2	5	5	8				
2	2	2	5	6	12				
2	2	2	5	7	6				
2	2	2	5	8	12				
2	2	2	5	9	8				
2	2	2	5	10	8				
2	2	2	5	J	8	9			
2	2	2	5	Q	8				
2	2	2	5	K	8				
2	2	2	6	6	8				
2	2	2	6	7	12				
2	2	2	6	8	6				
2	2	2	6	9	10				
2	2	2	6	10	6				
2	2	2	6	J	6	7			
2	2	2	6	Q	6				
2	2	2	6	K	6				
2	2	2	7	7	8				
2	2	2	7	8	8				
2	2	2	7	9	8				
2	2	2	7	10	6				

KEY TO CRIBBAGE.

Cards					Fifteens, Pairs & Seq.	With Jack of Turn-up	If Flush in Hand	If Flush with Turn-up	If Fl.& Jack of Turn-up
2	2	2	7	J	6	7			
2	2	2	7	Q	6				
2	2	2	7	K	6				
2	2	2	8	8	8				
2	2	2	8	9	8				
2	2	2	8	10	6				
2	2	2	8	J	6	7			
2	2	2	8	Q	6				
2	2	2	8	K	6				
2	2	2	9	9	12				
2	2	2	9	10	8				
2	2	2	9	J	8	9			
2	2	2	9	Q	8				
2	2	2	9	K	8				
2	2	2	10	10	8				
2	2	2	10	J	6	7			
2	2	2	10	Q	6				
2	2	2	10	K	6				
2	2	2	J	J	8	9			
2	2	2	J	Q	6	7			
2	2	2	J	K	6	7			
2	2	2	Q	Q	8				
2	2	2	Q	K	6				
2	2	2	K	K	8				
2	2	3	3	3	8				
2	2	3	3	4	16				
2	2	3	3	5	6				
2	2	3	3	6	4				
2	2	3	3	7	8				
2	2	3	3	8	8				
2	2	3	3	9	6				
2	2	3	3	10	12				
2	2	3	3	J	12	13			
2	2	3	3	Q	12				
2	2	3	3	K	12				
2	2	3	4	4	18				
2	2	3	4	5	10		14		
2	2	3	4	6	12		16		
2	2	3	4	7	10		14		
2	2	3	4	8	12		16		
2	2	3	4	9	12		16		
2	2	3	4	10	12	13	16		
2	2	3	4	J	12		16		
2	2	3	4	Q	12		16		
2	2	3	4	K	12		16		
2	2	3	5	5	8				
2	2	3	5	6	4		8		
2	2	3	5	7	4		8		
2	2	3	5	8	8		12		
2	2	3	5	9	2		6		
2	2	3	5	10	8		12		
2	2	3	5	J	8	9	12		
2	2	3	5	Q	8		12		
2	2	3	5	K	8		12		
2	2	3	6	6	6				
2	2	3	6	7	6		10		
2	2	3	6	8	4		8		
2	2	3	6	9	4		8		
2	2	3	6	10	6		10		
2	2	3	6	J	6	7	10		
2	2	3	6	Q	6		10		
2	2	3	6	K	6		10		
2	2	3	7	7	4				
2	2	3	7	8	6		10		
2	2	3	7	9	2		6		
2	2	3	7	10	6		10		
2	2	3	7	J	6	7	10		
2	2	3	7	Q	6		10		
2	2	3	7	K	6		10		
2	2	3	8	8	8				
2	2	3	8	9	4		8		
2	2	3	8	10	8		12		
2	2	3	8	J	8	9	12		
2	2	3	8	Q	8		12		
2	2	3	8	K	8		12		
2	2	3	9	9	4				
2	2	3	9	10	6		10		
2	2	3	9	J	6	7	10		

KEY TO CRIBBAGE.

Cards					Fifteens, Pairs & Seq.	With Jack of Turn-up.	If Flush in Hand......	If Flush with Turn-up.	If Fl& Jack of Turn-up		Cards					Fifteens, Pairs & Seq.	With Jack of Turn-up.	If Flush in Hand......	If Flush with Turn-up.	If Fl& Jack of Turn-up
2	2	3	9	Q	6	..	10	..	..		2	2	4	7	7	8	..	10	..	..
2	2	3	9	K	6	..	10	..	..		2	2	4	7	8	6	..	10	..	..
2	2	3	10	10	12	..	..	..	..		2	2	4	7	9	8	..	12	..	..
2	2	3	10	J	10	11	14	..	..		2	2	4	7	10	4	5	8	..	..
2	2	3	10	Q	10	..	14	..	..		2	2	4	7	J	4	5	8	..	..
2	2	3	10	K	10	..	14	..	..		2	2	4	7	Q	4	..	8	..	..
2	2	3	J	J	12	13	..	..	..		2	2	4	7	K	4	..	8	..	..
2	2	3	J	Q	10	11	14	..	..		2	2	4	8	8	4	..	..	..	..
2	2	3	J	K	10	11	14	..	..		2	2	4	8	9	6	..	10	..	..
2	2	3	Q	Q	12	..	..	..	..		2	2	4	8	10	2	..	6	..	..
2	2	3	Q	K	10	..	14	..	..		2	2	4	8	J	2	3	6	..	..
2	2	3	K	K	12	..	..	..	..		2	2	4	8	Q	2	..	6	..	..
2	2	4	4	4	8	..	..	..	..		2	2	4	8	K	2	..	6	..	..
2	2	4	4	5	8	..	..	..	..		2	2	4	9	9	12	..	..	..	..
2	2	4	4	6	4	..	..	..	..		2	2	4	9	10	6	..	10	..	..
2	2	4	4	7	10	..	..	..	..		2	2	4	9	J	6	7	10	..	..
2	2	4	4	8	4	..	..	..	..		2	2	4	9	Q	6	..	10	..	..
2	2	4	4	9	12	..	..	..	..		2	2	4	9	K	6	..	10	..	..
2	2	4	4	10	4	..	..	..	..		2	2	4	10	10	4	..	..	..	..
2	2	4	4	J	4	5	..	..	..		2	2	4	10	J	2	3	6	..	..
2	2	4	4	Q	4	..	..	..	..		2	2	4	10	Q	2	..	6	..	..
2	2	4	4	K	4	..	..	..	..		2	2	4	10	K	2	..	6	..	..
2	2	4	5	5	4	..	..	..	..		2	2	4	J	J	4	5	..	..	..
2	2	4	5	6	9	..	13	..	..		2	2	4	J	Q	2	3	6	..	..
2	2	4	5	7	4	..	8	..	..		2	2	4	J	K	2	3	6	..	..
2	2	4	5	8	6	..	10	..	..		2	2	4	Q	Q	4	..	..	..	..
2	2	4	5	9	6	..	10	..	..		2	2	4	Q	K	2	..	6	..	..
2	2	4	5	10	4	..	8	..	..		2	2	4	K	K	4	..	..	..	..
2	2	4	5	J	4	5	8	..	..		2	2	5	5	5	10	..	..	..	..
2	2	4	5	Q	4	..	8	..	..		2	2	5	5	6	8	..	..	..	..
2	2	4	5	K	4	..	8	..	..		2	2	5	5	7	4	..	..	..	..
2	2	4	6	6	4	..	..	..	..		2	2	5	5	8	12	..	..	..	..
2	2	4	6	7	8	..	12	..	..		2	2	5	5	9	4	..	..	..	..
2	2	4	6	8	2	..	6	..	..		2	2	5	5	10	8	..	..	..	..
2	2	4	6	9	8	..	12	..	..		2	2	5	5	J	8	9	..	..	..
2	2	4	6	10	2	..	6	..	..		2	2	5	5	Q	8	..	..	..	..
2	2	4	6	J	2	3	6	..	..		2	2	5	5	K	8	..	..	..	..
2	2	4	6	Q	2	..	6	..	..		2	2	5	6	6	8	..	..	..	..
2	2	4	6	K	2	..	6	..	..		2	2	5	6	7	11	..	15	.	..

KEY TO CRIBBAGE.

Cards					Fifteens, Pairs & Seq.	With Jack of Turn-up.	If Flush in Hand.	If Flush with Turn-up.	If Fl.& Jack of Turn-up
2	2	5	6	8	8		12		
2	2	5	6	9	6		10		
2	2	5	6	10	6		10		
2	2	5	6	J	6	7	10		
2	2	5	6	Q	6		10		
2	2	5	6	K	6		10		
2	2	5	7	7	4				
2	2	5	7	8	8		12		
2	2	5	7	9	2		6		
2	2	5	7	10	4		8		
2	2	5	7	J	4	5	8		
2	2	5	7	Q	4		8		
2	2	5	7	K	4		8		
2	2	5	8	8	12				
2	2	5	8	9	6		10		
2	2	5	8	10	8		12		
2	2	5	8	J	8	9	12		
2	2	5	8	Q	8		12		
2	2	5	8	K	8		12		
2	2	5	9	9	4				
2	2	5	9	10	4		8		
2	2	5	9	J	4	5	8		
2	2	5	9	Q	4		8		
2	2	5	9	K	4		8		
2	2	5	10	10	8				
2	2	5	10	J	6	7	10		
2	2	5	10	Q	6		10		
2	2	5	10	K	6		10		
2	2	5	J	J	8	9			
2	2	5	J	Q	6	7	10		
2	2	5	J	K	6	7	10		
2	2	5	Q	Q	8				
2	2	5	Q	K	6		10		
2	2	5	K	K	8				
2	2	6	6	6	8				
2	2	6	6	7	12				
2	2	6	6	8	4				
2	2	6	6	9	8				
2	2	6	6	10	4				
2	2	6	6	J	4	5			
2	2	6	6	Q	4				
2	2	6	6	K	4				
2	2	6	7	7	12				
2	2	6	7	8	11		15		
2	2	6	7	9	8		12		
2	2	6	7	10	6		10		
2	2	6	7	J	6	7	10		
2	2	6	7	Q	6		10		
2	2	6	7	K	6		10		
2	2	6	8	8	4				
2	2	6	8	9	4		8		
2	2	6	8	10	2		6		
2	2	6	8	J	2	3	6		
2	2	6	8	Q	2		6		
2	2	6	8	K	2		6		
2	2	6	9	9	8				
2	2	6	9	10	4		8		
2	2	6	9	J	4	5	8		
2	2	6	9	Q	4		8		
2	2	6	9	K	4		8		
2	2	6	10	10	4				
2	2	6	10	J	2	3	6		
2	2	6	10	Q	2		6		
2	2	6	10	K	2		6		
2	2	6	J	J	4	5			
2	2	6	J	Q	2	3	6		
2	2	6	J	K	2	3	6		
2	2	6	Q	Q	4				
2	2	6	Q	K	2		6		
2	2	6	K	K	4				
2	2	7	7	7	8				
2	2	7	7	8	8				
2	2	7	7	9	4				
2	2	7	7	10	4				
2	2	7	7	J	4	5			
2	2	7	7	Q	4				
2	2	7	7	K	4				
2	2	7	7	8	8				

KEY TO CRIBBAGE.

Cards					Fifteens, Pairs & Seq.	With Jack of Turn-up	If Flush in Hand	If Flush with Turn-up	If Fl& Jack of Turn-up
2	2	7	8	9	7		11		
2	2	7	8	10	4	4	8		
2	2	7	8	J	4	5	8		
2	2	7	8	Q	4		8		
2	2	7	8	K	4		8		
2	2	7	9	9	4				
2	2	7	9	10	2		6		
2	2	7	9	J	2	3	6		
2	2	7	9	Q	2		6		
2	2	7	9	K	2		6		
2	2	7	10	10	4				
2	2	7	10	J	2	3	6		
2	2	7	10	Q	2		6		
2	2	7	10	K	2		6		
2	2	7	J	J	4	5			
2	2	7	J	Q	2	3	6		
2	2	7	J	K	2	3	6		
2	2	7	Q	Q	4				
2	2	7	Q	K	2		6		
2	2	7	K	K	4				
2	2	8	8	8	8				
2	2	8	8	9	4				
2	2	8	8	10	4				
2	2	8	8	J	4	5			
2	2	8	8	Q	4				
2	2	8	8	K	4				
2	2	8	9	9	4				
2	2	8	9	10	5		9		
2	2	8	9	J	2	3	6		
2	2	8	9	Q	2		6		
2	2	8	9	K	2		6		
2	2	8	10	10	4				
2	2	8	10	J	2	3	6		
2	2	8	10	Q	2		6		
2	2	8	10	K	2		6		
2	2	8	J	J	4	5			
2	2	8	J	Q	2	3	6		
2	2	8	J	K	2	3	6		
2	2	8	Q	Q	4				

Cards					Fifteens, Pairs & Seq.	With Jack of Turn-up	If Flush in Hand	If Flush with Turn-up	If Fl& Jack of Turn-up
2	2	8	Q	K	2		6		
2	2	8	K	K	4				
2	2	9	9	9	8				
2	2	9	9	10	4				
2	2	9	9	J	4	5			
2	2	9	9	Q	4				
2	2	9	9	K	4				
2	2	9	10	10	4				
2	2	9	10	J	5	6	9		
2	2	9	10	Q	2		6		
2	2	9	10	K	2		6		
2	2	9	J	J	4	5			
2	2	9	J	Q	2	3	6		
2	2	9	J	K	2	3	6		
2	2	9	Q	Q	4				
2	2	9	Q	K	2		6		
2	2	9	K	K	4				
2	2	10	10	10	8				
2	2	10	10	J	4	5			
2	2	10	10	Q	4				
2	2	10	10	K	4				
2	2	10	J	J	4	5			
2	2	10	J	Q	5	6	9		
2	2	10	J	K	2	3	6		
2	2	10	Q	Q	4				
2	2	10	Q	K	2		6		
2	2	10	K	K	4				
2	2	J	J	J	8		9		
2	2	J	J	Q	4	5			
2	2	J	J	K	4	5			
2	2	J	Q	Q	4	5			
2	2	J	Q	K	5	6	9		
2	2	J	K	K	4	5			
2	2	Q	Q	Q	8				
2	2	Q	Q	K	4				
2	2	Q	K	K	4				
2	2	K	K	K	8				
2	3	3	3	3	12				
2	3	3	3	4	17				

KEY TO CRIBBAGE

Cards					Fifteens, Pairs & Seq..	With Jack of Turn-up	If Flush in Hand......	If Flush with Turn-up.	If Fl& Jack of Turn-up
2	3	3	3	5	6				
2	3	3	3	6	8				
2	3	3	3	7	12				
2	3	3	3	8	6				
2	3	3	3	9	12				
2	3	3	3	10	12				
2	3	3	3	J	12	13			
2	3	3	3	Q	12				
2	3	3	3	K	12				
2	3	3	4	4	16				
2	3	3	4	5	12		16		
2	3	3	4	6	12		16		
2	3	3	4	7	10		14		
2	3	3	4	8	12		16		
2	3	3	4	9	12		16		
2	3	3	4	10	12		16		
2	3	3	4	J	12	13	16		
2	3	3	4	Q	12		16		
2	3	3	4	K	12		16		
2	3	3	5	5	8				
2	3	3	5	6	2		6		
2	3	3	5	7	8		12		
2	3	3	5	8	4		8		
2	3	3	5	9	4		8		
2	3	3	5	10	8		12		
2	3	3	5	J	8	9	12		
2	3	3	5	Q	8		12		
2	3	3	5	K	8		12		
2	3	3	6	6	8				
2	3	3	6	7	6		10		
2	3	3	6	8	2		6		
2	3	3	6	9	6		10		
2	3	3	6	10	6		10		
2	3	3	6	J	6	7	10		
2	3	3	6	Q	6		10		
2	3	3	6	K	6		10		
2	3	3	7	7	8				
2	3	3	7	8	6		10		
2	3	3	7	9	6		10		
2	3	3	7	10	8		12		
2	3	3	7	J	8	9	12		
2	3	3	7	Q	8		12		
2	3	3	7	K	8		12		
2	3	3	8	8	4				
2	3	3	8	9	4		8		
2	3	3	8	10	6		10		
2	3	3	8	J	6	7	10		
2	3	3	8	Q	6		10		
2	3	3	8	K	6		10		
2	3	3	9	9	8				
2	3	3	9	10	8		12		
2	3	3	9	J	8	9	12		
2	3	3	9	Q	8		12		
2	3	3	9	K	8		12		
2	3	3	10	10	12				
2	3	3	10	J	10	11	14		
2	3	3	10	Q	10		14		
2	3	3	10	K	10		14		
2	3	3	J	J	12	13			
2	3	3	J	Q	10	11	14		
2	3	3	J	K	10	11	14		
2	3	3	Q	Q	12				
2	3	3	Q	K	10		14		
2	3	3	K	K	12				
2	3	4	4	4	17				
2	3	4	4	5	12		16		
2	3	4	4	6	12		16		
2	3	4	4	7	10		14		
2	3	4	4	8	12		16		
2	3	4	4	9	12		16		
2	3	4	4	10	10		14		
2	3	4	4	J	10	11	14		
2	3	4	4	Q	10		14		
2	3	4	4	K	10		14		
2	3	4	5	5	12		16		
2	3	4	5	6	9		13	14	
2	3	4	5	7	6		10	11	
2	3	4	5	8	8		12	13	

KEY TO CRIBBAGE.

CARDS					Fifteens, Pairs & Seq.	With Jack of Turn-up	If Flush in Hand	If Flush with Turn-up	If Fl& Jack of Turn-up
2	3	4	5	9	6	..	10	11	..
2	3	4	5	10	8	..	12	13	..
2	3	4	5	J	8	9	12	13	14
2	3	4	5	Q	8	..	12	13	..
2	3	4	5	K	8	..	12	13	..
2	3	4	6	6	11	..	15	..	..
2	3	4	6	7	7	..	11	12	..
2	3	4	6	8	7	..	11	12	..
2	3	4	6	9	9	..	13	14	..
2	3	4	6	10	7	..	11	12	..
2	3	4	6	J	7	8	11	12	13
2	3	4	6	Q	7	..	11	12	..
2	3	4	6	K	7	..	11	12	..
2	3	4	7	7	5	..	9	..	..
2	3	4	7	8	7	..	11	12	..
2	3	4	7	9	5	..	9	10	..
2	3	4	7	10	5	..	9	10	..
2	3	4	7	J	5	6	9	10	11
2	3	4	7	Q	5	..	9	10	..
2	3	4	7	K	5	..	9	10	..
2	3	4	8	8	9	..	13	..	..
2	3	4	8	9	7	..	11	12	..
2	3	4	8	10	7	..	11	12	..
2	3	4	8	J	7	8	11	12	13
2	3	4	8	Q	7	..	11	12	..
2	3	4	8	K	7	..	11	12	..
2	3	4	9	9	9	..	13	..	..
2	3	4	9	10	7	..	11	12	..
2	3	4	9	J	7	8	11	12	13
2	3	4	9	Q	7	..	11	12	..
2	3	4	9	K	9	..	11	12	..
2	3	4	10	10	9	..	13	..	..
2	3	4	10	J	7	8	11	12	13
2	3	4	10	Q	7	..	11	12	..
2	3	4	10	K	7	..	11	12	..
2	3	4	J	J	9	10	13	..	..
2	3	4	J	Q	7	8	11	12	13
2	3	4	J	K	7	8	11	12	13
2	3	4	Q	Q	9	..	13	..	..
2	3	4	Q	K	7	..	11	12	..
2	3	4	K	K	9	..	13	..	..
2	3	5	5	5	14	..	..	..	..
2	3	5	5	6	4	..	8	..	..
2	3	5	5	7	8	..	12	..	..
2	3	5	5	8	8	..	12	..	..
2	3	5	5	9	4	..	8	..	..
2	3	5	5	10	10	..	14	..	..
2	3	5	5	J	10	11	14	..	..
2	3	5	5	Q	10	..	14	..	..
2	3	5	5	K	10	..	14	..	..
2	3	5	6	6	4	..	8	..	..
2	3	5	6	7	7	..	11	12	..
2	3	5	6	8	2	..	6	7	..
2	3	5	6	9	2	..	6	7	..
2	3	5	6	10	4	..	8	9	..
2	3	5	6	J	4	5	8	9	10
2	3	5	6	Q	4	..	8	9	..
2	3	5	6	K	4	..	8	9	..
2	3	5	7	7	6	..	10	..	..
2	3	5	7	8	6	..	10	11	..
2	3	5	7	9	2	..	6	7	..
2	3	5	7	10	6	..	10	11	..
2	3	5	7	J	6	7	10	11	12
2	3	5	7	Q	6	..	10	11	..
2	3	5	7	K	6	..	10	11	..
2	3	5	8	9	2	..	6	7	..
2	3	5	8	10	6	..	10	11	..
2	3	5	8	J	6	7	10	11	12
2	3	5	8	Q	6	..	10	11	..
2	3	5	8	K	6	..	10	11	..
2	3	5	9	9	2	..	6	..	..
2	3	5	9	10	4	..	8	9	..
2	3	5	9	J	4	5	8	9	10
2	3	5	9	Q	4	..	8	9	..
2	3	5	9	K	4	..	8	9	..
2	3	5	10	10	10	..	14	..	..
2	3	5	10	J	8	9	12	13	14

KEY TO CRIBBAGE

CARDS.				Fifteens, Pairs & Seq..	With Jack of Turn-up...	If Flush in Hand......	If Flush with Turn-up.	If Fl& Jack of Turn-up
2	3	5	10	Q	8	..	12	13	..
2	3	5	10	K	8	..	12	13	..
2	3	5	J	J	10	11	14	..	..
2	3	5	J	Q	8	9	12	13	14
2	3	5	J	K	8	9	12	13	14
2	3	5	Q	Q	10	..	14	..	..
2	3	5	Q	K	8	..	12	13	..
2	3	5	K	K	10	..	14	..	..
2	3	6	6	6	12	..	..	..	..
2	3	6	6	7	8	..	12	..	..
2	3	6	6	8	4	..	8	..	..
2	3	6	6	9	8	..	12	..	..
2	3	6	6	10	6	..	10	..	..
2	3	6	6	J	6	7	10	..	..
2	3	6	6	Q	6	..	10	..	..
2	3	6	6	K	6	..	10	..	..
2	3	6	7	7	6	..	10	..	..
2	3	6	7	8	7	..	11	12	..
2	3	6	7	9	4	..	8	9	..
2	3	6	7	10	4	..	8	9	..
2	3	6	7	J	4	5	8	9	10
2	3	6	7	Q	4	..	8	9	..
2	3	6	7	K	4	..	8	9	..
2	3	6	8	8	2	..	6	..	..
2	3	6	8	9	2	..	6	7	..
2	3	6	8	10	2	..	6	7	..
2	3	6	8	J	2	3	6	7	8
2	3	6	8	Q	2	..	6	7	..
2	3	6	8	K	2	..	6	7	..
2	3	6	9	9	6	..	10	..	..
2	3	6	9	10	4	..	8	9	..
2	3	6	9	J	4	5	8	9	10
2	3	6	9	Q	4	..	8	9	..
2	3	6	9	K	4	..	8	9	..
2	3	6	10	10	6	..	10	..	..
2	3	6	10	J	4	5	8	9	10
2	3	6	10	Q	4	..	8	9	..
2	3	6	10	K	4	..	8	9	..
2	3	6	J	J	6	..	10	..	..

CARDS.				Fifteens, Pairs & Seq..	With Jack of Turn-up...	If Flush in Hand....	If Flush with Turn-up.	If Fl& Jack of Turn-up
2	3	6	J	Q	4	5	8	9	10
2	3	6	J	K	4	5	8	9	10
2	3	6	Q	Q	6	..	10	..	..
2	3	6	Q	K	4	..	8	9	..
2	3	6	K	K	6	..	10	..	..
2	3	7	7	7	6	..	..	..	..
2	3	7	7	8	6	..	10	..	..
2	3	7	7	9	2	..	6	..	..
2	3	7	7	10	4	..	8	..	..
2	3	7	7	J	4	5	8	..	..
2	3	7	7	Q	4	..	8	..	..
2	3	7	7	K	4	..	8	..	..
2	3	7	8	8	6	..	10	..	..
2	3	7	8	9	5	..	9	10	..
2	3	7	8	10	4	..	8	9	..
2	3	7	8	J	4	5	8	9	10
2	3	7	8	Q	4	..	8	9	..
2	3	7	8	K	4	..	8	9	..
2	3	7	9	9	2	..	6	..	..
2	3	7	9	10	2	..	6	7	..
2	3	7	9	J	2	3	6	7	8
2	3	7	9	Q	2	..	6	7	..
2	3	7	9	K	2	..	6	7	..
2	3	7	10	10	6	..	10	..	..
2	3	7	10	J	4	5	8	9	10
2	3	7	10	Q	4	..	8	9	..
2	3	7	10	K	4	..	8	9	..
2	3	7	J	J	6	7	10	..	..
2	3	7	J	Q	4	5	8	9	10
2	3	7	J	K	4	5	8	9	10
2	3	7	Q	Q	6	..	10	..	..
2	3	7	Q	K	4	..	8	9	..
2	3	7	K	K	6	..	10	..	..
2	3	8	8	8	6	..	..	..	..
2	3	8	8	9	2	..	6	..	..
2	3	8	8	10	4	..	8	..	..
2	3	8	8	J	4	5	8	..	..
2	3	8	8	Q	4	..	8	..	..
2	3	8	8	K	4	..	8	..	..

35   KEY TO CRIBBAGE.

Cards					Fifteens, Pairs & Seq.	With Jack of Turn-up.	If Flush in Hand.	If Flush with Turn-up.	If F.& Jack of Turn-up.
2	3	8	9	9	2		6		
2	3	8	9	10	5		6	9	10
2	3	8	9	J	2	3	6	7	8
2	3	8	9	Q	2		6	7	
2	3	8	9	K	2		6	7	
2	3	8	10	10	6		10		
2	3	8	10	J	4	5	8	9	10
2	3	8	10	Q	4		8	9	
2	3	8	10	K	4		8	9	
2	3	8	J	J	6	7	10		
2	3	8	J	Q	4	5	8	9	10
2	3	8	J	K	4	5	8	9	10
2	3	8	Q	Q	6		10		
2	3	8	Q	K	4		8	9	
2	3	8	K	K	6		10		
2	3	9	9	9	6				
2	3	9	9	10	4		8		
2	3	9	9	J	4	5	8		
2	3	9	9	Q	4		8		
2	3	9	9	K	4		8		
2	3	9	10	10	6		10		
2	3	9	10	J	7	8	11	12	13
2	3	9	10	Q	4		8	9	
2	3	9	10	K	4		8	9	
2	3	9	J	J	6	7	10		
2	3	9	J	Q	4	5	8	9	10
2	3	9	J	K	4	5	8	9	10
2	3	9	Q	Q	6		10		
2	3	9	Q	K	4		8	9	
2	3	9	K	K	6		10		
2	3	10	10	10	12				
2	3	10	10	J	8		9	12	
2	3	10	10	Q	8		12		
2	3	10	10	K	8		12		
2	3	10	J	J	8		9	12	
2	3	10	J	Q	9	10	13	14	15
2	3	10	J	K	6	7	10	11	12
2	3	10	Q	Q	8		12		
2	3	10	Q	K	6		10	11	
2	3	10	K	K	8		12		
2	3	J	J	J	12	13			
2	3	J	J	Q	8	9	12		
2	3	J	J	K	8	9	12		
2	3	J	Q	Q	8		12		
2	3	J	Q	K	8	10	13	14	15
2	3	J	K	K	8	9	12		
2	3	Q	Q	Q	12				
2	3	Q	Q	K	8		12		
2	3	Q	K	K	8		12		
2	3	K	K	K	12				
2	3	4	4	4	4				
2	3	4	4	5	6				
2	3	4	4	6	6				
2	3	4	4	7	8				
2	3	4	4	8	6				
2	3	4	4	9	6				
2	3	4	4	10	6	7			
2	3	4	4	J	6				
2	3	4	4	Q	6				
2	3	4	4	K	8				
2	3	4	5	5	6				
2	3	4	5	6	14		18		
2	3	4	5	7	6		10		
2	3	4	5	8	6		10		
2	3	4	5	9	8		12		
2	3	4	5	10	6		10		
2	3	4	5	J	6	7	10		
2	3	4	5	Q	6		10		
2	3	4	5	K	6		10		
2	3	4	6	6	4				
2	3	4	6	7	6		10		
2	3	4	6	8	2		6		
2	3	4	6	9	8		12		
2	3	4	6	10	2		6		
2	3	4	6	J	2		6	6	6
2	3	4	6	Q	2		6	6	6
2	3	4	6	K	2		6	6	
2	3	4	7	7	8				

KEY TO CRIBBAGE.

CARDS.					Fifteens, Pairs & Seq.	With Jack of Turn-up	If Flush in Hand	If Flush with Turn-up	If Fl & Jack of Turn up
2	4	4	7	8	6	..	10	..	..
2	4	4	7	9	8	..	12	..	..
2	4	4	7	10	4	..	8	..	..
2	4	4	7	J	4	5	8	..	..
2	4	4	7	Q	4	..	8	..	..
2	4	4	7	K	4	..	8	..	..
2	4	4	8	8	4	..	..	..	..
2	4	4	8	9	6	..	10	..	..
2	4	4	8	10	2	..	6	..	..
2	4	4	8	J	2	3	6	..	..
2	4	4	8	Q	2	..	6	..	..
2	4	4	8	K	2	..	6	..	..
2	4	4	9	9	12	..	..	..	..
2	4	4	9	10	6	..	10	..	..
2	4	4	9	J	6	7	10	..	..
2	4	4	9	Q	6	..	10	..	..
2	4	4	9	K	6	..	10	..	..
2	4	4	10	10	4	..	..	..	..
2	4	4	10	J	2	3	6	..	..
2	4	4	10	Q	2	..	6	..	..
2	4	4	10	K	2	..	6	..	..
2	4	4	J	J	4	5	..	..	..
2	4	4	J	Q	2	3	6	..	..
2	4	4	J	K	2	3	6	..	..
2	4	4	Q	Q	4	..	..	..	..
2	4	4	Q	K	2	..	6	..	..
2	4	4	K	K	4	..	..	..	..
2	4	5	5	5	8	..	10	..	..
2	4	5	5	6	12	..	10	..	..
2	4	5	5	7	2	..	6	..	..
2	4	5	5	8	6	..	10	..	..
2	4	5	5	9	4	..	8	..	..
2	4	5	5	10	6	..	10	..	..
2	4	5	5	J	6	7	10	..	..
2	4	5	5	Q	6	..	10	..	..
2	4	5	5	K	6	..	10	..	..
2	4	5	6	6	12	..	10	..	..
2	4	5	6	7	8	..	12	13	..
2	4	5	6	8	7	..	11	12	..

CARDS.					Fifteens, Pairs & Seq.	With Jack of Turn-up	If Flush in Hand	If Flush with Turn-up	If Fl & Jack of Turn up
2	4	5	6	9	9	..	13	14	..
2	4	5	6	10	7	..	11	12	..
2	4	5	6	J	7	8	11	12	13
2	4	5	6	Q	7	..	11	12	..
2	4	5	6	K	7	..	11	12	..
2	4	5	7	7	2	..	6	..	..
2	4	5	7	8	4	..	8	9	..
2	4	5	7	9	2	..	6	7	..
2	4	5	7	10	6	..	6	7	..
2	4	5	7	J	2	5	6	7	8
2	4	5	7	Q	2	..	6	7	..
2	4	5	7	K	2	..	6	7	..
2	4	5	8	8	6	..	10	..	..
2	4	5	8	9	4	..	8	9	..
2	4	5	8	10	4	..	8	9	..
2	4	5	8	J	4	5	8	9	10
2	4	5	8	Q	4	..	8	9	..
2	4	5	8	K	4	..	8	9	..
2	4	5	9	9	6	..	10	..	..
2	4	5	9	10	4	..	8	9	..
2	4	5	9	J	4	5	8	9	10
2	4	5	9	Q	4	..	8	9	..
2	4	5	9	K	4	..	8	9	..
2	4	5	10	10	6	..	10	..	..
2	4	5	10	J	4	5	8	9	10
2	4	5	10	Q	4	..	8	9	..
2	4	5	10	K	4	..	8	9	..
2	4	5	J	J	6	7	10	..	..
2	4	5	J	Q	4	5	8	9	10
2	4	5	J	K	4	5	8	9	10
2	4	5	Q	Q	6	..	10	..	..
2	4	5	Q	K	4	..	8	9	..
2	4	5	K	K	6	..	10	..	..
2	4	6	6	6	6	..	..	..	..
2	4	6	6	7	6	..	10	..	..
2	4	6	6	8	2	..	6	..	..
2	4	6	6	9	8	..	12	..	..
2	4	6	6	10	2	..	6	..	..
2	4	6	6	J	2	3	6	..	..

KEY TO CRIBBAGE.

Cards	Fifteens, Pairs & Seq.	With Jack of Turn-up	If Flush in Hand	If Flush with Turn-up	If Flush & Jack of Turn-up
2 4 6 6 Q	2		6		
2 4 6 6 K	2		6		
2 4 6 7 7	6		10		
2 4 6 7 8	7		11	12	
2 4 6 7 9	6		10	11	
2 4 6 7 10	2		6	7	
2 4 6 7 J	2	3	6	7	8
2 4 6 7 Q	2		6	7	
2 4 6 7 K	2		6	7	
2 4 6 8 8	2		6		
2 4 6 8 9	4		8	9	
2 4 6 8 10	0		4	5	
2 4 6 8 J	0	1	4	5	6
2 4 6 8 Q	0		4	5	
2 4 6 8 K	0		4	5	
2 4 6 9 9	10		14		
2 4 6 9 10	4		8	9	
2 4 6 9 J	4	5	8	9	10
2 4 6 9 Q	4		8	9	
2 4 6 9 K	4		8	9	
2 4 6 10 10	2		6		
2 4 6 10 J	0	1	4	5	6
2 4 6 10 Q	0		4	5	
2 4 6 10 K	0		4	5	
2 4 6 J J	2	3	6		
2 4 6 J Q	0	1	4	5	6
2 4 6 J K	0	1	4	5	6
2 4 6 Q Q	2		6		
2 4 6 Q K	0		4	5	
2 4 6 K K	2		6		
2 4 7 7 7	6				
2 4 7 7 8	6		10		
2 4 7 7 9	4		8		
2 4 7 7 10	2		6		
2 4 7 7 J	2	3	6		
2 4 7 7 Q	2		6		
2 4 7 7 K	2		6		
2 4 7 8 8	6		10		
2 4 7 8 9	7		11	12	
2 4 7 8 10	2		6	7	
2 4 7 8 J	2	3	6	7	8
2 4 7 8 Q	2		6	7	
2 4 7 8 K	2		6	7	
2 4 7 9 9	6		10		
2 4 7 9 10	2		6	7	
2 4 7 9 J	2	3	6	7	8
2 4 7 9 Q	2		6	7	
2 4 7 9 K	2		6	7	
2 4 7 10 10	2		6		
2 4 7 10 J	0	1	4	5	6
2 4 7 10 Q	0		4	5	
2 4 7 10 K	0		4	5	
2 4 7 J J	2	3	6		
2 4 7 J Q	0	1	4	5	6
2 4 7 J K	0	1	4	5	6
2 4 7 Q Q	2		6		
2 4 7 Q K	0		4	5	
2 4 7 K K	2		6		
2 4 8 8 8	6				
2 4 8 8 9	4		8		
2 4 8 8 10	2		6		
2 4 8 8 J	2	3	6		
2 4 8 8 Q	2		6		
2 4 8 8 K	2		6		
2 4 8 9 9	6		10		
2 4 8 9 10	5		9	10	
2 4 8 9 J	2	3	6	7	8
2 4 8 9 Q	2		6	7	
2 4 8 9 K	2		6	7	
2 4 8 10 10	2		6		
2 4 8 10 J	0	1	4	5	6
2 4 8 10 Q	0		4	5	
2 4 8 10 K	0		4	5	
2 4 8 J J	2	3	6		
2 4 8 J Q	0	1	4	5	6
2 4 8 J K	0	1	4	5	6
2 4 8 Q Q	2		6		
2 4 8 Q K	0		4	5	

KEY TO CRIBBAGE.

CARDS.					Fifteens, Pairs & Seq.	With Jack of Turn-up	If Flush in Hand	If Flush with Turn-up	If Fl& Jack of Turn-up
2	4	8	K	K	2		0		
2	4	9	9	9	12				
2	4	9	9	10	6		10		
2	4	9	9	J	6	7	10		
2	4	9	9	Q	6		10		
2	4	9	9	K	6		10		
2	4	9	10	10	4		8		
2	4	9	10	J	5	6	9	10	11
2	4	9	10	Q	2		6	7	
2	4	9	10	K	2		6	7	
2	4	9	J	J	4	5	8		8
2	4	9	J	Q	2	3	6	7	8
2	4	9	J	K	2	3	6	7	8
2	4	9	Q	Q	4		8		
2	4	9	Q	K	2		6	7	
2	4	9	K	K	4		8		
2	4	10	10	10	6				
2	4	10	10	J	2	3	6		
2	4	10	10	Q	2		6		
2	4	10	10	K	2		6		
2	4	10	J	J	2	3	6		
2	4	10	J	Q	3	4	7	8	9
2	4	10	J	K	0	1	4	5	6
2	4	10	Q	Q	2		6		
2	4	10	Q	K	0		4	5	
2	4	10	K	K	2		6		
2	4	J	J	J	6	7			
2	4	J	J	Q	2	3	6		
2	4	J	J	K	2	3	6		
2	4	J	Q	Q	2	3	6		
2	4	J	Q	K	3	4	7	8	9
2	4	J	K	K	2	3	6		
2	4	Q	Q	Q	6				
2	4	Q	Q	K	2		6		
2	4	Q	K	K	2		6		
2	4	K	K	K	6				
2	5	5	5	5	20				
2	5	5	5	6	8				
2	5	5	5	7	8				

CARDS.					Fifteens, Pairs & Seq.	With Jack of Turn-up	If Flush in Hand	If Flush with Turn-up	If Fl& Jack of Turn-up
2	5	5	5	8	14				
2	5	5	5	9	8				
2	5	5	5	10	14				
2	5	5	5	J	14	15			
2	5	5	5	Q	14				
2	5	5	5	K	14				
2	5	5	6	6	4				
2	5	5	6	7	10		14		
2	5	5	6	8	6		10		
2	5	5	6	9	4		8		
2	5	5	6	10	6		10		
2	5	5	6	J	6	7	10		
2	5	5	6	Q	6		10		
2	5	5	6	K	6		10		
2	5	5	7	7	4				
2	5	5	7	8	8		12		
2	5	5	7	9	2		6		
2	5	5	7	10	6		10		
2	5	5	7	J	6	7	10		
2	5	5	7	Q	6		10		
2	5	5	7	K	6		10		
2	5	5	8	8	12				
2	5	5	8	9	6		10		
2	5	5	8	10	10		14		
2	5	5	8	J	10	11	14		
2	5	5	8	Q	10		14		
2	5	5	8	K	10		14		
2	5	5	9	9	4				
2	5	5	9	10	6		10		
2	5	5	9	J	6	7	10		
2	5	5	9	Q	6		10		
2	5	5	9	K	6		10		
2	5	5	10	10	12				
2	5	5	10	J	10	11	14		
2	5	5	10	Q	10		14		
2	5	5	10	K	10		14		
2	5	5	J	J	12	13			
2	5	5	J	Q	10	11	14		
2	5	5	J	K	10	11	14		

KEY TO CRIBBAGE.

Cards					Fifteens, Pairs & Seq.	With Jack of Turn-up	If Flush in Hand	If Flush with Turn-up	If Fl& Jack of Turn-up
2	5	5	Q	Q	12		14		
2	5	5	Q	K	10		14		
2	5	5	K	K	12		14		
2	5	6	6	6	6				
2	5	6	6	7	12		16		
2	5	6	6	8	4		8		
2	5	6	6	9	6		10		
2	5	6	6	10	4		8		
2	5	6	6	J	4	5	8		
2	5	6	6	Q	4		8		
2	5	6	6	K	4		8		
2	5	6	7	7	12		16		
2	5	6	7	8	10		14	15	
2	5	6	7	9	7		11	12	
2	5	6	7	10	7		11	12	
2	5	6	7	J	7	8	11	12	13
2	5	6	7	Q	7		11	12	
2	5	6	7	K	7		11	12	
2	5	6	8	8	6		10		
2	5	6	8	9	4		8	9	
2	5	6	8	10	4		8	9	
2	5	6	8	J	4	5	8	9	10
2	5	6	8	Q	4		8	9	
2	5	6	8	K	4		8	9	
2	5	6	9	9	6		10		
2	5	6	9	10	4		8	9	
2	5	6	9	J	4	5	8	9	10
2	5	6	9	Q	4		8	9	
2	5	6	9	K	4		8	9	
2	5	6	10	10	6		10		
2	5	6	10	J	4	5	8	9	10
2	5	6	10	Q	4		8	9	
2	5	6	10	K	4		8	9	
2	5	6	J	J	6	7	10		
2	5	6	J	Q	4	5	8	9	10
2	5	6	J	K	4	5	8	9	10
2	5	6	Q	Q	6		10		
2	5	6	Q	K	4		8	9	
2	5	6	K	K	6		10		
2	5	7	7	7	6				
2	5	7	7	8	8		12		
2	5	7	7	9	2		6		
2	5	7	7	10	4		8		
2	5	7	7	J	4	5	8		
2	5	7	7	Q	4		8		
2	5	7	7	K	4		8		
2	5	7	8	8	10		14		
2	5	7	8	9	7		11	12	
2	5	7	8	10	6		10	11	
2	5	7	8	J	6	7	10	11	12
2	5	7	8	Q	6		10	11	
2	5	7	8	K	6		10	11	
2	5	7	9	9	2		6		
2	5	7	9	10	2		6	7	
2	5	7	9	J	2	3	6	7	8
2	5	7	9	Q	2		6	7	
2	5	7	9	K	2		6	7	
2	5	7	10	10	6		10		
2	5	7	10	J	4	5	8	9	10
2	5	7	10	Q	4		8	9	
2	5	7	10	K	4		8	9	
2	5	7	J	J	6	7	10		
2	5	7	J	Q	4	5	8	9	10
2	5	7	J	K	4	5	8	9	10
2	5	7	Q	Q	6		10		
2	5	7	Q	K	4		8	9	
2	5	7	K	K	6		10		
2	5	8	8	8	12				
2	5	8	8	9	6		10		
2	5	8	8	10	8		12		
2	5	8	8	J	8	9	12		
2	5	8	8	Q	8		12		
2	5	8	8	K	8		12		
2	5	8	9	9	4		8		
2	5	8	9	10	7		11	12	
2	5	8	9	J	4	5	8	9	10
2	5	8	9	Q	4		8	9	
2	5	8	9	K	4		8	9	

KEY TO CRIBBAGE.

The following table combines the two side-by-side blocks (left block first, then right block) into a single continuous sequence. The five scoring columns are, in order: *Fifteens, Pairs & Seq.* · *With Jack of Turn-up* · *If Flush in Hand* · *If Flush with Turn-up* · *If Fl. & Jack of Turn-up.*

Cards					Fifteens, Pairs & Seq.	With Jack of Turn-up	If Flush in Hand	If Flush with Turn-up	If Fl. & Jack of Turn-up
2	5	8	10	10	8	..	12	..	..
2	5	8	10	J	6	7	10	11	12
2	5	8	10	Q	6	..	10	11	..
2	5	8	10	K	6	..	10	11	..
2	5	8	J	J	8	9	12	..	..
2	5	8	J	Q	6	7	10	11	12
2	5	8	J	K	6	7	10	11	12
2	5	8	Q	Q	8	..	12	..	..
2	5	8	Q	K	6	..	10	11	..
2	5	8	K	K	8	..	12	..	..
2	5	9	9	9	6	..	..	..	..
2	5	9	9	10	4	..	8	..	..
2	5	9	9	J	4	5	8	..	..
2	5	9	9	Q	4	..	8	..	..
2	5	9	9	K	4	..	8	..	..
2	5	9	10	10	6	..	10	..	..
2	5	9	10	J	7	8	11	12	13
2	5	9	10	Q	4	..	8	9	..
2	5	9	10	K	4	..	8	9	..
2	5	9	J	J	6	7	10	..	..
2	5	9	J	Q	4	5	8	9	10
2	5	9	J	K	4	5	8	9	10
2	5	9	Q	Q	6	..	10	..	..
2	5	9	Q	K	4	..	8	9	..
2	5	9	K	K	6	..	10	..	..
2	5	10	10	10	12	..	..	..	..
2	5	10	10	J	8	9	12	..	..
2	5	10	10	Q	8	..	12	..	..
2	5	10	10	K	8	..	12	..	..
2	5	10	J	J	8	9	12	..	..
2	5	10	J	Q	9	10	13	14	15
2	5	10	J	K	6	7	10	11	12
2	5	10	Q	Q	8	..	12	..	..
2	5	10	Q	K	6	..	10	11	..
2	5	10	K	K	8	..	12	..	..
2	5	J	J	J	12	13	..	..	..
2	5	J	J	Q	8	9	12	..	..
2	5	J	J	K	8	9	12	..	..
2	5	J	Q	Q	8	9	12	..	..
2	5	J	Q	K	9	10	13	14	15
2	5	J	K	K	8	9	12	..	..
2	5	Q	Q	Q	12	..	..	..	..
2	5	Q	Q	K	8	..	12	..	..
2	5	Q	K	K	8	..	12	..	..
2	5	K	K	K	12	..	..	..	..
2	6	6	6	6	12	..	..	..	..
2	6	6	6	7	12	..	..	..	..
2	6	6	6	8	6	..	..	..	..
2	6	6	6	9	12	..	..	..	..
2	6	6	6	10	6	..	..	..	..
2	6	6	6	J	6	7	..	..	..
2	6	6	6	Q	6	..	..	..	..
2	6	6	6	K	6	..	..	..	..
2	6	6	7	7	12	..	..	..	..
2	6	6	7	8	14	..	18	..	..
2	6	6	7	9	10	..	14	..	..
2	6	6	7	10	6	..	10	..	..
2	6	6	7	J	6	7	10	..	..
2	6	6	7	Q	6	..	10	..	..
2	6	6	7	K	6	..	10	..	..
2	6	6	8	8	4	..	..	..	..
2	6	6	8	9	6	..	10	..	..
2	6	6	8	10	2	..	6	..	..
2	6	6	8	J	2	3	6	..	..
2	6	6	8	Q	2	..	6	..	..
2	6	6	8	K	2	..	6	..	..
2	6	6	9	9	12	..	..	..	..
2	6	6	9	10	6	..	10	..	..
2	6	6	9	J	6	7	10	..	..
2	6	6	9	Q	6	..	10	..	..
2	6	6	9	K	6	..	10	..	..
2	6	6	10	10	4	..	..	..	..
2	6	6	10	J	2	3	6	..	..
2	6	6	10	Q	2	..	6	..	..
2	6	6	10	K	2	..	6	..	..
2	6	6	J	J	4	5	..	..	..
2	6	6	J	Q	2	3	6	..	..
2	6	6	J	K	2	3	6	..	..

KEY TO CRIBBAGE.

Cards					Fifteens, Pairs & Seq.	With Jack of Turn-up	If Flush in Hand	If Flush with Turn-up	If Fl& Jack of Turn-up
2	6	6	Q	Q	4				
2	6	6	Q	K	2		6		
2	6	6	K	K	4				
2	6	7	7	7	12				
2	6	7	7	8	16		20		
2	6	7	7	9	8		12		
2	6	7	7	10	6		10		
2	6	7	7	J	6	7	10		
2	6	7	7	Q	6		10		
2	6	7	7	K	6		10		
2	6	7	8	8	14		18		
2	6	7	8	9	10		14	15	
2	6	7	8	10	7		11	12	
2	6	7	8	J	7	8	11	12	13
2	6	7	8	Q	7		11	12	
2	6	7	8	K	7		11	12	
2	6	7	9	9	8		12		
2	6	7	9	10	4		8	9	
2	6	7	9	J	4	5	8	9	10
2	6	7	9	Q	4		8	9	
2	6	7	9	K	4		8	9	
2	6	7	10	10	4		8		
2	6	7	10	J	2	3	6	7	8
2	6	7	10	Q	2		6	7	
2	6	7	10	K	2		6	7	
2	6	7	J	J	4	5	8		
2	6	7	J	Q	2	3	6	7	8
2	6	7	J	K	2	3	6	7	8
2	6	7	Q	Q	4		8		
2	6	7	Q	K	2		6	7	
2	6	7	K	K	4		8		
2	6	8	8	8	6				
2	6	8	8	9	4		8		
2	6	8	8	10	2		6		
2	6	8	8	J	2	3	6		
2	6	8	8	Q	2		6		
2	6	8	8	K	2		6		
2	6	8	9	9	6		10		
2	6	8	9	10	5		9	10	
2	6	8	9	J	2	3	6	7	8
2	6	8	9	Q	2		6	7	
2	6	8	9	K	2		6	7	
2	6	8	10	10	2		6		
2	6	8	10	J	0	1	4	5	6
2	6	8	10	Q	0		4	5	
2	6	8	10	K	0		4	5	
2	6	8	J	J	2	3	6		
2	6	8	J	Q	0	1	4	5	6
2	6	8	J	K	0	1	4	5	6
2	6	8	Q	Q	2		6		
2	6	8	Q	K	0		4	5	
2	6	8	K	K	2		6		
2	6	9	9	9	12		10		
2	6	9	9	10	6		10		
2	6	9	9	J	6	7	10		
2	6	9	9	Q	6		10		
2	6	9	9	K	6		10		
2	6	9	10	10	4		8		
2	6	9	10	J	5	6	9	10	11
2	6	9	10	Q	2		6	7	
2	6	9	10	K	2		6	7	
2	6	9	J	J	4	5	8		
2	6	9	J	Q	2	3	6	7	8
2	6	9	J	K	2	3	6	7	8
2	6	9	Q	Q	4		8		
2	6	9	Q	K	2		6	7	
2	6	9	K	K	4		8		
2	6	10	10	10	6				
2	6	10	10	J	2	3	6		
2	6	10	10	Q	2		6		
2	6	10	10	K	2		6		
2	6	10	J	J	2	3	6		
2	6	10	J	Q	0	1	4	5	6
2	6	10	J	K	0	1	4	5	6
2	6	10	Q	Q	2		6		
2	6	10	Q	K	0		4	5	
2	6	10	K	K	2		6		
2	6	J	J	J	6				

KEY TO CRIBBAGE.

CARDS.	Fifteens, Pairs & Seq.	With Jack of Turn-up	If Flush in Hand	If Flush with Turn-up	If Fl & Jack of Turn-up
2 6 J J Q	2	3	6		
2 6 J J K	2	3	6		
2 6 J Q Q	2	3	6		
2 6 J Q K	3	4	7	8	9
2 6 J K K	2	3	6		
2 6 Q Q Q	6				
2 6 Q Q K	2		6		
2 6 Q K K	2		6		
2 6 K K K	6				
2 7 7 7 7	12				
2 7 7 7 8	12				
2 7 7 7 9	6				
2 7 7 7 10	6				
2 7 7 7 J	6	7			
2 7 7 7 Q	6				
2 7 7 7 K	6				
2 7 7 8 8	12				
2 7 7 8 9	12		16		
2 7 7 8 10	6		10		
2 7 7 8 J	6	7	10		
2 7 7 8 Q	6		10		
2 7 7 8 K	6		10		
2 7 7 9 9	4				
2 7 7 9 10	2		6		
2 7 7 9 J	2	3	6		
2 7 7 9 Q	2		6		
2 7 7 9 K	2		6		
2 7 7 10 10	4				
2 7 7 10 J	2	3	6		
2 7 7 10 Q	2		6		
2 7 7 10 K	2		6		
2 7 7 J J	4	5			
2 7 7 J Q	2	3	6		
2 7 7 J K	2	3	6		
2 7 7 Q Q	4				
2 7 7 Q K	2		6		
2 7 7 K K	4				
2 7 8 8 8	12				
2 7 8 8 9	12		16		
2 7 8 8 10	6		10		
2 7 8 8 J	6	7	10		
2 7 8 8 Q	6		10		
2 7 8 8 K	6		10		
2 7 8 9 9	10		14		
2 7 8 9 10	6		10	11	
2 7 8 9 J	5	6	9	10	11
2 7 8 9 Q	5		9	10	
2 7 8 9 K	5		9	10	
2 7 8 10 10	4		8		
2 7 8 10 J	2	3	6	7	8
2 7 8 10 Q	2		6	7	
2 7 8 10 K	2		6	7	
2 7 8 J J	4	5	6		
2 7 8 J Q	2	3	6	7	8
2 7 8 J K	2	3	6	7	8
2 7 8 Q Q	4		8		
2 7 8 Q K	2		6	7	
2 7 8 K K	4		8		
2 7 9 9 9	6				
2 7 9 9 10	2		6		
2 7 9 9 J	2	3	6		
2 7 9 9 Q	2		6		
2 7 9 9 K	2		6		
2 7 9 10 10	2		6		
2 7 9 10 J	3	4	7	8	9
2 7 9 10 Q	0		4	5	
2 7 9 10 K	0		4	5	
2 7 9 J J	2	3	6		
2 7 9 J Q	0	1	4	5	6
2 7 9 J K	0	1	4	5	6
2 7 9 Q Q	2		6		
2 7 9 Q K	2		4	5	
2 7 9 K K	2		6		
2 7 10 10 10	2		6		
2 7 10 10 J	2	3	6		
2 7 10 10 Q	2		6		
2 7 10 10 K	2		6		
2 7 10 J J	2	3			

KEY TO CRIBBAGE.

CARDS.					Fifteens, Pairs & Seq.	With Jack of Turn-up.	If Flush in Hand.	If Flush with Turn-up.	If Fl.& Jack of Turn-up.
2	7	10	J	Q	3			4 1	7 4 8 5 9 6
2	7	10	J	K	3 0 2 0		1		
2	7	10	Q	K	0 2		4 6	4 6 5	
2	7	10	K	K	0 2		4 6		
2	7	J	J	J	6	7			
2	7	J	J	Q	2	3	6		
2	7	J	J	K	2	3	6		
2	7	J	Q	Q	2	3	6		
2	7	J	Q	K	3	4	7 6	8	9
2	7	J	K	K	2	3	6		
2	7	Q	Q	Q	6			6	
2	7	Q	Q	K	2				
2	7	Q	K	K	2		6		
2	7	K	K	K	6				
2	8	8	8	8	12				
2	8	8	8	9	6				
2	8	8	8	10	6				
2	8	8	8	J	6	7			
2	8	8	8	Q	6				
2	8	8	9	9	4				
2	8	8	9	10	8		12		
2	8	8	9	J	2	3	6		
2	8	8	9	Q	2		6		
2	8	8	9	K	2		6		
2	8	8	10	10	4				
2	8	8	10	J	2	3	6		
2	8	8	10	Q	2		6		
2	8	8	10	K	2		6		
2	8	8	J	J	4	5			
2	8	8	J	Q	2	3	6		
2	8	8	J	K	2	3	6		
2	8	8	Q	Q	4				
2	8	8	Q	K	2		6		
2	8	8	K	K	4				
2	8	9	K	9	6				
2	8	9	9	9	8		12		
2	8	9	9	J	2	3	6		

CARDS.					Fifteens, Pairs &c.	With Jack of Turn-up.	If Flush in Hand.	If Flush with Turn-up.	If Fl.& Jack of Turn-up.
2	8	9	9	Q	2 2		6		
2	8	9	9	K	2 2		6		
2	8	9	10	10	8		12		
2	8	9	10	J	4 3	5	8 7	9 8	10
2	8	9	10	Q	3 3		7 6	8	
2	8	9	10	K	2	3	6		
2	8	9	J	J	0	3	4 6	5	6
2	8	9	J	Q	0	1	4 4	5	6
2	8	9	J	K	2		6		
2	8	9	Q	Q	0		4 6	5	
2	8	9	Q	K	2		6		
2	8	9	K	K	2		6		
2	8	10	10	10	6				
2	8	10	10	J	2	3	6		
2	8	10	10	Q	2		6		
2	8	10	10	K	2		6		
2	8	10	J	J	2	3	6		
2	8	10	J	Q	3	4	7	8	9
2	8	10	J	K	0	1	4	5	6
2	8	10	Q	Q	2		6		
2	8	10	Q	K	0		4	5	
2	8	10	K	K	2		6		
2	8	J	J	J	6	7			
2	8	J	J	Q	2	3	6		
2	8	J	J	K	2	3	6		
2	8	J	Q	Q	2	3	6		
2	8	J	Q	K	3	4	7	8	9
2	8	J	K	K	2	3	6		
2	8	Q	Q	Q	6			6	
2	8	Q	Q	K	2		6		
2	8	Q	K	K	2		6		
2	8	K	K	K	6				
2	9	9	9	9	12				
2	9	9	9	10	6				
2	9	9	9	J	6	7			
2	9	9	9	Q	6				
2	9	9	9	K	6				
2	9	9	10	10	4		9	12	
2	9	9	10	J	8		9		

KEY TO CRIBBAGE.

CARDS.					Fifteens, Pairs & Seq.	With Jack of Turn-up	If Flush in Hand	If Flush with Turn-up	If Fl& Jack of Turn-up
2	9	9	10	Q	2		6		
2	9	9	10	K	2		6		
2	9	9	J	J	4	5			
2	9	9	J	Q	2	3	6		
2	9	9	J	K	2	3	6		
2	9	9	Q	Q	4				
2	9	9	Q	K	2		6		
2	9	9	K	K	4				
2	9	10	10	10	6				
2	9	10	10	J	8	9	12		
2	9	10	10	Q	2		6		
2	9	10	10	K	2		6		
2	9	10	J	J	8	9	12		
2	9	10	J	Q	4	5	8	9	10
2	9	10	J	K	3	4	7	8	9
2	9	10	Q	Q	2		6		
2	9	10	Q	K	0		4	5	
2	9	10	K	K	2		6		
2	9	J	J	J	6	7			
2	9	J	J	Q	2	3	6		
2	9	J	J	K	2	3	6		
2	9	J	Q	Q	2	3	6		
2	9	J	Q	K	3	4	7	8	9
2	9	J	K	K	2	3	6		
2	9	Q	Q	Q	6				
2	9	Q	Q	K	2		6		
2	9	Q	K	K	2		6		
2	9	K	K	K	6				
2	10	10	10	10	12				
2	10	10	10	J	6	7			
2	10	10	10	Q	6				
2	10	10	10	K	6				
2	10	10	J	J	4	5			
2	10	10	J	Q	8	9	12		
2	10	10	J	K	2	3	6		
2	10	10	Q	Q	4				
2	10	10	Q	K	2		6		
2	10	10	K	K	4				
2	10	J	J	J	6	7			

CARDS.					Fifteens, Pairs & Seq.	With Jack of Turn-up	If Flush in Hand	If Flush with Turn-up	If Fl& Jack of Turn-up
2	10	J	J	Q	8	9	12		
2	10	J	J	K	2	3	6		
2	10	J	Q	Q	8	9	12		
2	10	J	Q	K	4	5	8	9	10
2	10	J	K	K	2	3	6		
2	10	Q	Q	Q	6				
2	10	Q	Q	K	2		6		
2	10	Q	K	K	2		6		
2	10	K	K	K	6				
2	J	J	J	J	12	13			
2	J	J	J	Q	6	7			
2	J	J	J	K	6	7			
2	J	J	Q	Q	4	5			
2	J	J	Q	K	8	9	12		
2	J	J	K	K	4	5			
2	J	Q	Q	Q	6	7			
2	J	Q	Q	K	8	9	12		
2	J	Q	K	K	8	9	12		
2	J	K	K	K	6	7			
2	Q	Q	Q	Q	12				
2	Q	Q	Q	K	6				
2	Q	Q	K	K	4				
2	Q	K	K	K	6				
2	K	K	K	K	12				
3	3	3	3	4	12				
3	3	3	3	5	12				
3	3	3	3	6	20				
3	3	3	3	7	12				
3	3	3	3	8	12				
3	3	3	3	9	24				
3	3	3	3	10	12				
3	3	3	3	J	12	13			
3	3	3	3	Q	12				
3	3	3	3	K	12				
3	3	3	4	4	8				
3	3	3	4	5	21				
3	3	3	4	6	8				
3	3	3	4	7	6				
3	3	3	4	8	12				

KEY TO CRIBBAGE.

CARDS					Fifteens, Pairs & Seq.	With Jack of Turn-up	If Flush in Hand	If Flush with Turn-up	If Fl& Jack of Turn-up
3	3	3	4	9	12				
3	3	3	4	10	6				
3	3	3	4	J	6	7			
3	3	3	4	Q	6				
3	3	3	4	K	6				
3	3	3	5	5	8				
3	3	3	5	6	8				
3	3	3	5	7	12				
3	3	3	5	8	6				
3	3	3	5	9	12				
3	3	3	5	10	8				
3	3	3	5	J	8	9			
3	3	3	5	Q	8				
3	3	3	5	K	8				
3	3	3	6	6	18				
3	3	3	6	7	8				
3	3	3	6	8	8				
3	3	3	6	9	16				
3	3	3	6	10	8				
3	3	3	6	J	8	9			
3	3	3	6	Q	8				
3	3	3	6	K	8				
3	3	3	7	7	8				
3	3	3	7	8	8				
3	3	3	7	9	12				
3	3	3	7	10	6				
3	3	3	7	J	6	7			
3	3	3	7	Q	6				
3	3	3	7	K	6				
3	3	3	8	8	8				
3	3	3	8	9	12				
3	3	3	8	10	6				
3	3	3	8	J	6	7			
3	3	3	8	Q	6				
3	3	3	8	K	6				
3	3	3	9	9	20				
3	3	3	9	10	12				
3	3	3	9	J	12	13			
3	3	3	9	Q	12				
3	3	3	9	K	12				
3	3	3	10	10	8				
3	3	3	10	J	6	7			
3	3	3	10	Q	6				
3	3	3	10	K	6				
3	3	3	J	J	8	9			
3	3	3	J	Q	6	7			
3	3	3	J	K	6	7			
3	3	3	Q	Q	8				
3	3	3	Q	K	6				
3	3	3	K	K	8				
3	3	4	4	4	12				
3	3	4	4	5	20				
3	3	4	4	6	4				
3	3	4	4	7	6				
3	3	4	4	8	12				
3	3	4	4	9	6				
3	3	4	4	10	4				
3	3	4	4	J	4	5			
3	3	4	4	Q	4				
3	3	4	4	K	4				
3	3	4	5	5	20				
3	3	4	5	6	14		18		
3	3	4	5	7	14		18		
3	3	4	5	8	14		18		
3	3	4	5	9	12		16		
3	3	4	5	10	12		16		
3	3	4	5	J	12	13	16		
3	3	4	5	Q	12		16		
3	3	4	5	K	12		16		
3	3	4	6	6	8				
3	3	4	6	7	2			6	
3	3	4	6	8	6			10	
3	3	4	6	9	6			10	
3	3	4	6	10	2			6	
3	3	4	6	J	2	3		6	6
3	3	4	6	Q	2			6	6
3	3	4	6	K	2				
3	3	4	7	7	4				

KEY TO CRIBBAGE.

Cards					Fifteens, Pairs & Seq.	With Jack of Turn-up	If Flush in Hand	If Flush with Turn-up	If Fl & Jack of Turn-up
3	3	4	7	8	8		12		
3	3	4	7	9	4		8		
3	3	4	7	10	2		6		
3	3	4	7	J	2	3	6		
3	3	4	7	Q	2		6		
3	3	4	7	K	2		6		
3	3	4	8	8	12				
3	3	4	8	9	8		12		
3	3	4	8	10	6		10		
3	3	4	8	J	6	7	10		
3	3	4	8	Q	6		10		
3	3	4	8	K	6		10		
3	3	4	9	9	8				
3	3	4	9	10	4		8		
3	3	4	9	J	4	5	8		
3	3	4	9	Q	4		8		
3	3	4	9	K	4		8		
3	3	4	10	10	4				
3	3	4	10	J	2	3	6		
3	3	4	10	Q	2		6		
3	3	4	10	K	2		6		
3	3	4	J	J	4	5			
3	3	4	J	Q	2	3	6		
3	3	4	J	K	2	3	6		
3	3	4	Q	Q	4				
3	3	4	Q	K	2		6		
3	3	4	K	K	4				
3	3	5	5	5	10				
3	3	5	5	6	4				
3	3	5	5	7	12				
3	3	5	5	8	4				
3	3	5	5	9	6				
3	3	5	5	10	8				
3	3	5	5	J	8	9			
3	3	5	5	Q	8				
3	3	5	5	K	8				
3	3	5	6	6	8				
3	3	5	6	7	9		13		
3	3	5	6	8	2		6		
3	3	5	6	9	6		10		
3	3	5	6	10	4		8		
3	3	5	6	J	4	5	8		
3	3	5	6	Q	4		8		
3	3	5	6	K	4		8		
3	3	5	7	7	12				
3	3	5	7	8	8		12		
3	3	5	7	9	8		12		
3	3	5	7	10	8		12		
3	3	5	7	J	8	9	12		
3	3	5	7	Q	8		12		
3	3	5	7	K	8		12		
3	3	5	8	8	4				
3	3	5	8	9	4		8		
3	3	5	8	10	4		8		
3	3	5	8	J	4	5	8		
3	3	5	8	Q	4		8		
3	3	5	8	K	4		8		
3	3	5	9	9	8				
3	3	5	9	10	6		10		
3	3	5	9	J	6	7	10		
3	3	5	9	Q	6		10		
3	3	5	9	K	6		10		
3	3	5	10	10	8				
3	3	5	10	J	6	7	10		
3	3	5	10	Q	6		10		
3	3	5	10	K	6		10		
3	3	5	J	J	8	9			
3	3	5	J	Q	6	7	10		
3	3	5	J	K	6	7	10		
3	3	5	Q	Q	8				
3	3	5	Q	K	6		10		
3	3	5	K	K	8				
3	3	6	6	6	20				
3	3	6	6	7	8				
3	3	6	6	8	8				
3	3	6	6	9	14				
3	3	6	6	10	8				
3	3	6	6	J	8	9			

KEY TO CRIBBAGE.

Cards					Fifteens, Pairs & Seq.	With Jack of Turn-up	If Flush in Hand	If Flush with Turn-up	If Fl& Jack of Turn-up
3	3	6	6	Q	8				
3	3	6	6	K	8				
3	3	6	6	7	4				
3	3	6	7	7	4				
3	3	6	7	8	7		11		
3	3	6	7	9	6		10		
3	3	6	7	10	2		6		
3	3	6	7	J	2	3	6		
3	3	6	7	Q	2		6		
3	3	6	7	K	2		6		
3	3	6	8	9	4				
3	3	6	8	10	6		10		
3	3	6	8	J	2	3	6		
3	3	6	8	Q	2		6		
3	3	6	8	K	2		6		
3	3	6	9	10	12				
3	3	6	9	J	6	7	10		
3	3	6	9	Q	6		10		
3	3	6	9	K	6		10		
3	3	6	10	10	4				
3	3	6	10	J	2	3	6		
3	3	6	10	Q	2		6		
3	3	6	10	K	2		6		
3	3	6	J	J	4	5	3	6	
3	3	6	J	Q	2		3	6	
3	3	6	J	K	2			6	
3	3	6	Q	Q	4				
3	3	6	Q	K	2			6	
3	3	6	K	K	4				
3	3	7	7	7	8				
3	3	7	7	8	8				
3	3	7	7	9	6				
3	3	7	7	10	4				
3	3	7	7	J	4	5			
3	3	7	7	Q	4				
3	3	7	8	8	8				
3	3	7	8	9	9		13		
3	3	7	8	10	4		8		
3	3	7	8	J	4	5	8		
3	3	7	8	Q	4		8		
3	3	7	8	K	4		8		
3	3	7	9	9	8		8		
3	3	7	9	10	4		8		
3	3	7	9	J	4	5	8		
3	3	7	9	Q	4		8		
3	3	7	9	K	4		8		
3	3	7	10	10	4		8		
3	3	7	10	J	2	3	6		
3	3	7	10	Q	2		6		
3	3	7	10	K	2		6		
3	3	7	J	J	4	5			
3	3	7	J	Q	2	3	6		
3	3	7	J	K	2		6		
3	3	7	Q	Q	4				
3	3	7	Q	K	2		6		
3	3	7	K	K	4				
3	3	8	8	8	8				
3	3	8	8	9	6				
3	3	8	8	10	4				
3	3	8	8	J	4	5			
3	3	8	8	Q	4				
3	3	8	9	9	8				
3	3	8	9	10	7		11		
3	3	8	9	J	4	5	8		
3	3	8	9	Q	4		8		
3	3	8	9	K	4		8		
3	3	8	10	10	4				
3	3	8	10	J	2	3	6		
3	3	8	10	Q	2		6		
3	3	8	10	K	2		6		
3	3	8	J	J	4	5		6	
3	3	8	J	Q	2	3	6		
3	3	8	J	K	2		6		
3	3	8	Q	Q	4				
3	3	8	Q	K	2		6		

KEY TO CRIBBAGE.

CARDS.					Fifteens, Pairs & Seq.	With Jack of Turn-up.	If Flush in Hand.	If Flush with Turn-up.	If Fl& Jack of Turn-up.	CARDS.					Fifteens, Pairs & Seq.	With Jack of Turn-up.	If Flush in Hand.	If Flush with Turn-up.	If Fl& Jack of Turn-up.
3	3	8	K	K	4	.	.	.	.	3	4	4	4	7	14	.	.	.	.
3	3	9	9	9	14	.	.	.	.	3	4	4	4	8	14	.	.	.	.
3	3	9	9	10	8	.	.	.	.	3	4	4	4	9	8	.	.	.	.
3	3	9	9	J	8	9	.	.	.	3	4	4	4	10	8	.	.	.	.
3	3	9	9	Q	8	.	.	.	.	3	4	4	4	J	8	9	.	.	.
3	3	9	9	K	8	.	.	.	.	3	4	4	4	Q	8	.	.	.	.
3	3	9	10	10	6	.	.	.	.	3	4	4	4	K	8	.	.	.	.
3	3	9	10	J	7	8	11	.	.	3	4	4	5	5	16	.	.	.	.
3	3	9	10	Q	4	.	8	.	.	3	4	4	5	6	14	.	18	.	.
3	3	9	10	K	4	.	8	.	.	3	4	4	5	7	12	.	16	.	.
3	3	9	J	J	6	7	.	.	.	3	4	4	5	8	12	.	16	.	.
3	3	9	J	Q	4	5	8	.	.	3	4	4	5	9	8	.	12	.	.
3	3	9	J	K	4	5	8	.	.	3	4	4	5	10	16	.	14	.	.
3	3	9	Q	Q	6	.	.	.	.	3	4	4	5	J	16	11	14	.	.
3	3	9	Q	K	4	.	8	.	.	3	4	4	5	Q	10	.	14	.	.
3	3	9	K	K	6	.	.	.	.	3	4	4	5	K	10	.	14	.	.
3	3	10	10	10	8	.	.	.	.	3	4	4	6	6	6	.	.	.	.
3	3	10	10	J	4	5	.	.	.	3	4	4	6	7	4	.	8	.	.
3	3	10	10	Q	4	.	.	.	.	3	4	4	6	8	6	.	10	.	.
3	3	10	10	K	4	.	.	.	.	3	4	4	6	9	4	.	8	.	.
3	3	10	J	J	4	5	.	.	.	3	4	4	6	10	2	.	6	.	.
3	3	10	J	Q	5	6	9	.	.	3	4	4	6	J	2	3	6	.	.
3	3	10	J	K	2	3	6	.	.	3	4	4	6	Q	2	.	6	.	.
3	3	10	Q	Q	4	.	.	.	.	3	4	4	6	K	2	.	6	.	.
3	3	10	Q	K	2	.	6	.	.	3	4	4	7	7	8	.	.	.	.
3	3	10	K	K	4	.	.	.	.	3	4	4	7	8	10	.	14	.	.
3	3	J	J	J	8	9	.	.	.	3	4	4	7	9	4	.	8	.	.
3	3	J	J	Q	4	5	.	.	.	3	4	4	7	10	4	.	8	.	.
3	3	J	J	K	4	5	.	.	.	3	4	4	7	J	4	5	8	.	.
3	3	J	Q	Q	4	5	.	.	.	3	4	4	7	Q	4	.	8	.	.
3	3	J	Q	K	5	6	9	.	.	3	4	4	7	K	4	.	8	.	.
3	3	J	K	K	4	5	.	.	.	3	4	4	8	8	12	.	.	.	.
3	3	Q	Q	Q	8	.	.	.	.	3	4	4	8	9	6	.	10	.	.
3	3	Q	Q	K	4	.	.	.	.	3	4	4	8	10	6	.	10	.	.
3	3	Q	K	K	4	.	.	.	.	3	4	4	8	J	6	7	10	.	.
3	3	K	K	K	8	.	.	.	.	3	4	4	8	Q	6	.	10	.	.
3	4	4	4	4	20	.	.	.	.	3	4	4	8	K	6	.	10	.	.
3	4	4	4	5	17	.	.	.	.	3	4	4	9	9	4	.	.	.	.
3	4	4	4	6	8	.	.	.	.	3	4	4	9	10	2	.	6	.	.

KEY TO CRIBBAGE.

CARDS.	Fifteens, Pairs & Seq..	With Jack of Turn-up..	If Flush in Hand....	If Flush with Turn-up.	If Fl& Jack of Turn-up
3 4 4 9 J	2	3	6		
3 4 4 9 Q	2	2		6	
3 4 4 9 K	2	2		6	
3 4 4 10 10	4				
3 4 4 10 J	2	3	6		
3 4 4 10 Q	2		6		
3 4 4 10 K	2		6		
3 4 4 J J	4	5			
3 4 4 J Q	2	3	6		
3 4 4 J K	2	3	6		
3 4 4 Q Q	4				
3 4 4 Q K	2		6		
3 4 4 K K	4				
3 4 5 5 5	17				
3 4 5 5 6	14		18		
3 4 5 5 7	12		16		
3 4 5 5 8	10		14		
3 4 5 5 9	8		12		
3 4 5 5 10	12		16		
3 4 5 5 J	12	13	16		
3 4 5 5 Q	12		16		
3 4 5 5 K	12		16		
3 4 5 6 6	16		20		
3 4 5 6 7	9		13	14	
3 4 5 6 8	8		12	13	
3 4 5 6 9	8		12	13	
3 4 5 6 10	8		12	13	
3 4 5 6 J	8	9	12	13	14
3 4 5 6 Q	8		12	13	
3 4 5 6 K	8		12	13	
3 4 5 7 7	9		13		
3 4 5 7 8	9		13	14	
3 4 5 7 9	5		9	10	
3 4 5 7 10	7		11	12	
3 4 5 7 J	7	8	11	12	13
3 4 5 7 Q	7		11	12	
3 4 5 7 K	7		11	12	
3 4 5 8 8	9		13		
3 4 5 8 9	5		9	10	

CARDS.	Fifteens, Pairs & Seq..	With Jack of Turn-up..	If Flush in Hand....	If Flush with Turn-up.	If Fl& Jack of Turn-up
3 4 5 8 10	7		11	12	
3 4 5 8 J	7	8	11	12	13
3 4 5 8 Q	7		11	12	
3 4 5 8 K	7		11	12	
3 4 5 9 9	5		9		
3 4 5 9 10	5		9	10	
3 4 5 9 J	5	6	9	10	11
3 4 5 9 Q	5		9	10	
3 4 5 9 K	5		9	10	
3 4 5 10 10	9		13		
3 4 5 10 J	7	8	11	12	13
3 4 5 10 Q	7		11	12	
3 4 5 10 K	7		11	12	
3 4 5 J J	9	10	13		
3 4 5 J Q	7	8	11	12	13
3 4 5 J K	7	8	11	12	13
3 4 5 Q Q	9		13		
3 4 5 Q K	7		11	12	
3 4 5 K K	9		13		
3 4 6 6 6	12				
3 4 6 6 7	4		8		
3 4 6 6 8	6		10		
3 4 6 6 9	8		12		
3 4 6 6 10	4		8		
3 4 6 6 J	4	5	8		
3 4 6 6 Q	4		8		
3 4 6 6 K	4		8		
3 4 6 7 7	2		6		
3 4 6 7 8	2		11	12	
3 4 6 7 9	2		6		
3 4 6 7 10	0		4	5	
3 4 6 7 J	0	1	4	5	6
3 4 6 7 Q	0		4	5	
3 4 6 7 K	0		4	5	
3 4 6 8 8	6		10		
3 4 6 8 9	4		8	9	
3 4 6 8 10	6		6	6	
3 4 6 8 J	2	2	3	6	6
3 4 6 8 Q	2	2		6	7

KEY TO CRIBBAGE.

Cards	Fifteens, Pairs & Seq..	With Jack of Turn-up..	If Flush in Hand......	If Flush with Turn-up..	If Fl& Jack of Turn-up
3 4 6 8 K	2	..	6	7	..
3 4 6 9 9	6	..	10	..	..
3 4 6 9 10	2	..	6	7	..
3 4 6 9 J	2	3	6	7	8
3 4 6 9 Q	2	..	6	7	..
3 4 6 9 K	2	..	6	7	..
3 4 6 10 10	2	..	6	..	..
3 4 6 10 J	0	1	4	5	6
3 4 6 10 Q	0	..	4	5	..
3 4 6 10 K	0	..	4	5	..
3 4 6 J J	2	3	6	..	..
3 4 6 J Q	0	1	4	5	6
3 4 6 J K	0	1	4	5	6
3 4 6 Q Q	2	..	6	..	..
3 4 6 Q K	0	..	4	5	..
3 4 6 K K	2	..	6	..	..
3 4 7 7 7	6	..	..	..	..
3 4 7 7 8	8	..	12	..	..
3 4 7 7 9	2	..	6	..	..
3 4 7 7 10	2	..	6	..	..
3 4 7 7 J	2	3	6	..	..
3 4 7 7 Q	2	..	6	..	..
3 4 7 7 K	2	..	6	..	..
3 4 7 8 8	10	..	14	..	..
3 4 7 8 9	7	..	11	12	..
3 4 7 8 10	4	..	8	9	..
3 4 7 8 J	4	5	8	9	10
3 4 7 8 Q	4	..	8	9	..
3 4 7 8 K	4	..	8	9	..
3 4 7 9 9	2	..	6	..	..
3 4 7 9 10	0	..	4	5	..
3 4 7 9 J	0	1	4	5	6
3 4 7 9 Q	0	..	4	5	..
3 4 7 9 K	0	..	4	5	..
3 4 7 10 10	2	..	6	..	..
3 4 7 10 J	0	1	4	5	6
3 4 7 10 Q	0	..	4	5	..
3 4 7 10 K	0	..	4	5	..
3 4 7 J J	2	3	6	..	..

Cards	Fifteens, Pairs & Seq..	With Jack of Turn-up..	If Flush in Hand......	If Flush with Turn-up..	If Fl& Jack of Turn-up
3 4 7 J Q	0	1	4	5	6
3 4 7 J K	0	1	4	5	6
3 4 7 Q Q	2	..	6	..	..
3 4 7 Q K	0	..	4	5	..
3 4 7 K K	2	..	6	..	..
3 4 8 8 8	12	..	..	..	..
3 4 8 8 9	6	..	10	..	..
3 4 8 8 10	6	..	10	..	..
3 4 8 8 J	6	7	10	..	..
3 4 8 8 Q	6	..	10	..	..
3 4 8 8 K	6	..	10	..	..
3 4 8 9 9	4	..	8	..	..
3 4 8 9 10	5	..	9	10	..
3 4 8 9 J	2	3	6	7	8
3 4 8 9 Q	2	..	6	7	..
3 4 8 9 K	2	..	6	7	..
3 4 8 10 10	4	..	8	..	..
3 4 8 10 J	2	3	6	7	8
3 4 8 10 Q	2	..	6	7	..
3 4 8 10 K	2	..	6	7	..
3 4 8 J J	4	5	8	..	..
3 4 8 J Q	2	3	6	7	8
3 4 8 J K	2	3	6	7	8
3 4 8 Q Q	4	..	8	..	..
3 4 8 Q K	2	..	6	7	..
3 4 8 K K	4	..	8	..	..
3 4 9 9 9	6	..	..	..	..
3 4 9 9 10	2	..	6	..	..
3 4 9 9 J	2	3	6	..	..
3 4 9 9 Q	2	..	6	..	..
3 4 9 9 K	2	..	6	..	..
3 4 9 10 10	2	..	6	..	..
3 4 9 10 J	3	4	7	8	9
3 4 9 10 Q	0	..	4	5	..
3 4 9 10 K	0	..	4	5	..
3 4 9 J J	2	3	6	..	..
3 4 9 J Q	0	1	4	5	6
3 4 9 J K	0	1	4	5	6
3 4 9 Q Q	2	..	6	..	..

KEY TO CRIBBAGE.

CARDS.					Fifteens, Pairs & Seq..	With Jack of Turn-up..	If Flush in Hand......	If Flush with Turn-up.	If Fl & Jack of Turn-up
3	4	9	Q	K	0	..	4	5	..
3	4	9	K	K	2	..	6	..	..
3	4	10	10	10	6	..	6	..	..
3	4	10	10	J	2	3	6	..	..
3	4	10	10	Q	2	..	6	..	..
3	4	10	10	K	2	..	6	..	..
3	4	10	J	J	2	3	6	..	..
3	4	10	J	Q	3	4	7	8	9
3	4	10	J	K	0	1	4	5	6
3	4	10	Q	Q	2	..	6	..	..
3	4	10	Q	K	0	..	4	5	..
3	4	10	K	K	2	..	6	..	..
3	4	J	J	J	6	7	..	..	..
3	4	J	J	Q	2	3	6	..	..
3	4	J	J	K	2	3	6	..	..
3	4	J	Q	Q	2	3	6	..	..
3	4	J	Q	K	3	4	7	8	9
3	4	J	K	K	2	3	6	..	..
3	4	Q	Q	Q	6	..	..	..	..
3	4	Q	Q	K	2	..	6	..	..
3	4	Q	K	K	2	..	6	..	..
3	4	K	K	K	6	..	..	..	..
3	5	5	5	5	20	..	..	..	..
3	5	5	5	6	8	..	..	..	..
3	5	5	5	7	14	..	..	..	..
3	5	5	5	8	8	..	..	..	..
3	5	5	5	9	8	..	..	..	..
3	5	5	5	10	14	..	..	..	..
3	5	5	5	J	14	15	..	..	..
3	5	5	5	Q	14	..	..	..	..
3	5	5	5	K	14	..	..	..	..
3	5	5	6	6	6	..	..	..	..
3	5	5	6	7	12	..	16	..	..
3	5	5	6	8	2	..	6	..	..
3	5	5	6	9	4	..	8	..	..
3	5	5	6	10	6	..	10	..	..
3	5	5	6	J	6	7	10	..	..
3	5	5	6	Q	6	..	10	..	..
3	5	5	6	K	6	..	10	..	..

CARDS.					Fifteens, Pairs & Seq..	With Jack of Turn-up..	If Flush in Hand......	If Flush with Turn-up.	If Fl & Jack of Turn-up
3	5	5	7	7	12	..	..	..	..
3	5	5	7	8	8	..	12	..	..
3	5	5	7	9	6	..	10	..	..
3	5	5	7	10	10	..	14	..	..
3	5	5	7	J	10	11	14	..	..
3	5	5	7	Q	10	..	14	..	..
3	5	5	7	K	10	..	14	..	..
3	5	5	8	8	4	..	..	..	..
3	5	5	8	9	2	..	6	..	..
3	5	5	8	10	6	..	10	..	..
3	5	5	8	J	6	7	10	..	..
3	5	5	8	Q	6	..	10	..	..
3	5	5	8	K	6	..	10	..	..
3	5	5	9	9	4	..	..	..	..
3	5	5	9	10	6	..	10	..	..
3	5	5	9	J	6	7	10	..	..
3	5	5	9	Q	6	..	10	..	..
3	5	5	9	K	6	..	10	..	..
3	5	5	10	10	12	..	..	..	..
3	5	5	10	J	10	11	14	..	..
3	5	5	10	Q	10	..	14	..	..
3	5	5	10	K	10	..	14	..	..
3	5	5	J	J	12	13	..	..	..
3	5	5	J	Q	10	11	14	..	..
3	5	5	J	K	10	11	14	..	..
3	5	5	Q	Q	12	..	..	..	..
3	5	5	Q	K	10	..	14	..	..
3	5	5	K	K	12	..	..	..	..
3	5	6	6	6	12	..	..	..	..
3	5	6	6	7	12	..	16	..	..
3	5	6	6	8	4	..	8	..	..
3	5	6	6	9	8	..	12	..	..
3	5	6	6	10	6	..	10	..	..
3	5	6	6	J	6	7	10	..	..
3	5	6	6	Q	6	..	10	..	..
3	5	6	6	K	6	..	10	..	..
3	5	6	7	7	12	..	16	..	..
3	5	6	7	8	8	..	12	13	..
3	5	6	7	9	7	..	11	12	..

KEY TO CRIBBAGE.

CARDS					Fifteens, Pairs & Seq..	With Jack of Turn-up..	If Flush in Hand......	If Flush with Turn-up.	If Fl& Jack of Turn-up
3	5	6	7	10	7	..	11	12	..
3	5	6	7	J	7	8	11	12	13
3	5	6	7	Q	7	..	11	12	..
3	5	6	7	K	7	..	11	12	..
3	5	6	8	8	2	..	6	..	..
3	5	6	8	9	2	..	6	7	..
3	5	6	8	10	2	..	6	7	..
3	5	6	8	J	2	3	6	7	8
3	5	6	8	Q	2	..	6	7	..
3	5	6	8	K	2	..	6	7	..
3	5	6	9	9	6	..	10	..	..
3	5	6	9	10	4	..	8	9	..
3	5	6	9	J	4	5	8	9	10
3	5	6	9	Q	4	..	8	9	..
3	5	6	9	K	4	..	8	9	..
3	5	6	10	10	6	..	10	..	..
3	5	6	10	J	4	5	8	9	10
3	5	6	10	Q	4	..	8	9	..
3	5	6	10	K	4	..	8	9	..
3	5	6	J	J	6	7	10	..	..
3	5	6	J	Q	4	5	8	9	10
3	5	6	J	K	4	5	8	9	10
3	5	6	Q	Q	6	..	10	..	..
3	5	6	Q	K	4	..	8	9	..
3	5	6	K	K	6	..	10	..	..
3	5	7	7	7	12	..	..	..	..
3	5	7	7	8	10	..	14	..	..
3	5	7	7	9	6	..	10	..	..
3	5	7	7	10	8	..	12	..	..
3	5	7	7	J	8	9	12	..	..
3	5	7	7	Q	8	..	12	..	..
3	5	7	7	K	8	..	12	..	..
3	5	7	8	8	8	..	12	..	..
3	5	7	8	9	7	..	11	12	..
3	5	7	8	10	6	..	10	11	..
3	5	7	8	J	6	7	10	11	12
3	5	7	8	Q	6	..	10	11	..
3	5	7	8	K	6	..	10	11	..
3	5	7	9	9	4	..	8	..	..
3	5	7	9	10	4	..	8	9	..
3	5	7	9	J	4	5	8	9	10
3	5	7	9	Q	4	..	8	9	..
3	5	7	9	K	4	..	8	9	..
3	5	7	10	10	8	..	12	..	..
3	5	7	10	J	6	7	10	11	12
3	5	7	10	Q	6	..	10	11	..
3	5	7	10	K	6	..	10	11	..
3	5	7	J	J	8	9	12	..	..
3	5	7	J	Q	6	7	10	11	12
3	5	7	J	K	6	7	10	11	12
3	5	7	Q	Q	8	..	12	..	..
3	5	7	Q	K	6	..	10	11	..
3	5	7	K	K	8	..	12	..	..
3	5	8	8	8	6	..	..	..	..
3	5	8	8	9	2	..	6	..	..
3	5	8	8	10	4	..	8	..	..
3	5	8	8	J	4	5	8	..	..
3	5	8	8	Q	4	..	8	..	..
3	5	8	8	K	4	..	8	..	..
3	5	8	9	9	2	..	6	..	..
3	5	8	9	10	5	..	9	10	..
3	5	8	9	J	2	3	6	7	8
3	5	8	9	Q	2	..	6	7	..
3	5	8	9	K	2	..	6	7	..
3	5	8	10	10	6	..	10	..	..
3	5	8	10	J	4	5	8	9	10
3	5	8	10	Q	4	..	8	9	..
3	5	8	10	K	4	..	8	9	..
3	5	8	J	J	6	7	10	..	..
3	5	8	J	Q	4	5	8	9	10
3	5	8	J	K	4	5	8	9	10
3	5	8	Q	Q	6	..	10	..	..
3	5	8	Q	K	4	..	8	9	..
3	5	8	K	K	6	..	10	..	..
3	5	9	9	9	6	..	..	..	..
3	5	9	9	10	4	..	8	..	..
3	5	9	9	J	4	5	8	8	..
3	5	9	9		4	..	8	8	..

KEY TO CRIBBAGE.

CARDS.					Fifteens, Pairs & Seq..	With Jack of Turn-up..	If Flush in Hand......	If Flush with Turn-up.	If Fl& Jack of Turn-up
3	5	9	9	K	4		8		
3	5	9	10	10	6		10		
3	5	9	10	J	7	8	11	12	13
3	5	9	10	Q	4		8	9	
3	5	9	10	K	4		8	9	
3	5	9	J	J	6	7	10		
3	5	9	J	Q	4	5	8	9	10
3	5	9	J	K	4	5	8	9	10
3	5	9	Q	Q	6		10		
3	5	9	Q	K	4		8	9	
3	5	9	K	K	6		10		
3	5	10	10	10	12				
3	5	10	10	J	8	9	12		
3	5	10	10	Q	8		12		
3	5	10	10	K	8		12		
3	5	10	J	J	8	9	12		
3	5	10	J	Q	9	10	13	14	15
3	5	10	J	K	6	7	10	11	12
3	5	10	Q	Q	8		12		
3	5	10	Q	K	6		10	11	
3	5	10	K	K	8		12		
3	5	J	J	J	12	13			
3	5	J	J	Q	8	9	12		
3	5	J	J	K	8	9	12		
3	5	J	Q	Q	8	9	12		
3	5	J	Q	K	9	10	13	14	15
3	5	J	K	K	8	9	12		
3	5	Q	Q	Q	12				
3	5	Q	Q	K	8		12		
3	5	Q	K	K	8		12		
3	5	K	K	K	12				
3	6	6	6	6	24				
3	6	6	6	7	12				
3	6	6	6	8	12				
3	6	6	6	9	18				
3	6	6	6	10	12				
3	6	6	6	J	12	13			
3	6	6	6	Q	12				
3	6	6	6	K	12				

CARDS.					Fifteens, Pairs & Seq..	With Jack of Turn-up..	If Flush in Hand......	If Flush with Turn-up.	If Fl& Jack of Turn-up
3	6	6	7	7	6		10		
3	6	6	7	8	12		16		
3	6	6	7	9	8		12		
3	6	6	7	10	4	5	8		
3	6	6	7	J	4		8		
3	6	6	7	Q	4		8		
3	6	6	8	8	6				
3	6	6	8	9	8		12		
3	6	6	8	10	4		8		
3	6	6	8	J	4	5	8		
3	6	6	8	Q	4		8		
3	6	6	8	K	4		8		
3	6	6	9	9	14				
3	6	6	9	10	8		12		
3	6	6	9	J	8	9	12		
3	6	6	9	Q	8		12		
3	6	6	9	K	8		12		
3	6	6	10	10	6				
3	6	6	10	J	4	5	8		
3	6	6	10	Q	4		8		
3	6	6	10	K	4		8		
3	6	6	J	J	6	7			
3	6	6	J	Q	4	5	8		
3	6	6	J	K	4	5	8		
3	6	6	Q	Q	6				
3	6	6	Q	K	4		8		
3	6	6	K	K	6				
3	6	7	7	7	6				
3	6	7	7	8	12		16		
3	6	7	7	9	4		8		
3	6	7	7	10	2		6		
3	6	7	7	J	2	3	6		
3	6	7	7	Q	2		6		
3	6	7	7	K	2		6		
3	6	7	8	8	12		16		
3	6	7	8	9	8		12	13	
3	6	7	8	10	5		9	10	11
3	6	7	8	J	5	6	9	10	11

KEY TO CRIBBAGE.

Cards					Fifteens, Pairs & Seq..	With Jack of Turn-up...	If Flush in Hand.....	If Flush with Turn-up.	If Fl& Jack of Turn-up		Cards					Fifteens, Pairs & Seq..	With Jack of Turn-up...	If Flush in Hand.....	If Flush with Turn-up.	If Fl& Jack of Turn-up
3	6	7	8	Q	5	..	9	10	..		3	6	9	9	10	6	..	10	..	..
3	6	7	8	K	5	..	9	10	..		3	6	9	9	J	6	7	10	..	..
3	6	7	9	9	6	..	10	.	..		3	6	9	9	Q	6	..	10	..	..
3	6	7	9	10	2	..	6	7	..		3	6	9	9	K	6	..	10	..	..
3	6	7	9	J	2	3	6	7	8		3	6	9	10	10	4	..	8	..	..
3	6	7	9	Q	2	..	6	7	..		3	6	9	10	J	5	6	9	10	11
3	6	7	9	K	2	..	6	7	..		3	6	9	10	Q	2	..	6	7	..
3	6	7	10	10	2	..	6	.	..		3	6	9	10	K	2	..	6	7	..
3	6	7	10	J	0	1	4	5	6		3	6	9	J	J	4	5	8	..	..
3	6	7	10	Q	0	..	4	5	..		3	6	9	J	Q	2	3	6	7	8
3	6	7	10	K	0	..	4	5	..		3	6	9	J	K	2	3	6	7	8
3	6	7	J	J	2	3	6	..	..		3	6	9	Q	Q	4	..	8	..	..
3	6	7	J	Q	0	1	4	5	6		3	6	9	Q	K	2	..	6	7	..
3	6	7	J	K	0	1	4	5	6		3	6	9	K	K	4	..	8	..	..
3	6	7	Q	Q	2	..	6	.	..		3	6	10	10	10	6	..	.	..	..
3	6	7	Q	K	0	..	4	5	..		3	6	10	10	J	2	3	6	..	..
3	6	7	K	K	2	..	6	.	..		3	6	10	10	Q	2	..	6	..	..
3	6	8	8	8	6	..	.	.	..		3	6	10	10	K	2	..	6	..	..
3	6	8	8	9	4	..	8	.	..		3	6	10	J	J	2	3	6	..	..
3	6	8	8	10	2	..	6	.	..		3	6	10	J	Q	3	4	7	8	9
3	6	8	8	J	2	3	6	.	..		3	6	10	J	K	0	1	4	5	6
3	6	8	8	Q	2	..	6	.	..		3	6	10	Q	Q	2	..	6	..	..
3	6	8	8	K	2	..	6	.	..		3	6	10	Q	K	0	..	4	5	..
3	6	8	9	9	6	..	10	.	..		3	6	10	K	K	2	..	6	..	..
3	6	8	9	10	5	..	9	10	..		3	6	J	J	J	6	7	.	..	..
3	6	8	9	J	2	3	6	7	8		3	6	J	J	Q	2	3	6	..	..
3	6	8	9	Q	2	..	6	7	..		3	6	J	J	K	2	3	6	..	..
3	6	8	9	K	2	..	6	7	..		3	6	J	Q	Q	2	3	6	..	..
3	6	8	10	10	2	..	6	.	..		3	6	J	Q	K	3	4	7	8	9
3	6	8	10	J	0	1	4	5	6		3	6	J	K	K	2	3	6	..	..
3	6	8	10	Q	0	..	4	5	..		3	6	Q	Q	Q	6	..	.	..	..
3	6	8	10	K	0	..	4	5	..		3	6	Q	Q	K	2	..	6	..	..
3	6	8	J	J	2	3	6	.	..		3	6	Q	K	K	2	..	6	..	..
3	6	8	J	Q	0	1	4	5	6		3	6	K	K	K	6	..	.	..	..
3	6	8	J	K	0	1	4	5	6		3	7	7	7	7	12	..	.	..	..
3	6	8	Q	Q	2	..	6	.	..		3	7	7	7	8	12	..	.	..	..
3	6	8	Q	K	0	..	4	5	..		3	7	7	7	9	6	..	.	..	..
3	6	8	K	K	2	..	6	.	..		3	7	7	7	10	6	6	.	..	..
3	6	9	9	9	12	..	.	.	..		3	7	7	7	J	6	7	.	..	..

KEY TO CRIBBAGE.

Cards					Fifteens, Pairs & Seq.	With Jack of Turn-up	If Flush in Hand	If Flush with Turn-up	If Fl& Jack of Turn-up
3	7	7	7	Q	6				
3	7	7	7	K	6				
3	7	7	8	8	12				
3	7	7	8	9	12		16		
3	7	7	8	10	6		10		
3	7	7	8	J	6	7	10		
3	7	7	8	Q	6		10		
3	7	7	8	K	6		10		
3	7	7	9	9	4				
3	7	7	9	10	2		6		
3	7	7	9	J	2	3	6		
3	7	7	9	Q	2		6		
3	7	7	9	K	2		6		
3	7	7	10	10	4				
3	7	7	10	J	2	3	6		
3	7	7	10	Q	2		6		
3	7	7	10	K	2		6		
3	7	7	J	J	4	5			
3	7	7	J	Q	2	3	6		
3	7	7	J	K	2	3	6		
3	7	7	Q	Q	4				
3	7	7	Q	K	2		6		
3	7	7	K	K	4				
3	7	8	8	8	12				
3	7	8	8	9	12		16		
3	7	8	8	10	6		10		
3	7	8	8	J	6	7	10		
3	7	8	8	Q	6		10		
3	7	8	8	K	6		10		
3	7	8	9	9	10		14		
3	7	8	9	10	6		10	11	
3	7	8	9	J	5	6	9	10	11
3	7	8	9	Q	5		9	10	
3	7	8	9	K	5		9	10	
3	7	8	10	10	4		8		
3	7	8	10	J	2	3	6	7	8
3	7	8	10	Q	2		6	7	
3	7	8	10	K	2		6	7	
3	7	8	J	J	4	5	8		
3	7	8	J	Q	2	3	6	7	8
3	7	8	J	K	2	3	6		7
3	7	8	Q	Q	4		8		
3	7	8	Q	K	2		6		7
3	7	8	K	K	4		8		
3	7	9	9	9	6				
3	7	9	9	10	2		6		
3	7	9	9	J	2	3	6		
3	7	9	9	Q	2		6		
3	7	9	9	K	2		6		
3	7	9	10	10	2		6		
3	7	9	10	J	3	4	7	8	9
3	7	9	10	Q	0		4	5	
3	7	9	10	K	0		4	5	
3	7	9	J	J	2	3	6		
3	7	9	J	Q	0	3	4	5	6
3	7	9	J	K	0	1	4	5	6
3	7	9	Q	Q	2		6		
3	7	9	Q	K	0		4	5	
3	7	9	K	K	2		6		
3	7	10	10	10	6				
3	7	10	10	J	2	3	6		
3	7	10	10	Q	2		6		
3	7	10	10	K	2		6		
3	7	10	J	J	2	3	6		
3	7	10	J	Q	3	4	7	8	9
3	7	10	J	K	0	1	4	5	6
3	7	10	Q	Q	2		6		
3	7	10	Q	K	0		4	5	
3	7	10	K	K	2		6		
3	7	J	J	J	6	7			
3	7	J	J	Q	2	3	6		
3	7	J	J	K	2	3	6		
3	7	J	Q	Q	2	3	6		
3	7	J	Q	K	3	4	7	8	9
3	7	J	K	K	2	3	6		
3	7	Q	Q	Q	6				
3	7	Q	Q	K	2		6		
3	7	Q	K	K	2		6		
3	7	K	K	K	6				

KEY TO CRIBBAGE.

CARDS					Fifteens, Pairs & Seq.	With Jack of Turn-up	If Flush in Hand	If Flush with Turn-up	If Fl & Jack of Turn-up
3	7	K	K	K	6				
3	8	8	8	8	12				
3	8	8	8	9	6				
3	8	8	8	10	6				
3	8	8	8	J	6	7			
3	8	8	8	Q	6				
3	8	8	8	K	6				
3	8	8	9	9	4				
3	8	8	9	10	8		12		
3	8	8	9	J	2	3	6		
3	8	8	9	Q	2		6		
3	8	8	9	K	2		6		
3	8	8	10	10	4				
3	8	8	10	J	2	3	6		
3	8	8	10	Q	2		6		
3	8	8	10	K	2		6		
3	8	8	J	J	4	5			
3	8	8	J	Q	2	3	6		
3	8	8	J	K	2	3	6		
3	8	8	Q	Q	4				
3	8	8	Q	K	2		6		
3	8	8	K	K	4				
3	8	9	9	9	6				
3	8	9	9	10	8		12		
3	8	9	9	J	2	3	6		
3	8	9	9	Q	2		6		
3	8	9	9	K	2		6		
3	8	9	10	10	8		12		
3	8	9	10	J	4	5	8	9	10
3	8	9	10	Q	3		7	8	
3	8	9	10	K	3		7	8	
3	8	9	J	J	2	3	6		
3	8	9	J	Q	0	1	4	5	6
3	8	9	J	K	0	1	4	5	6
3	8	9	Q	Q	2		6		
3	8	9	Q	K	0		4	5	
3	8	9	K	K	2		6		
3	8	10	10	10	6				
3	8	10	10	J	2	3	6		
3	8	10	10	Q	2		6		
3	8	10	10	K	2		6		
3	8	10	J	J	2	3	6		
3	8	10	J	Q	3	4	7	8	9
3	8	10	J	K	0	1	4	5	6
3	8	10	Q	Q	2		6		
3	8	10	Q	K	0		4	5	
3	8	10	K	K	2		6		
3	8	J	J	J	6	7			
3	8	J	J	Q	2	3	6		
3	8	J	J	K	2	3	6		
3	8	J	Q	Q	2	3	6		
3	8	J	Q	K	3	4	7	8	9
3	8	J	K	K	2	3	6		
3	8	Q	Q	Q	6				
3	8	Q	Q	K	2		6		
3	8	Q	K	K	2		6		
3	8	K	K	K	6				
3	9	9	9	9	12				
3	9	9	9	10	6				
3	9	9	9	J	6	7			
3	9	9	9	Q	6				
3	9	9	9	K	6				
3	9	9	10	10	4				
3	9	9	10	J	8	9	12		
3	9	9	10	Q	2		6		
3	9	9	10	K	2		6		
3	9	9	J	J	4	5			
3	9	9	J	Q	2	3	6		
3	9	9	J	K	2	3	6		
3	9	9	Q	Q	4				
3	9	9	Q	K	2		6		
3	9	9	K	K	4				
3	9	10	10	10	6				
3	9	10	10	J	8	9	12		
3	9	10	10	Q	2		6		
3	9	10	10	K	2		6		
3	9	10	J	J	8	9	12		
3	9	10	J	Q	4	5	8	9	10

KEY TO CRIBBAGE.

Cards					Fifteens, Pairs & Seq.	With Jack of Turn-up	If Flush in Hand	If Flush with Turn-up	If Fl. & Jack of Turn-up
3	9	10	J	K	3	4	7	8	9
3	9	10	Q	Q	2		6		
3	9	10	Q	K	0		4	5	
3	9	10	K	K	2		6		
3	9	J	J	J	6	7			
3	9	J	J	Q	2	3	6		
3	9	J	J	K	2	3	6		
3	9	J	Q	Q	2	3	6		
3	9	J	Q	K	3	4	7	8	9
3	9	J	K	K	2	3	6		
3	9	Q	Q	Q	6				
3	9	Q	Q	K	2		6		
3	9	Q	K	K	2		6		
3	9	K	K	K	6				
3	10	10	10	10	12				
3	10	10	10	J	6	7			
3	10	10	10	Q	6				
3	10	10	10	K	6				
3	10	10	J	J	4	5			
3	10	10	J	Q	8	9	12		
3	10	10	J	K	2	3	6		
3	10	10	Q	Q	4				
3	10	10	Q	K	2		6		
3	10	10	K	K	4				
3	10	J	J	J	6	7			
3	10	J	J	Q	8	9	12		
3	10	J	J	K	2	3	6		
3	10	J	Q	Q	8	9	12		
3	10	J	Q	K	4	5	8	9	10
3	10	J	K	K	2	3	6		
3	10	Q	Q	Q	6				
3	10	Q	Q	K	2		6		
3	10	Q	K	K	2		6		
3	10	K	K	K	6				
3	J	J	J	J	12	13			
3	J	J	J	Q	6	7			
3	J	J	J	K	6	7			
3	J	J	Q	Q	4	5			
3	J	J	Q	K	8	9	12		

Cards					Fifteens, Pairs & Seq.	With Jack of Turn-up	If Flush in Hand	If Flush with Turn-up	If Fl. & Jack of Turn-up
3	J	J	K	K	4	5			
3	J	Q	Q	Q	6	7			
3	J	Q	Q	K	8	9	12		
3	J	Q	K	K	8	9	12		
3	J	K	K	K	6	7			
3	Q	Q	Q	Q	12				
3	Q	Q	Q	K	6				
3	Q	Q	K	K	4				
3	Q	K	K	K	6				
3	K	K	K	K	12				
4	4	4	4	5	12				
4	4	4	4	6	12				
4	4	4	4	7	24				
4	4	4	4	8	12				
4	4	4	4	9	12				
4	4	4	4	10	12				
4	4	4	4	J	12	13			
4	4	4	4	Q	12				
4	4	4	4	K	12				
4	4	4	5	5	8				
4	4	4	5	6	21				
4	4	4	5	7	12				
4	4	4	5	8	6				
4	4	4	5	9	6				
4	4	4	5	10	8				
4	4	4	5	J	8	9			
4	4	4	5	Q	8				
4	4	4	5	K	8				
4	4	4	6	6	8				
4	4	4	6	7	12				
4	4	4	6	8	6				
4	4	4	6	9	8				
4	4	4	6	10	6				
4	4	4	6	J	6	7			
4	4	4	6	Q	6				
4	4	4	6	K	6				
4	4	4	7	7	20				
4	4	4	7	8	14				
4	4	4	7	9	12				

KEY TO CRIBBAGE.

CARDS.					Fifteens, Pairs & Seq.	With Jack of Turn-up.	If Flush in Hand.	If Flush with Turn-up.	If Fl& Jack of Turn-up.
4	4	4	7	10	12				
4	4	4	7	J	12	13			
4	4	4	7	Q	12				
4	4	4	7	K	12				
4	4	4	8	8	8				
4	4	4	8	9	6				
4	4	4	8	10	6				
4	4	4	8	J	6	7			
4	4	4	8	Q	6				
4	4	4	8	K	6				
4	4	4	9	9	8				
4	4	4	9	10	6				
4	4	4	9	J	6	7			
4	4	4	9	Q	6				
4	4	4	9	K	6				
4	4	4	10	10	8				
4	4	4	10	J	6	7			
4	4	4	10	Q	6				
4	4	4	10	K	6				
4	4	4	J	J	8	9			
4	4	4	J	Q	6	7			
4	4	4	J	K	6	7			
4	4	4	Q	Q	8				
4	4	4	Q	K	6				
4	4	4	K	K	8				
4	4	5	5	5	10				
4	4	5	5	6	24				
4	4	5	5	7	6				
4	4	5	5	8	4				
4	4	5	5	9	4				
4	4	5	5	10	8				
4	4	5	5	J	8	9			
4	4	5	5	Q	8				
4	4	5	5	K	8				
4	4	5	6	6	24				
4	4	5	6	7	16		20		
4	4	5	6	8	12		16		
4	4	5	6	9	14		18		
4	4	5	6	10	14		18		

CARDS.					Fifteens, Pairs & Seq.	With Jack of Turn-up.	If Flush in Hand.	If Flush with Turn-up.	If Fl& Jack of Turn-up.
4	4	5	6	J	14	15	18		
4	4	5	6	Q	14		18		
4	4	5	6	K	14		18		
4	4	5	7	7	8		10		
4	4	5	7	8	6		10		
4	4	5	7	9	4		8		
4	4	5	7	10	6		10		
4	4	5	7	J	6	7	10		
4	4	5	7	Q	6		10		
4	4	5	7	K	6		10		
4	4	5	8	8	4				
4	4	5	8	9	2		6		
4	4	5	8	10	4		8		
4	4	5	8	J	4	5	8		
4	4	5	8	Q	4		8		
4	4	5	8	K	4		8		
4	4	5	9	9	4				
4	4	5	9	10	4		8		
4	4	5	9	J	4	5	8		
4	4	5	9	Q	4		8		
4	4	5	9	K	4		8		
4	4	5	10	10	8				
4	4	5	10	J	6	7	10		
4	4	5	10	Q	6		10		
4	4	5	10	K	6		10		
4	4	5	J	J	8	9	10		
4	4	5	J	Q	6	7	10		
4	4	5	J	K	6	7	10		
4	4	5	Q	Q	8				
4	4	5	Q	K	6		10		
4	4	5	K	K	8				
4	4	6	6	6	8				
4	4	6	6	7	6				
4	4	6	6	8	4				
4	4	6	6	9	8				
4	4	6	6	10	4				
4	4	6	6	J	4	5			
4	4	6	6	Q	4				
4	4	6	6	K	4				

KEY TO CRIBBAGE.

CARDS					Fifteens, Pairs & Seq..	With Jack of Turn-up..	If Flush in Hand......	If Flush with Turn-up..	If Fl& Jack of Turn-up
4	4	6	7	7	8				
4	4	6	7	8	9		13		
4	4	6	7	9	6		10		
4	4	6	7	10	4		8		
4	4	6	7	J	4	5	8		
4	4	6	7	Q	4		8		
4	4	6	7	K	4		8		
4	4	6	8	8	4				
4	4	6	8	9	4		8		
4	4	6	8	10	2		6		
4	4	6	8	J	2	3	6		
4	4	6	8	Q	2		6		
4	4	6	8	K	2		6		
4	4	6	9	9	8				
4	4	6	9	10	4		8		
4	4	6	9	J	4	5	8		
4	4	6	9	Q	4		8		
4	4	6	9	K	4		8		
4	4	6	10	10	4				
4	4	6	10	J	2	3	6		
4	4	6	10	Q	2		6		
4	4	6	10	K	2		6		
4	4	6	J	J	4	5			
4	4	6	J	Q	2	3	6		
4	4	6	J	K	2	3	6		
4	4	6	Q	Q	4				
4	4	6	Q	K	2		6		
4	4	6	K	K	4				
4	4	7	7	7	14				
4	4	7	7	8	12				
4	4	7	7	9	8				
4	4	7	7	10	8				
4	4	7	7	J	8	9			
4	4	7	7	Q	8				
4	4	7	7	K	8				
4	4	7	8	8	10				
4	4	7	8	9	9		13		
4	4	7	8	10	6		10		
4	4	7	8	J	6	7	10		

CARDS					Fifteens, Pairs & Seq..	With Jack of Turn-up..	If Flush in Hand......	If Flush with Turn-up..	If Fl& Jack of Turn-up
4	4	7	8	Q	6		10		
4	4	7	8	K	6		10		
4	4	7	9	9	6				
4	4	7	9	10	4		8		
4	4	7	9	J	4	5	8		
4	4	7	9	Q	4		8		
4	4	7	9	K	4		8		
4	4	7	10	10	6				
4	4	7	10	J	4	5	8		
4	4	7	10	Q	4		8		
4	4	7	10	K	4		8		
4	4	7	J	J	6	7			
4	4	7	J	Q	4	5	8		
4	4	7	J	K	4	5	8		
4	4	7	Q	Q	6				
4	4	7	Q	K	4		8		
4	4	7	K	K	6				
4	4	8	8	8	8				
4	4	8	8	9	4				
4	4	8	8	10	4				
4	4	8	8	J	4	5			
4	4	8	8	Q	4				
4	4	8	8	K	4				
4	4	8	9	9	4				
4	4	8	9	10	5		9		
4	4	8	9	J	2	3	6		
4	4	8	9	Q	2		6		
4	4	8	9	K	2		6		
4	4	8	10	10	4				
4	4	8	10	J	2	3	6		
4	4	8	10	Q	2		6		
4	4	8	10	K	2		6		
4	4	8	J	J	4	5	6		
4	4	8	J	Q	2	3	6		
4	4	8	J	K	2	3	6		
4	4	8	Q	Q	4		6		
4	4	8	Q	K	2		6		
4	4	8	K	K	4				
4	4	9	9	9	8				

KEY TO CRIBBAGE.

CARDS.					Fifteens, Pairs & Seq..	With Jack of Turn-up......	If Flush in Hand......	If Flush with Turn-up.	If Fl& Jack of Turn up
4	4	9	9	10	4				
4	4	9	9	J	4	5			
4	4	9	9	Q	4				
4	4	9	9	K	4				
4	4	9	10	10	4				
4	4	9	10	J	5	6	9		
4	4	9	10	Q	2		6		
4	4	9	10	K	2		6		
4	4	9	J	J	4	5			
4	4	9	J	Q	2	3	6		
4	4	9	J	K	2	3	6		
4	4	9	Q	Q	4				
4	4	9	Q	K	2		6		
4	4	9	K	K	4				
4	4	10	10	10	8				
4	4	10	10	J	4	5			
4	4	10	10	Q	4				
4	4	10	10	K	4				
4	4	10	J	J	8	9			
4	4	10	J	Q	5	6	6		
4	4	10	J	K	5		6		
4	4	10	Q	Q	4				
4	4	10	Q	K	2			6	
4	4	10	K	K	4				
4	4	J	J	J	8	9			
4	4	J	J	Q	4	5			
4	4	J	J	K	4	5			
4	4	J	Q	Q	4	5			
4	4	J	Q	K	5	6	6		
4	4	J	K	K	4	5			
4	4	Q	Q	Q	8				
4	4	Q	Q	K	4				
4	4	Q	K	K	4				
4	4	K	K	K	8				
4	5	5	5	5	20				
4	5	5	5	6	23				
4	5	5	5	7	8				
4	5	5	5	8	8				
4	5	5	5	9	8				

CARDS.					Fifteens, Pairs & Seq..	With Jack of Turn-up......	If Flush in Hand......	If Flush with Turn-up.	If Fl& Jack of Turn up
4	5	5	5	10	14				
4	5	5	5	J	14	15			
4	5	5	5	Q	14				
4	5	5	5	K	14				
4	5	5	6	6	24				
4	5	5	6	7	14		18		
4	5	5	6	8	12		16		
4	5	5	6	9	14		18		
4	5	5	6	10	16		20		
4	5	5	6	J	16	17	20		
4	5	5	6	Q	16		20		
4	5	5	6	K	16		20		
4	5	5	7	7	4				
4	5	5	7	8	4		8		
4	5	5	7	9	2		6		
4	5	5	7	10	6		10		
4	5	5	7	J	6	7	10		
4	5	5	7	Q	6		10		
4	5	5	7	K	6		10		
4	5	5	8	8	4				
4	5	5	8	9	2		6		
4	5	5	8	10	6		10		
4	5	5	8	J	6	7	10		
4	5	5	8	Q	6		10		
4	5	5	8	K	6		10		
4	5	5	9	9	4				
4	5	5	9	10	6		10		
4	5	5	9	J	6	7	10		
4	5	5	9	Q	6		10		
4	5	5	9	K	6		10		
4	5	5	10	10	12				
4	5	5	10	J	10	11	14		
4	5	5	10	Q	10		14		
4	5	5	10	K	10		14		
4	5	5	J	J	12	13			
4	5	5	J	Q	10	11	14		
4	5	5	J	K	10	11	14		
4	5	5	Q	Q	12				
4	5	5	Q	K	10		14		

KEY TO CRIBBAGE.

CARDS.					Fifteens, Pairs & Seq..	With Jack of Turn-up..	If Flush in Hand.....	If Flush with Turn-up.	If Fl& Jack of Turn-up
4	5	5	K	K	12				
4	5	6	6	6	21				
4	5	6	6	7	14		18		
4	5	6	6	8	12		16		
4	5	6	6	9	16		20		
4	5	6	6	10	14		18		
4	5	6	6	J	14	15	18		
4	5	6	6	Q	14		18		
4	5	6	6	K	14		18		
4	5	6	7	7	12		16		
4	5	6	7	8	9		13	14	
4	5	6	7	9	8		12	13	
4	5	6	7	10	8		12	13	
4	5	6	7	J	8	9	12	13	14
4	5	6	7	Q	8		12	13	
4	5	6	7	K	8		12	13	
4	5	6	8	8	7		11		
4	5	6	8	9	7		11	12	
4	5	6	8	10	7		11	12	
4	5	6	8	J	7	8	11	12	13
4	5	6	8	Q	7		11	12	
4	5	6	8	K	7		11	12	
4	5	6	9	9	11		15		
4	5	6	9	10	9		13	14	
4	5	6	9	J	9	10	13	14	15
4	5	6	9	Q	9		13	14	
4	5	6	9	K	9		13	14	
4	5	6	10	10	11		15		
4	5	6	10	J	9	10	13	14	15
4	5	6	10	Q	9		13	14	
4	5	6	10	K	9		13	14	
4	5	6	J	J	11	12	15		
4	5	6	J	Q	9	10	13	14	15
4	5	6	J	K	9	10	13	14	15
4	5	6	Q	Q	11		15		
4	5	6	Q	K	9		13	14	
4	5	6	K	K	11		15		
4	5	7	7	7	6				
4	5	7	7	8	6		10		

CARDS.					Fifteens, Pairs & Seq..	With Jack of Turn-up..	If Flush in Hand.....	If Flush with Turn-up.	If Fl& Jack of Turn-up
4	5	7	7	9	2		6		
4	5	7	7	10	4		8		
4	5	7	7	J	4	5	8		
4	5	7	7	Q	4		8		
4	5	7	7	K	4		8		
4	5	7	8	8	6		10		
4	5	7	8	9	5		9	10	
4	5	7	8	10	4		8	9	
4	5	7	8	J	4	5	8	9	10
4	5	7	8	Q	4		8	9	
4	5	7	8	K	4		8	9	
4	5	7	9	9	2		6		
4	5	7	9	10	2		6	7	
4	5	7	9	J	2	3	6	7	8
4	5	7	9	Q	2		6	7	
4	5	7	9	K	2		6	7	
4	5	7	10	10	6		10		
4	5	7	10	J	4	5	8	9	10
4	5	7	10	Q	4		8	9	
4	5	7	10	K	4		8	9	
4	5	7	J	J	6	7	10		
4	5	7	J	Q	4	5	8	9	10
4	5	7	J	K	4	5	8	9	10
4	5	7	Q	Q	6		10		
4	5	7	Q	K	4		8	9	
4	5	7	K	K	6		10		
4	5	8	8	8	2		6		
4	5	8	8	9	4		8		
4	5	8	8	10	4	5	8		
4	5	8	8	J	4		8		
4	5	8	8	Q	4		8		
4	5	8	8	K	4		8		
4	5	8	9	9	2		6		
4	5	8	9	10	5		9	10	
4	5	8	9	J	2	3	6	7	8
4	5	8	9	Q	2		6	7	
4	5	8	9	K	2		6	7	
4	5	8	10	10	6		10		
4	5	8	10	J	4	5	8	9	10

KEY TO CRIBBAGE.

Cards					Fifteens, Pairs & Seq.	With Jack of Turn-up	If Flush in Hand	If Flush with Turn-up	If Fl & Jack of Turn-up
4	5	8	10	Q	4		8	9	
4	5	8	10	K	4		8	9	
4	5	8	J	J	6	7	10		
4	5	8	J	Q	4	5	8	9	10
4	5	8	J	K	4	5	8	9	10
4	5	8	Q	Q	6		10		
4	5	8	Q	K	4		8	9	
4	5	8	K	K	6		10		
4	5	9	9	9	6				
4	5	9	9	10	4		8		
4	5	9	9	J	4	5	8		
4	5	9	9	Q	4		8		
4	5	9	9	K	4		8		
4	5	9	10	10	6		10		
4	5	9	10	J	7	8	11	12	13
4	5	9	10	Q	4		8	9	
4	5	9	10	K	4		8	9	
4	5	9	J	J	6	7	10		
4	5	9	J	Q	4	5	8	9	10
4	5	9	J	K	4	5	8	9	10
4	5	9	Q	Q	6		10		
4	5	9	Q	K	4		8	9	
4	5	9	K	K	6		10		
4	5	10	10	10	12				
4	5	10	10	J	8	9	12		
4	5	10	10	Q	8		12		
4	5	10	10	K	8		12		
4	5	10	J	J	8	9	12		
4	5	10	J	Q	9	10	13	14	15
4	5	10	J	K	6	7	10	11	12
4	5	10	Q	Q	8		12		
4	5	10	Q	K	6		10	11	
4	5	10	K	K	8		12		
4	5	J	J	J	12	13			
4	5	J	J	Q	8	9	12		
4	5	J	J	K	8	9	12		
4	5	J	Q	Q	8	9	12		
4	5	J	Q	K	9	10	13	14	15
4	5	J	K	K	8	9	12		

Cards					Fifteens, Pairs & Seq.	With Jack of Turn-up	If Flush in Hand	If Flush with Turn-up	If Fl & Jack of Turn-up
4	5	Q	Q	Q	12				
4	5	Q	Q	K	8		12		
4	5	Q	K	K	8		12		
4	5	K	K	K	12				
4	6	6	6	6	12				
4	6	6	6	7	6				
4	6	6	6	8	6				
4	6	6	6	9	12				
4	6	6	6	10	6				
4	6	6	6	J	6	7			
4	6	6	6	Q	6				
4	6	6	6	K	6				
4	6	6	7	7	4				
4	6	6	7	8	10		14		
4	6	6	7	9	6		10		
4	6	6	7	10	2		6		
4	6	6	7	J	2	3	6		
4	6	6	7	Q	2		6		
4	6	6	7	K	2		6		
4	6	6	8	8	4				
4	6	6	8	9	6		10		
4	6	6	8	10	2		6		
4	6	6	8	J	2	3	6		
4	6	6	8	Q	2		6		
4	6	6	8	K	2		6		
4	6	6	9	9	12				
4	6	6	9	10	6		10		
4	6	6	9	J	6	7	10		
4	6	6	9	Q	6		10		
4	6	6	9	K	6		10		
4	6	6	10	10	4				
4	6	6	10	J	2	3	6		
4	6	6	10	Q	2		6		
4	6	6	10	K	2		6		
4	6	6	J	J	4	5			
4	6	6	J	Q	2	3	6		
4	6	6	J	K	2	3	6		
4	6	6	Q	Q	4				
4	6	6	Q	K	2		6		

KEY TO CRIBBAGE.

Cards					Fifteens, Pairs & Seq.	With Jack of Turn-up	If Flush in Hand	If Flush with Turn-up	If Fl & Jack of Turn-up
4	6	6	K	K	4				
4	6	7	7	7	6				
4	6	7	7	8	12		16		
4	6	7	7	9	4		8		
4	6	7	7	10	2		6		
4	6	7	7	J	2	3	6		
4	6	7	7	Q	2		6		
4	6	7	7	K	2		6		
4	6	7	8	8	12		16		
4	6	7	8	9	8		12	13	
4	6	7	8	10	5		9	10	
4	6	7	8	J	5	6	9	10	11
4	6	7	8	Q	5		9	10	
4	6	7	8	K	5		9	10	
4	6	7	9	9	6		10		
4	6	7	9	10	2		6	7	
4	6	7	9	J	2	3	6	7	8
4	6	7	9	Q	2		6	7	
4	6	7	9	K	2		6	7	
4	6	7	10	10	2		6		
4	6	7	10	J	0	1	4	5	6
4	6	7	10	Q	0		4	5	
4	6	7	10	K	0		4	5	
4	6	7	J	J	2	3	6		
4	6	7	J	Q	0	1	4	5	6
4	6	7	J	K	0	1	4	5	6
4	6	7	Q	Q	2		6		
4	6	7	Q	K	0		4	5	
4	6	7	K	K	2		6		
4	6	8	8	8	6				
4	6	8	8	9	4		8		
4	6	8	8	10	2		6		
4	6	8	8	J	2	3	6		
4	6	8	8	Q	2		6		
4	6	8	8	K	2		6		
4	6	8	9	9	6		10		
4	6	8	9	10	5		9	10	
4	6	8	9	J	2	3	6	7	8
4	6	8	9	Q	2		6	7	
4	6	8	9	K	2		6	7	
4	6	8	10	10	2		6		
4	6	8	10	J	0	1	4	5	6
4	6	8	10	Q	0		4	5	
4	6	8	10	K	0		4	5	
4	6	8	J	J	2	3	6		
4	6	8	J	Q	0	1	4	5	6
4	6	8	J	K	0	1	4	5	6
4	6	8	Q	Q	2		6		
4	6	8	Q	K	0		4	5	
4	6	8	K	K	2		6		
4	6	9	9	9	12				
4	6	9	9	10	6		10		
4	6	9	9	J	6	7	10		
4	6	9	9	Q	6		10		
4	6	9	9	K	6		10		
4	6	9	10	10	4		8		
4	6	9	10	J	5	6	9	10	11
4	6	9	10	Q	2		6	7	
4	6	9	10	K	2		6	7	
4	6	9	J	J	4	5	8		
4	6	9	J	Q	2	3	6	7	8
4	6	9	J	K	2	3	6	7	8
4	6	9	Q	Q	4		8		
4	6	9	Q	K	2		6	7	
4	6	9	K	K	4		8		
4	6	10	10	10	6		6		
4	6	10	10	J	2	3	6		
4	6	10	10	Q	2		6		
4	6	10	10	K	2		6		
4	6	10	J	J	2	3	6		
4	6	10	J	Q	3	4	7	8	9
4	6	10	J	K	0	1	4	5	6
4	6	10	Q	Q	2		6		
4	6	10	Q	K	0		4	5	
4	6	10	K	K	2		6		
4	6	J	J	J	6		6		
4	6	J	J	Q	2	3	6		
4	6	J	J	K	2	3	6		

KEY TO CRIBBAGE.

Cards					Fifteens, Pairs & Seq.	With Jack of Turn-up	If Flush in Hand	If Flush with Turn-up	If Fl & Jack of Turn-up
4	6	J	Q	Q	2	3	6		
4	6	J	Q	K	3	4	6	8	9
4	6	J	K	K	2	3	6		
4	6	Q	Q	Q	6		6		
4	6	Q	Q	K	2		6		
4	6	Q	K	K	2		6		
4	6	K	K	K	6				
4	7	7	7	7	12				
4	7	7	7	8	12				
4	7	7	7	9	6				
4	7	7	7	10	6				
4	7	7	7	J	6	7			
4	7	7	7	Q	6				
4	7	7	7	K	6				
4	7	7	8	8	12				
4	7	7	8	9	12		16		
4	7	7	8	10	6		10		
4	7	7	8	J	6	7	10		
4	7	7	8	Q	6		10		
4	7	7	8	K	6		10		
4	7	7	9	9	4				
4	7	7	9	10	2		6		
4	7	7	9	J	2	3	6		
4	7	7	9	Q	2		6		
4	7	7	10	10	4				
4	7	7	10	J	2		3	6	
4	7	7	10	Q	2		6		
4	7	7	10	K	2		6		
4	7	7	J	J	4	5			
4	7	7	J	Q	2	3	6		
4	7	7	J	K	2		3	6	
4	7	7	Q	Q	4				
4	7	7	Q	K	4	2		6	
4	7	7	K	K	4				
4	7	8	8	8	12		16		
4	7	8	8	9	12		16		
4	7	8	8	10	6		10		
4	7	8	8	J	6	7	10		

Cards					Fifteens, Pairs & Seq.	With Jack of Turn-up	If Flush in Hand	If Flush with Turn-up	If Fl & Jack of Turn-up
4	7	8	8	Q	6		10		
4	7	8	8	K	6		10		
4	7	8	9	9	10		14		
4	7	8	9	10	6		10	11	
4	7	8	9	J	5	6	9	10	11
4	7	8	9	Q	5		9	10	
4	7	8	9	K	5		9	10	
4	7	8	10	10	4		8		
4	7	8	10	J	2	3	6	7	8
4	7	8	10	Q	2		6	7	
4	7	8	10	K	2		6	7	
4	7	8	J	J	4	5	8		
4	7	8	J	Q	2	3	6	7	8
4	7	8	J	K	2	3	6	7	8
4	7	8	Q	Q	4		8		
4	7	8	Q	K	2		6	7	
4	7	8	K	K	4		8		
4	7	9	9	9	6				
4	7	9	9	10	2		6		
4	7	9	9	J	2	3	6		
4	7	9	9	Q	2		6		
4	7	9	9	K	2		6		
4	7	9	10	10	2		6		
4	7	9	10	J	3	4	7	8	9
4	7	9	10	Q	0		4	5	
4	7	9	10	K	0		4	5	
4	7	9	J	J	0		3	4	5
4	7	9	J	Q	0	1	4	5	6
4	7	9	J	K	0	1	4	5	6
4	7	9	Q	Q	2		6		
4	7	9	Q	K	0		4	5	
4	7	9	K	K	2		6		
4	7	10	10	10	6				
4	7	10	10	J	2	3	6		
4	7	10	10	Q	2		6		
4	7	10	10	K	2		6		
4	7	10	J	J	2	3	6		
4	7	10	J	Q	2	2	3	4	1
4	7	10	J	K	2	3	6	7	8
4	7	J	J	Q	2	3	0		8 5
4	7	J	J	K	0		6 7 4		9 6

KEY TO CRIBBAGE.

CARDS.					Fifteens, Pairs & Seq..	With Jack of Turn-up..	If Flush in Hand......	If Flush with Turn-up.	If Fl& Jack of Turn-up
4	7	10	Q	Q	2		6		
4	7	10	Q	K	0		4	5	
4	7	10	K	K	2		6		
4	7	J	J	J	6	7			
4	7	J	J	Q	2	3	6		
4	7	J	J	K	2	3	6		
4	7	J	Q	Q	2	3	6		
4	7	J	Q	K	3	4	7	8	9
4	7	J	K	K	2	3	6		
4	7	Q	Q	Q	6				
4	7	Q	Q	K	2		6		
4	7	Q	K	K	2		6		
4	7	K	K	K	6				
4	8	8	8	8	12				
4	8	8	8	9	6				
4	8	8	8	10	6				
4	8	8	8	J	6	7			
4	8	8	8	Q	6				
4	8	8	8	K	6				
4	8	8	9	9	4				
4	8	8	9	10	8		12		
4	8	8	9	J	2	3	6		
4	8	8	9	Q	2		6		
4	8	8	9	K	2		6		
4	8	8	10	10	4				
4	8	8	10	J	2	3	6		
4	8	8	10	Q	2		6		
4	8	8	10	K	2		6		
4	8	8	J	J	4	5			
4	8	8	J	Q	2	3	6		
4	8	8	J	K	2	3	6		
4	8	8	Q	Q	4				
4	8	8	Q	K	2		6		
4	8	8	K	K	4				
4	8	9	9	9	6				
4	8	9	9	10	8		12		
4	8	9	9	J	2	3	6		
4	8	9	9	Q	2		6		
4	8	9	9	K	2		6		

CARDS.					Fifteens, Pairs & Seq..	With Jack of Turn-up..	If Flush in Hand......	If Flush with Turn-up.	If Fl& Jack of Turn-up
4	8	9	10	10	8		12		
4	8	9	10	J	4	5	8	9	10
4	8	9	10	Q	3		7	8	
4	8	9	10	K	3		7	8	
4	8	9	J	J	2	3	6		
4	8	9	J	Q	0	1	4	5	6
4	8	9	J	K	0	1	4	5	6
4	8	9	Q	Q	2		6		
4	8	9	Q	K	0		4	5	
4	8	9	K	K	2		6		
4	8	10	10	10	6				
4	8	10	10	J	2	3	6		
4	8	10	10	Q	2		6		
4	8	10	10	K	2		6		
4	8	10	J	J	2	3	6		
4	8	10	J	Q	3	4	7	8	9
4	8	10	J	K	0	1	4	5	6
4	8	10	Q	Q	2		6		
4	8	10	Q	K	0		4	5	
4	8	10	K	K	2		6		
4	8	J	J	J	6	7			
4	8	J	J	Q	2	3	6		
4	8	J	J	K	2	3	6		
4	8	J	Q	Q	2	3	6		
4	8	J	Q	K	3	4	7	8	9
4	8	J	K	K	2	3	6		
4	8	Q	Q	Q	6				
4	8	Q	Q	K	2		6		
4	8	Q	K	K	2		6		
4	8	K	K	K	6				
4	9	9	9	9	12				
4	9	9	9	10	6				
4	9	9	9	J	6	7			
4	9	9	9	Q	6				
4	9	9	9	K	6				
4	9	9	10	10	4				
4	9	9	10	J	8	9	12		
4	9	9	10	Q	2		6		
4	9	9	10	K	2		6		

KEY TO CRIBBAGE.

CARDS				Fifteens, Pairs & Seq.	With Jack of Turn-up.	If Flush in Hand.	If Flush with Turn-up.	If Fl & Jack of Turn-up
4 9 9	J	J		4	5	.	.	.
4 9 9	J	Q		2	3	6	.	.
4 9 9	J	K		2	3	6	.	.
4 9 9	Q	Q		4	.	.	.	.
4 9 9	Q	K		2	.	6	.	.
4 9 9	K	K		4	.	.	.	.
4 9 10 10	10			6	.	.	.	.
4 9 10 10	J			8	9	12	.	.
4 9 10 10	Q			2	.	6	.	.
4 9 10 10	K			2	.	6	.	.
4 9 10	J	J		8	9	12	.	.
4 9 10	J	Q		4	5	8	9	10
4 9 10	J	K		3	4	7	8	9
4 9 10	Q	Q		2	.	6	.	.
4 9 10	Q	K		0	.	4	5	.
4 9 10	K	K		2	.	6	.	.
4 9	J J	J		6	7	.	.	.
4 9	J J	Q		2	3	6	.	.
4 9	J J	K		2	3	6	.	.
4 9	J	Q Q		2	3	6	.	.
4 9	J	Q K		3	4	7	8	9
4 9	J	K K		2	3	6	.	.
4 9	Q Q	Q		6	.	.	.	.
4 9	Q Q	K		2	.	6	.	.
4 9	Q	K K		2	.	6	.	.
4 9	K K	K		6	.	.	.	.
4 10 10 10	10			12	.	.	.	.
4 10 10 10	J			6	7	.	.	.
4 10 10 10	Q			6	.	.	.	.
4 10 10 10	K			6	.	.	.	.
4 10 10	J	J		4	5	.	.	.
4 10 10	J	Q		8	9	12	.	.
4 10 10	J	K		2	3	6	.	.
4 10 10	Q	Q		4	.	.	.	.
4 10 10	Q	K		2	.	6	.	.
4 10 10	K	K		4	.	.	.	.
4 10	J J	J		6	7	.	.	.
4 10	J J	Q		8	9	12	.	.
4 10	J J	K		2	3	6	.	.

CARDS				Fifteens, Pairs & Seq.	With Jack of Turn-up.	If Flush in Hand.	If Flush with Turn-up.	If Fl & Jack of Turn-up
4 10	J	Q Q		8	9	12	.	.
4 10	J	Q K		4	5	8	9	10
4 10	J	K K		2	3	6	.	.
4 10	Q Q	Q		6	.	.	.	.
4 10	Q Q	K		2	.	6	.	.
4 10	Q	K K		2	.	6	.	.
4 10	K K	K		6	.	.	.	.
4	J J J	J		12	13	.	.	.
4	J J J	Q		6	7	.	.	.
4	J J J	K		6	7	.	.	.
4	J J	Q Q		4	5	.	.	.
4	J J	Q K		8	9	12	.	.
4	J J	K K		4	5	.	.	.
4	J	Q Q Q		6	7	.	.	.
4	J	Q Q K		8	9	12	.	.
4	J	Q K K		8	9	12	.	.
4	J	K K K		6	7	.	.	.
4	Q Q Q	Q		12	.	.	.	.
4	Q Q Q	K		6	.	.	.	.
4	Q Q	K K		4	.	.	.	.
4	Q	K K K		6	.	.	.	.
4	K K K	K		12	.	.	.	.
5 5 5 5	6			20	.	.	.	.
5 5 5 5	7			20	.	.	.	.
5 5 5 5	8			20	.	.	.	.
5 5 5 5	9			20	.	.	.	.
5 5 5 5	10			28	.	.	.	.
5 5 5 5	J			28	29	.	.	.
5 5 5 5	Q			28	.	.	.	.
5 5 5 5	K			28	.	.	.	.
5 5 5	6	6		10	.	.	.	.
5 5 5	6	7		17	.	.	.	.
5 5 5	6	8		8	.	.	.	.
5 5 5	6	9		10	.	.	.	.
5 5 5	6	10		14	.	.	.	.
5 5 5	6	J		14	15	.	.	.
5 5 5	6	Q		14	.	.	.	.
5 5 5	6	K		14	.	.	.	.
5 5 5	7	7		10	.	.	.	.

KEY TO CRIBBAGE.

Cards					Fifteens, Pairs & Seq.	With Jack of Turn-up	If Flush in Hand	If Flush with Turn-up	If Fl& Jack of Turn-up
5	5	5	7	8	10				
5	5	5	7	9	8				
5	5	5	7	10	14				
5	5	5	7	J	14	15			
5	5	5	7	Q	14				
5	5	5	7	K	14				
5	5	5	8	8	10				
5	5	5	8	9	8				
5	5	5	8	10	14				
5	5	5	8	J	14	15			
5	5	5	8	Q	14				
5	5	5	8	K	14				
5	5	5	9	9	10				
5	5	5	9	10	14				
5	5	5	9	J	14	15			
5	5	5	9	Q	14				
5	5	5	9	K	14				
5	5	5	10	10	22				
5	5	5	10	J	20	21			
5	5	5	10	Q	20				
5	5	5	10	K	20				
5	5	5	J	J	22	23			
5	5	5	J	Q	20	21			
5	5	5	J	K	20	21			
5	5	5	Q	Q	22				
5	5	5	Q	K	20				
5	5	5	K	K	22				
5	5	6	6	6	8				
5	5	6	6	7	16				
5	5	6	6	8	4				
5	5	6	6	9	8				
5	5	6	6	10	8				
5	5	6	6	J	8	9			
5	5	6	6	Q	8				
5	5	6	6	K	8				
5	5	6	7	7	16				
5	5	6	7	8	12		16		
5	5	6	7	9	10		14		
5	5	6	7	10	12		16		

Cards					Fifteens, Pairs & Seq.	With Jack of Turn-up	If Flush in Hand	If Flush with Turn-up	If Fl& Jack of Turn-up
5	5	6	7	J	12	13	16		
5	5	6	7	Q	12		16		
5	5	6	7	K	12		16		
5	5	6	8	8	4				
5	5	6	8	9	4		8		
5	5	6	8	10	6		10		
5	5	6	8	J	6	7	10		
5	5	6	8	Q	6		10		
5	5	6	8	K	6		10		
5	5	6	9	9	8				
5	5	6	9	10	8		12		
5	5	6	9	J	8	9	12		
5	5	6	9	Q	8		12		
5	5	6	9	K	8		12		
5	5	6	10	10	12				
5	5	6	10	J	10	11	14		
5	5	6	10	Q	10		14		
5	5	6	10	K	10		14		
5	5	6	J	J	12	13			
5	5	6	J	Q	10	11	14		
5	5	6	J	K	10	11	14		
5	5	6	Q	Q	12				
5	5	6	Q	K	10		14		
5	5	6	K	K	12				
5	5	7	7	7	8				
5	5	7	7	8	8				
5	5	7	7	9	4				
5	5	7	7	10	8				
5	5	7	7	J	8	9			
5	5	7	7	Q	8				
5	5	7	7	K	8				
5	5	7	8	8	8				
5	5	7	8	9	7		11		
5	5	7	8	10	8		12		
5	5	7	8	J	8	9	12		
5	5	7	8	Q	8		12		
5	5	7	8	K	8		12		
5	5	7	9	9	4				
5	5	7	9	10	6		10		

KEY TO CRIBBAGE.

CARDS.					Fifteens, Pairs & Seq..	With Jack of Turn-up......	If Flush in Hand.	If Flush with Turn-up.	If Fl & Jack of Turn up
5	5	7	9	J	6	7	10	..	..
5	5	7	9	Q	6	..	10	..	..
5	5	7	9	K	6	..	10	..	..
5	5	7	10	10	12	..	..	..	..
5	5	7	10	J	10	11	14	..	..
5	5	7	10	Q	10	..	14	..	..
5	5	7	10	K	10	..	14	..	..
5	5	7	J	J	12	13	..	..	..
5	5	7	J	Q	10	11	14	..	..
5	5	7	J	K	10	11	14	..	..
5	5	7	Q	Q	12	..	..	..	..
5	5	7	Q	K	10	..	14	..	..
5	5	7	K	K	12	..	..	..	..
5	5	8	8	8	8	..	..	..	..
5	5	8	8	9	4	..	..	..	..
5	5	8	8	10	8	..	..	..	..
5	5	8	8	J	8	..	9	..	..
5	5	8	8	Q	8	..	..	..	..
5	5	8	8	K	8	..	..	..	..
5	5	8	9	9	4	..	..	..	..
5	5	8	9	10	9	..	13	..	..
5	5	8	9	J	6	7	10	..	..
5	5	8	9	Q	6	..	10	..	..
5	5	8	9	K	6	..	10	..	..
5	5	8	10	10	12	..	..	..	..
5	5	8	10	J	10	11	14	..	..
5	5	8	10	Q	10	..	14	..	..
5	5	8	10	K	10	..	14	..	..
5	5	8	J	J	12	13	..	..	..
5	5	8	J	Q	10	11	14	..	..
5	5	8	J	K	10	11	14	..	..
5	5	8	Q	Q	12	..	..	..	..
5	5	8	Q	K	10	..	14	..	..
5	5	8	K	K	12	..	..	..	..
5	5	9	9	9	8	..	..	..	..
5	5	9	9	10	8	..	..	..	..
5	5	9	9	J	8	..	9	..	..
5	5	9	9	Q	8	..	..	..	..
5	5	9	9	K	8	..	..	..	..

CARDS.					Fifteens, Pairs & Seq..	With Jack of Turn-up......	If Flush in Hand......	If Flush with Turn-up	If Fl & Jack of Turn-up
5	5	9	10	10	12	..	..	..	..
5	5	9	10	J	13	14	17	..	..
5	5	9	10	Q	10	..	14	..	..
5	5	9	10	K	10	..	14	..	..
5	5	9	J	J	12	13	..	..	..
5	5	9	J	Q	10	11	14	..	..
5	5	9	J	K	10	11	14	..	..
5	5	9	Q	Q	12	..	..	..	..
5	5	9	Q	K	10	..	14	..	..
5	5	9	K	K	12	..	..	..	..
5	5	10	10	10	20	..	..	..	..
5	5	10	10	J	16	17	..	..	..
5	5	10	10	Q	16	..	..	..	..
5	5	10	10	K	16	..	..	..	..
5	5	10	J	J	16	17	..	..	..
5	5	10	J	Q	17	18	21	..	..
5	5	10	J	K	14	15	18	..	..
5	5	10	Q	Q	16	..	..	..	..
5	5	10	Q	K	14	..	18	..	..
5	5	10	K	K	16	..	..	..	..
5	5	J	J	J	20	21	..	..	..
5	5	J	J	Q	16	17	..	..	..
5	5	J	J	K	16	17	..	..	..
5	5	J	Q	Q	16	17	..	..	..
5	5	J	Q	K	17	18	21	..	..
5	5	J	K	K	16	17	..	..	..
5	5	Q	Q	Q	20	..	..	..	..
5	5	Q	Q	K	16	..	..	..	..
5	5	Q	K	K	16	..	..	..	..
5	5	K	K	K	20	..	..	..	..
5	6	6	6	6	12	..	..	..	..
5	6	6	6	7	15	..	..	..	..
5	6	6	6	8	6	..	..	..	..
5	6	6	6	9	12	..	..	..	..
5	6	6	6	10	8	9	..	..	..
5	6	6	6	J	8	..	..	..	..
5	6	6	6	Q	8	..	..	..	..
5	6	6	6	K	8	..	..	..	..
5	6	6	7	7	16	..	..	..	..

KEY TO CRIBBAGE.

CARDS.					Fifteens, Pairs & Seq..	With Jack of Turn-up..	If Flush in Hand..	If Flush with Turn-up.	If Fl& Jack of Turn-up	CARDS.					Fifteens, Pairs & Seq..	With Jack of Turn-up..	If Flush in Hand..	If Flush with Turn-up.	If Fl& Jack of Turn-up
5	6	6	7	8	12	..	16	..	..	5	6	7	8	K	8	..	12	13	..
5	6	6	7	9	12	..	16	..	..	5	6	7	9	9	9	..	13	..	..
5	6	6	7	10	10	..	14	..	..	5	6	7	9	10	7	..	11	12	..
5	6	6	7	J	10	11	14	..	..	5	6	7	9	J	7	8	11	12	13
5	6	6	7	Q	10	..	14	..	..	5	6	7	9	Q	7	..	11	12	..
5	6	6	7	K	10	..	14	..	..	5	6	7	9	K	7	..	11	12	..
5	6	6	8	8	4	..	..	..	..	5	6	7	10	10	9	..	13	..	..
5	6	6	8	9	6	..	10	..	..	5	6	7	10	J	7	8	11	12	13
5	6	6	8	10	4	..	8	..	..	5	6	7	10	Q	7	..	11	12	..
5	6	6	8	J	4	5	8	..	..	5	6	7	10	K	7	..	11	12	..
5	6	6	8	Q	4	..	8	..	..	5	6	7	J	J	9	10	13	..	..
5	6	6	8	K	4	..	8	..	..	5	6	7	J	Q	7	8	11	12	13
5	6	6	9	9	12	..	..	..	..	5	6	7	J	K	7	8	11	12	13
5	6	6	9	10	8	..	12	..	..	5	6	7	Q	Q	9	..	13	..	..
5	6	6	9	J	8	9	12	..	..	5	6	7	Q	K	7	..	11	12	..
5	6	6	9	Q	8	..	12	..	..	5	6	7	K	K	9	..	13	..	..
5	6	6	10	10	8	..	..	..	..	5	6	8	8	8	6	..	..	..	..
5	6	6	10	J	6	7	10	..	..	5	6	8	8	9	4	..	8	..	..
5	6	6	10	Q	6	..	10	..	..	5	6	8	8	10	4	..	8	..	..
5	6	6	10	K	6	..	10	..	..	5	6	8	8	J	4	5	8	..	..
5	6	6	J	J	8	9	..	..	..	5	6	8	8	Q	4	..	8	..	..
5	6	6	J	Q	6	7	10	..	..	5	6	8	8	K	4	..	8	..	..
5	6	6	J	K	6	7	10	..	..	5	6	8	9	9	6	..	10	..	..
5	6	6	Q	Q	8	..	..	..	..	5	6	8	9	10	7	..	11	12	..
5	6	6	Q	K	6	..	10	..	..	5	6	8	9	J	4	5	8	9	10
5	6	6	K	K	8	..	..	..	..	5	6	8	9	Q	4	..	8	9	..
5	6	7	7	7	15	..	..	..	..	5	6	8	9	K	4	..	8	9	..
5	6	7	7	8	14	..	18	..	..	5	6	8	10	10	6	..	10	..	..
5	6	7	7	9	10	..	14	..	..	5	6	8	10	J	4	5	8	9	10
5	6	7	7	10	10	..	14	..	..	5	6	8	10	Q	4	..	8	9	..
5	6	7	7	J	10	11	14	..	..	5	6	8	10	K	4	..	8	9	..
5	6	7	7	Q	10	..	14	..	..	5	6	8	J	J	6	7	10	..	..
5	6	7	7	K	10	..	14	..	..	5	6	8	J	Q	4	5	8	9	10
5	6	7	8	8	14	..	18	..	..	5	6	8	J	K	4	5	8	9	10
5	6	7	8	9	9	..	13	14	..	5	6	8	Q	Q	6	..	10	..	..
5	6	7	8	10	8	..	12	13	..	5	6	8	Q	K	4	..	8	..	9
5	6	7	8	J	8	9	12	13	14	5	6	8	K	K	6	..	10	..	..
5	6	7	8	Q	8	..	12	13	..	5	6	9	9	9	12	..	..	..	..
										5	6	9	9	10	8	..	12	..	..

KEY TO CRIBBAGE.

Cards					Fifteens, Pairs & Seq.	With Jack of Turn-up	If Flush in Hand	If Flush with Turn-up	If Fl& Jack of Turn-up
5	6	9	9	J	8	9	12	..	..
5	6	9	9	Q	8	..	12	..	..
5	6	9	9	K	8	..	12	..	..
5	6	9	10	10	8	..	12	..	..
5	6	9	10	J	9	10	13	14	15
5	6	9	10	Q	6	..	10	11	..
5	6	9	10	K	6	..	10	11	..
5	6	9	J	J	8	9	12	..	..
5	6	9	J	Q	6	7	10	11	12
5	6	9	J	K	6	7	10	11	12
5	6	9	Q	Q	8	..	12	..	..
5	6	9	Q	K	6	..	10	11	..
5	6	9	K	K	8	..	12	..	..
5	6	10	10	10	12	..	..	..	..
5	6	10	10	J	8	9	12	..	..
5	6	10	10	Q	8	..	12	..	..
5	6	10	10	K	8	..	12	..	..
5	6	10	J	J	8	9	12	..	..
5	6	10	J	Q	9	10	13	14	15
5	6	10	J	K	6	7	10	11	12
5	6	10	Q	Q	8	..	12	..	..
5	6	10	Q	K	6	..	10	11	..
5	6	10	K	K	8	..	12	..	..
5	6	J	J	J	12	13	..	..	..
5	6	J	J	Q	8	9	12	..	..
5	6	J	J	K	8	9	12	..	..
5	6	J	Q	Q	8	9	12	..	..
5	6	J	Q	K	9	10	13	14	15
5	6	J	K	K	8	9	12	..	..
5	6	Q	Q	Q	12	..	..	..	..
5	6	Q	Q	K	8	..	12	..	..
5	6	Q	K	K	8	..	12	..	..
5	6	K	K	K	12	..	..	..	..
5	7	7	7	7	12	..	..	..	..
5	7	7	7	8	12	..	..	..	..
5	7	7	7	9	6	..	..	..	..
5	7	7	7	10	8	..	..	..	..
5	7	7	7	J	8	9	..	..	..
5	7	7	7	Q	8	..	..	..	..
5	7	7	7	K	8	..	..	..	..
5	7	7	8	8	12	..	..	..	..
5	7	7	8	9	12	..	16	..	..
5	7	7	8	10	8	..	12	..	..
5	7	7	8	J	8	9	12	..	..
5	7	7	8	Q	8	..	12	..	..
5	7	7	8	K	8	..	12	..	..
5	7	7	9	9	4	..	..	..	..
5	7	7	9	10	4	..	8	..	..
5	7	7	9	J	4	5	8	..	..
5	7	7	9	Q	4	..	8	..	..
5	7	7	9	K	4	..	8	..	..
5	7	7	10	10	8	..	..	..	..
5	7	7	10	J	6	7	10	..	..
5	7	7	10	Q	6	..	10	..	..
5	7	7	10	K	6	..	10	..	..
5	7	7	J	J	8	9	..	..	..
5	7	7	J	Q	6	7	10	..	..
5	7	7	J	K	6	7	10	..	..
5	7	7	Q	Q	8	..	..	..	..
5	7	7	Q	K	6	..	10	..	..
5	7	7	K	K	8	..	..	..	..
5	7	8	8	8	12	..	..	..	..
5	7	8	8	9	12	..	16	..	..
5	7	8	8	10	8	..	12	..	..
5	7	8	8	J	8	9	12	..	..
5	7	8	8	Q	8	..	12	..	..
5	7	8	8	K	8	..	12	..	..
5	7	8	9	9	10	..	14	..	..
5	7	8	9	10	8	..	12	13	..
5	7	8	9	J	7	8	11	12	13
5	7	8	9	Q	7	..	11	12	..
5	7	8	9	K	7	..	11	12	..
5	7	8	10	10	8	..	12	..	..
5	7	8	10	J	6	7	10	11	12
5	7	8	10	Q	6	..	10	11	..
5	7	8	10	K	6	..	10	11	..
5	7	8	J	J	8	9	12	..	..
5	7	8	J	Q	6	7	10	11	12

KEY TO CRIBBAGE.

CARDS					Fifteens, Pairs & Seq.	With Jack of Turn up	If Flush in Hand	If Flush with Turn-up	If Fl& Jack of Turn-up
5	7	8	J	K	6	7	10	11	12
5	7	8	Q	Q	8		12		
5	7	8	Q	K	6		10	11	
5	7	8	K	K	4		12		
5	7	9	9	9	6				
5	7	9	9	10	4		8		
5	7	9	9	J	4	5	8		
5	7	9	9	Q	4		8		
5	7	9	9	K	4		8		
5	7	9	10	10	6		10		
5	7	9	10	J	7	8	11	12	13
5	7	9	10	Q	4		8	9	
5	7	9	10	K	4		8	9	
5	7	9	J	J	6	7	10		
5	7	9	J	Q	4	5	8	9	10
5	7	9	J	K	4	5	8	9	10
5	7	9	Q	Q	6		10		
5	7	9	Q	K	4		8	9	
5	7	9	K	K	6		10		
5	7	10	10	10	12				
5	7	10	10	J	8	9	12		
5	7	10	10	Q	8		12		
5	7	10	10	K	8		12		
5	7	10	J	J	8	9	12		
5	7	10	J	Q	9	10	13	14	15
5	7	10	J	K	6	7	10	11	12
5	7	10	Q	Q	8		12		
5	7	10	Q	K	6		10	11	
5	7	10	K	K	8		12		
5	7	J	J	J	12	13			
5	7	J	J	Q	8	9	12		
5	7	J	J	K	8	9	12		
5	7	J	Q	Q	8	9	12		
5	7	J	Q	K	9	10	13	14	15
5	7	J	K	K	8	9	12		
5	7	Q	Q	Q	12				
5	7	Q	Q	K	8		12		
5	7	Q	K	K	8		12		
5	7	K	K	K	12				

CARDS					Fifteens, Pairs & seq.	With Jack of Turn-un	If Flush in Hand	If Flush with Turn-up	If Fl& Jack of Turn-up
5	8	8	8	8	12				
5	8	8	8	9	6				
5	8	8	8	10	8				
5	8	8	8	J	8	9			
5	8	8	8	Q	8				
5	8	8	8	K	8				
5	8	8	9	9	4				
5	8	8	9	10	10		14		
5	8	8	9	J	4	5	8		
5	8	8	9	Q	4		8		
5	8	8	9	K	4		8		
5	8	8	10	10	8				
5	8	8	10	J	6	7	10		
5	8	8	10	Q	6		10		
5	8	8	10	K	6		10		
5	8	8	J	J	8	9			
5	8	8	J	Q	6	7	10		
5	8	8	J	K	6	7	10		
5	8	8	Q	Q	8				
5	8	8	Q	K	6		10		
5	8	8	K	K	8				
5	8	9	9	9	6				
5	8	9	9	10	10		14		
5	8	9	9	J	4	5	8		
5	8	9	9	Q	4		8		
5	8	9	9	K	4		8		
5	8	9	10	10	12		16		
5	8	9	10	J	8	9	12	13	14
5	8	9	10	Q	7		11	12	
5	8	9	10	K	7		11	12	
5	8	9	J	J	6	7	10		
5	8	9	J	Q	4	5	8	9	10
5	8	9	J	K	4	5	8	9	10
5	8	9	Q	Q	6		10		
5	8	9	Q	K	4		8	9	
5	8	9	K	K	6		10		
5	8	10	10	10	12				
5	8	10	10	J	8	9	12		
5	8	10	10	Q	8		12		

KEY TO CRIBBAGE.

CARDS.				Fifteens, Pairs & Seq..	With Jack of Turn-up..	If Flush in Hand......	If Flush with Turn-up.	If Fl& Jack of Turn-up
5	8	10	10	K	8		12		
5	8	10	J	J	8	9	12		
5	8	10	J	Q	9	10	13	14	15
5	8	10	J	K	6	7	10	11	12
5	8	10	Q	Q	8		12		
5	8	10	Q	K	6		10	11	
5	8	10	K	K	8		12		
5	8	J	J	J	12	13			
5	8	J	J	Q	8	9	12		
5	8	J	J	K	8	9	12		
5	8	J	Q	Q	8	9	12		
5	8	J	Q	K	9	10	13	14	15
5	8	J	K	K	8	9	12		
5	8	Q	Q	Q	12				
5	8	Q	Q	K	8		12		
5	8	Q	K	K	8		12		
5	8	K	K	K	12				
5	9	9	9	9	12				
5	9	9	9	10	8				
5	9	9	9	J	8	9			
5	9	9	9	Q	8				
5	9	9	9	K	8				
5	9	9	10	10	8				
5	9	9	10	J	12	13	16		
5	9	9	10	Q	6		10		
5	9	9	10	K	6		10		
5	9	9	J	J	8	9			
5	9	9	J	Q	6	7	10		
5	9	9	J	K	6	7	10		
5	9	9	Q	Q	8				
5	9	9	Q	K	6		10		
5	9	9	K	K	8				
5	9	10	10	10	12				
5	9	10	10	J	14	15	18		
5	9	10	10	Q	8		12		
5	9	10	10	K	8		12		
5	9	10	J	J	14	15	18		
5	9	10	J	Q	10	11	14	15	16
5	9	10	J	K	9	10	13	14	15

CARDS.				Fifteens, Pairs & Seq..	With Jack of Turn-up..	If Flush in Hand......	If Flush with Turn-up.	If Fl&Jack of Turn-up
5	9	10	Q	Q	8		12		
5	9	10	Q	K	6		10	11	
5	9	10	K	K	8		12		
5	9	J	J	J	12	13			
5	9	J	J	Q	8	9	12		
5	9	J	J	K	8	9	12		
5	9	J	Q	Q	8	9	12		
5	9	J	Q	K	9	10	13	14	15
5	9	J	K	K	8	9	12		
5	9	Q	Q	Q	12				
5	9	Q	Q	K	8		12		
5	9	Q	K	K	8		12		
5	9	K	K	K	12				
5	10	10	10	10	20				
5	10	10	10	J	14	15			
5	10	10	10	Q	14				
5	10	10	10	K	14				
5	10	10	J	J	12	15			
5	10	10	J	Q	16	17	20		
5	10	10	J	K	10	11	14		
5	10	10	Q	Q	12				
5	10	10	Q	K	10		14		
5	10	10	K	K	12				
5	10	J	J	J	14	15			
5	10	J	J	Q	16	17	20		
5	10	J	J	K	10	11	14		
5	10	J	Q	Q	16	17	20		
5	10	J	Q	K	12	13	16	17	18
5	10	J	K	K	10	11	14		
5	10	Q	Q	Q	14				
5	10	Q	Q	K	10		14		
5	10	Q	K	K	10		14		
5	10	K	K	K	14				
5	J	J	J	J	20	21			
5	J	J	J	Q	14	15			
5	J	J	J	K	14	15			
5	J	J	Q	Q	12	13			
5	J	J	Q	K	16	17	20		
5	J	J	K	K	12	13			

KEY TO CRIBBAGE.

Cards					Fifteens, Pairs & Seq.	With Jack of Turn-up.	If Flush in Hand.	If Flush with Turn-up.	If Fl. & Jack of Turn-up.
5	J	Q	Q	Q	14	15			
5	J	Q	Q	K	16	17	20		
5	J	Q	K	K	16	17	20		
5	J	K	K	K	14	15			
5	Q	Q	Q	Q	20				
5	Q	Q	Q	K	14				
5	Q	Q	K	K	12				
5	Q	K	K	K	14				
5	K	K	K	K	20				
6	6	6	6	7	12				
6	6	6	6	8	12				
6	6	6	6	9	20				
6	6	6	6	10	12				
6	6	6	6	J	12	13			
6	6	6	6	Q	12				
6	6	6	6	K	12				
6	6	6	7	7	8				
6	6	6	7	8	17				
6	6	6	7	9	12				
6	6	6	7	10	6				
6	6	6	7	J	6	7			
6	6	6	7	Q	6				
6	6	6	7	K	6				
6	6	6	8	8	8				
6	6	6	8	9	12				
6	6	6	8	10	6				
6	6	6	8	J	6	7			
6	6	6	8	Q	6				
6	6	6	8	K	6				
6	6	6	9	9	20				
6	6	6	9	10	12				
6	6	6	9	J	12	13			
6	6	6	9	Q	12				
6	6	6	9	K	12				
6	6	6	10	10	8				
6	6	6	10	J	6	7			
6	6	6	10	Q	6				
6	6	6	10	K	6				
6	6	6	J	J	8	9			
6	6	6	J	Q	6	7			
6	6	6	J	K	6	7			
6	6	6	Q	Q	8				
6	6	6	Q	K	6				
6	6	6	K	K	8				
6	6	7	7	7	8				
6	6	7	7	8	20				
6	6	7	7	9	8				
6	6	7	7	10	4				
6	6	7	7	J	4	5			
6	6	7	7	Q	4				
6	6	7	7	K	4				
6	6	7	8	8	20				
6	6	7	8	9	16		20		
6	6	7	8	10	10		14		
6	6	7	8	J	10	11	14		
6	6	7	8	Q	10		14		
6	6	7	8	K	10		14		
6	6	7	9	9	12				
6	6	7	9	10	6		10		
6	6	7	9	J	6	7	10		
6	6	7	9	Q	6		10		
6	6	7	9	K	6		10		
6	6	7	10	10	4				
6	6	7	10	J	2	3	6		
6	6	7	10	Q	2		6		
6	6	7	10	K	2		6		
6	6	7	J	J	4	5			
6	6	7	J	Q	2	3	6		
6	6	7	J	K	2	3	6		
6	6	7	Q	Q	4				
6	6	7	Q	K	2		6		
6	6	7	K	K	4				
6	6	8	8	8	8				
6	6	8	8	9	8				
6	6	8	8	10	4				
6	6	8	8	J	4	5			
6	6	8	8	Q	4				
6	6	8	8	K	4				

KEY TO CRIBBAGE.

Cards					Fifteens, Pairs & Seq.	With Jack of Turn-up.	If Flush in Hand.	If Flush with Turn-up.	If Fl & Jack of Turn-up.
6	6	8	9	9	12				
6	6	8	9	10	9		13		
6	6	8	9	J	6	7	10		
6	6	8	9	Q	6		10		
6	6	8	9	K	6		10		
6	6	8	10	10	4				
6	6	8	10	J	2	3	6		
6	6	8	10	Q	2		6		
6	6	8	10	K	2		6		
6	6	8	J	J	4	5			
6	6	8	J	Q	2	3	6		
6	6	8	J	K	2	3	6		
6	6	8	Q	Q	4				
6	6	8	Q	K	2		6		
6	6	8	K	K	4				
6	6	9	9	9	20				
6	6	9	9	10	12				
6	6	9	9	J	12	13			
6	6	9	9	Q	12				
6	6	9	9	K	12				
6	6	9	10	10	8				
6	6	9	10	J	9	10	13		
6	6	9	10	Q	6		10		
6	6	9	10	K	6		10		
6	6	9	J	J	8	9			
6	6	9	J	Q	6	7	10		
6	6	9	J	K	6	7	10		
6	6	9	Q	Q	8				
6	6	9	Q	K	6		10		
6	6	9	K	K	8				
6	6	10	10	10	8				
6	6	10	10	J	4	5			
6	6	10	10	Q	4				
6	6	10	10	K	4				
6	6	10	J	J	4	5			
6	6	10	J	Q	5	6	9		
6	6	10	J	K	2	3	6		
6	6	10	Q	Q	4				
6	6	10	Q	K	2		6		
6	6	10	K	K	4				
6	6	J	J	J	8	9			
6	6	J	J	Q	4	5			
6	6	J	J	K	4	5			
6	6	J	Q	Q	4	5			
6	6	J	Q	K	5	6	9		
6	6	J	K	K	4	5			
6	6	Q	Q	Q	8				
6	6	Q	Q	K	4				
6	6	Q	K	K	4				
6	6	K	K	K	8				
6	7	7	7	7	12				
6	7	7	7	8	21				
6	7	7	7	9	8				
6	7	7	7	10	6				
6	7	7	7	J	6	7			
6	7	7	7	Q	6				
6	7	7	7	K	6				
6	7	7	8	8	24				
6	7	7	8	9	16		20		
6	7	7	8	10	12		16		
6	7	7	8	J	12	13	16		
6	7	7	8	Q	12		16		
6	7	7	8	K	12		16		
6	7	7	9	9	8				
6	7	7	9	10	4		8		
6	7	7	9	J	4	5	8		
6	7	7	9	Q	4		8		
6	7	7	9	K	4		8		
6	7	7	10	10	4				
6	7	7	10	J	2	3	6		
6	7	7	10	Q	2		6		
6	7	7	10	K	2		6		
6	7	7	J	J	4	5			
6	7	7	J	Q	2	3	6		
6	7	7	J	K	2	3	6		
6	7	7	Q	Q	4				
6	7	7	Q	K	2		6		
6	7	7	K	K	4				

KEY TO CRIBBAGE.

Cards	Fifteens, Pairs & Seq.	With Jack of Turn-up	If Flush in Hand	If Flush with Turn-up	If Fl. & Jack of Turn-up
6 7 8 8 8	21		20		
6 7 8 8 9	16		20		
6 7 8 8 10	12		16		
6 7 8 8 J	12	13	16		
6 7 8 8 Q	12		16		
6 7 8 8 K	12		16		
6 7 8 9 9	16		20		
6 7 8 9 10	9		13	14	
6 7 8 9 J	8	9	12	13	14
6 7 8 9 Q	8		12	13	
6 7 8 9 K	8		12	13	
6 7 8 10 10	7		11		
6 7 8 10 J	5	6	9	10	11
6 7 8 10 Q	5		9	10	
6 7 8 10 K	5		9	10	
6 7 8 J J	7	8	11		
6 7 8 J Q	5	6	9	10	11
6 7 8 J K	5	6	9	10	11
6 7 8 Q Q	7		11		
6 7 8 Q K	5		9	10	
6 7 8 K K	7		11		
6 7 9 9 9	12				
6 7 9 9 10	6		10		
6 7 9 9 J	6	7	10		
6 7 9 9 Q	6		10		
6 7 9 9 K	6		10		
6 7 9 10 10	4		8		
6 7 9 10 J	5	6	9	10	11
6 7 9 10 Q	2		6	7	
6 7 9 10 K	2		6	7	
6 7 9 J J	4	5	8		
6 7 9 J Q	2	3	6	7	8
6 7 9 J K	2	3	6	7	8
6 7 9 Q Q	4		8		
6 7 9 Q K	2		6	7	
6 7 9 K K	4		8		
6 7 10 10 10	6				
6 7 10 10 J	2	3	6		
6 7 10 10 Q	2		6		
6 7 10 10 K	2		6		
6 7 10 J J	2	3	6		
6 7 10 J Q	3	4	7	8	9
6 7 10 J K	0	1	4	5	6
6 7 10 Q Q	2		6		
6 7 10 Q K	0		4	5	
6 7 10 K K	2		6		
6 7 J J J	6	7			
6 7 J J Q	2	3	6		
6 7 J J K	2	3	6		
6 7 J Q Q	2	3	6		
6 7 J Q K	3	4	7	8	9
6 7 J K K	2	3	6		
6 7 Q Q K	2		6		
6 7 Q K K	2		6		
6 7 K K K	6				
6 8 8 8 8	12				
6 8 8 8 9	8				
6 8 8 8 10	6				
6 8 8 8 J	6	7			
6 8 8 8 Q	6				
6 8 8 8 K	6				
6 8 8 9 9	8				
6 8 8 9 10	10		14		
6 8 8 9 J	4	5	8		
6 8 8 9 Q	4		8		
6 8 8 9 K	4		8		
6 8 8 10 10	4				
6 8 8 10 J	2	3	6		
6 8 8 10 Q	2		6		
6 8 8 10 K	2		6		
6 8 8 J J	4	5	6		
6 8 8 J Q	2	3	6		
6 8 8 J K	2	3	6		
6 8 8 Q Q	4		6		
6 8 8 Q K	2		6		
6 8 8 K K	4		6		
6 8 9 9 9	12				

KEY TO CRIBBAGE.

Cards					Fifteens, Pairs & Seq.	With Jack of Turn-up	If Flush in Hand	If Flush with Turn-up	If Fl & Jack of Turn-up
6	8	9	9	10	12		16		
6	8	9	9	J	6	7	10		
6	8	9	9	Q	6		10		
6	8	9	9	K	6		10		
6	8	9	10	10	10		14		
6	8	9	10	J	6	7	10	11	12
6	8	9	10	Q	5		9	10	
6	8	9	10	K	5		9	10	
6	8	9	J	J	4	5	8		
6	8	9	J	Q	2	3	6	7	8
6	8	9	J	K	2	3	6	7	8
6	8	9	Q	Q	4		8		
6	8	9	Q	K	2		6	7	
6	8	9	K	K	4		8		
6	8	10	10	10	6				
6	8	10	10	J	2	3	6		
6	8	10	10	Q	2		6		
6	8	10	10	K	2		6		
6	8	10	J	J	2	3	6		
6	8	10	J	Q	3	4	7	8	9
6	8	10	J	K	0	1	4	5	6
6	8	10	Q	Q	2		6		
6	8	10	Q	K	0		4	5	
6	8	10	K	K	2		6		
6	8	J	J	J	6	7			
6	8	J	J	Q	2	3	6		
6	8	J	J	K	2	3	6		
6	8	J	Q	Q	2	3	6		
6	8	J	Q	K	3	4	7	8	9
6	8	J	K	K	2	3	6		
6	8	Q	Q	Q	6				
6	8	Q	Q	K	2		6		
6	8	Q	K	K	2		6		
6	8	K	K	K	6				
6	9	9	9	9	20				
6	9	9	9	10	12				
6	9	9	9	J	12	13			
6	9	9	9	Q	12				
6	9	9	9	K	12				

Cards					Fifteens, Pairs & Seq.	With Jack of Turn-up	If Flush in Hand	If Flush with Turn-up	If Fl & Jack of Turn-up
6	9	9	10	10	8				
6	9	9	10	J	12	13	16		
6	9	9	10	Q	6		10		
6	9	9	10	K	6		10		
6	9	9	J	J	8	9			
6	9	9	J	Q	6	7	10		
6	9	9	J	K	6	7	10		
6	9	9	Q	Q	8				
6	9	9	Q	K	6		10		
6	9	9	K	K	8				
6	9	10	10	10	8				
6	9	10	10	J	10	11	14		
6	9	10	10	Q	4		8		
6	9	10	10	K	4		8		
6	9	10	J	J	10	11	14		
6	9	10	J	Q	6	7	10	11	12
6	9	10	J	K	5	6	9	10	11
6	9	10	Q	Q	4		8		
6	9	10	Q	K	2		6	7	
6	9	10	K	K	4		8		
6	9	J	J	J	8	9			
6	9	J	J	Q	4	5	8		
6	9	J	J	K	4	5	8		
6	9	J	Q	Q	4	5	8		
6	9	J	Q	K	5	6	9	10	11
6	9	J	K	K	4	5	8		
6	9	Q	Q	Q	8				
6	9	Q	Q	K	4		8		
6	9	Q	K	K	4		8		
6	9	K	K	K	8				
6	10	10	10	10	12				
6	10	10	10	J	6	7			
6	10	10	10	Q	6				
6	10	10	10	K	6				
6	10	10	J	J	4	5			
6	10	10	J	Q	8	9	12		
6	10	10	J	K	2	3	6		
6	10	10	Q	Q	4		8		
6	10	10	Q	K	2		6		

KEY TO CRIBBAGE.

Cards					Fifteens, Pairs & seq.	With Jack of Turn-up	If Flush in Hand	If Flush with Turn-up	If Fl & Jack of Turn-up
6	10	10	K	K	4				
6	10	J	J	J	6	7			
6	10	J	J	Q	8	9	12		
6	10	J	J	K	2	3	6		
6	10	J	Q	Q	8	9	12		
6	10	J	Q	K	4	5	8	9	10
6	10	J	K	K	2	3	6		
6	10	Q	Q	Q	6				
6	10	Q	Q	K	2		6		
6	10	Q	K	K	2		6		
6	10	K	K	K	6				
6	J	J	J	J	12	13			
6	J	J	J	Q	6	7			
6	J	J	J	K	6				
6	J	J	Q	Q	4	5			
6	J	J	Q	K	8	9	12		
6	J	J	K	K	4	5			
6	J	Q	Q	Q	6	7			
6	J	Q	Q	K	8	9	12		
6	J	Q	K	K	8	9	12		
6	J	K	K	K	6	7			
6	Q	Q	Q	Q	12				
6	Q	Q	Q	K	6				
6	Q	Q	K	K	4				
6	Q	K	K	K	6				
6	K	K	K	K	12				
7	7	7	7	8	20				
7	7	7	7	9	12				
7	7	7	7	10	12				
7	7	7	7	J	12	13			
7	7	7	7	Q	12				
7	7	7	7	K	12				
7	7	7	8	8	20				
7	7	7	8	9	21				
7	7	7	8	10	12				
7	7	7	8	J	12	13			
7	7	7	8	Q	12				
7	7	7	8	K	12				
7	7	7	9	9	8				
7	7	7	9	10	6				
7	7	7	9	J	6	7			
7	7	7	9	Q	6				
7	7	7	9	K	6				
7	7	7	10	10	8				
7	7	7	10	J	6	7			
7	7	7	10	Q	6				
7	7	7	10	K	6				
7	7	7	J	J	8	9			
7	7	7	J	Q	6	7			
7	7	7	J	K	6	7			
7	7	7	Q	Q	8				
7	7	7	Q	K	6				
7	7	7	K	K	8				
7	7	8	8	8	20				
7	7	8	8	9	24				
7	7	8	8	10	12				
7	7	8	8	J	12	13			
7	7	8	8	Q	12				
7	7	8	8	K	12				
7	7	8	9	9	20				
7	7	8	9	10	14		18		
7	7	8	9	J	12	13	16		
7	7	8	9	Q	12		16		
7	7	8	9	K	12		16		
7	7	8	10	10	8				
7	7	8	10	J	6	7	10		
7	7	8	10	Q	6		10		
7	7	8	10	K	6		10		
7	7	8	J	J	8	9			
7	7	8	J	Q	6	7	10		
7	7	8	J	K	6	7	10		
7	7	8	Q	Q	8				
7	7	8	Q	K	6		10		
7	7	8	K	K	8				
7	7	9	9	9	8				
7	7	9	9	10	4				
7	7	9	9	J	4	5			
7	7	9	9	Q	4				

KEY TO CRIBBAGE.

CARDS.					Fifteens, Pairs & Seq.	With Jack of Turn-up.	If Flush in Hand.	If Flush with Turn-up.	If Fl& Jack of Turn-up
7	7	9	9	K	4	..	..	..	..
7	7	9	10	10	4	..	..	..	..
7	7	9	10	J	5	6	9	..	..
7	7	9	10	Q	2	..	6	..	..
7	7	9	10	K	2	..	6	..	..
7	7	9	J	J	4	5	..	..	..
7	7	9	J	Q	2	3	6	..	..
7	7	9	J	K	2	3	6	..	..
7	7	9	Q	Q	4	..	..	..	..
7	7	9	Q	K	2	..	6	..	..
7	7	9	K	K	4	..	..	..	..
7	7	10	10	10	8	..	..	..	..
7	7	10	10	J	4	5	..	..	..
7	7	10	10	Q	4	..	..	..	..
7	7	10	10	K	4	..	..	..	..
7	7	10	J	J	4	5	..	..	..
7	7	10	J	Q	5	6	9	..	..
7	7	10	J	K	2	3	6	..	..
7	7	10	Q	Q	4	..	..	..	..
7	7	10	Q	K	2	..	6	..	..
7	7	10	K	K	4	..	..	..	..
7	7	J	J	J	8	9	..	..	..
7	7	J	J	Q	4	5	..	..	..
7	7	J	J	K	4	5	..	..	..
7	7	J	Q	Q	4	5	..	..	..
7	7	J	Q	K	5	6	9	..	..
7	7	J	K	K	4	5	..	..	..
7	7	Q	Q	Q	8	..	..	..	..
7	7	Q	Q	K	4	..	..	..	..
7	7	Q	K	K	4	..	..	..	..
7	7	K	K	K	8	..	..	..	..
7	8	8	8	8	20	..	..	..	..
7	8	8	8	9	21	..	..	..	..
7	8	8	8	10	12	..	..	..	..
7	8	8	8	J	12	13	..	..	..
7	8	8	8	Q	12	..	..	..	..
7	8	8	8	K	12	..	..	..	..
7	8	8	9	9	20	..	..	..	..
7	8	8	9	10	14	..	18	..	..

CARDS.					Fifteens, Pairs & Seq.	With Jack of Turn-up.	It Flush in Hand.	If Tlush with Turn-up.	If Fl& Jack of Turn-up
7	8	8	9	J	12	13	16	..	..
7	8	8	9	Q	12	..	16	..	..
7	8	8	9	K	12	..	16	..	..
7	8	8	10	10	8	..	..	..	..
7	8	8	10	J	6	7	10	..	..
7	8	8	10	Q	6	..	10	..	..
7	8	8	10	K	6	..	10	..	..
7	8	8	J	J	8	9	..	..	..
7	8	8	J	Q	6	7	10	..	..
7	8	8	J	K	6	7	10	..	..
7	8	8	Q	Q	8	..	..	..	..
7	8	8	Q	K	6	..	10	..	..
7	8	8	K	K	8	..	..	..	..
7	8	9	9	9	17	..	..	..	..
7	8	9	9	10	12	..	16	..	..
7	8	9	9	J	10	11	14	..	..
7	8	9	9	Q	10	..	14	..	..
7	8	9	9	K	10	..	14	..	..
7	8	9	10	10	12	..	16	..	..
7	8	9	10	J	7	8	11	12	13
7	8	9	10	Q	6	..	10	11	..
7	8	9	10	K	6	..	10	11	..
7	8	9	J	J	7	8	11	..	..
7	8	9	J	Q	5	6	9	10	11
7	8	9	J	K	5	6	9	10	11
7	8	9	Q	Q	7	..	11	..	..
7	8	9	Q	K	5	..	9	10	..
7	8	9	K	K	7	..	11	..	..
7	8	10	10	10	8	..	..	..	..
7	8	10	10	J	4	5	8	..	..
7	8	10	10	Q	4	..	8	..	..
7	8	10	10	K	4	..	8	..	..
7	8	10	J	J	4	5	8	..	..
7	8	10	J	Q	5	6	9	10	11
7	8	10	J	K	2	3	6	7	8
7	8	10	Q	Q	4	..	8	..	..
7	8	10	Q	K	2	..	6	7	..
7	8	10	K	K	4	..	8	..	..
7	8	J	J	J	8	9	..	..	..

KEY TO CRIBBAGE.

Cards					Fifteens, Pairs & Seq.	With Jack of Turn-up	If Flush in Hand	If Flush with Turn-up	If Fl. & Jack of Turn-up
7	8	J	J	Q	4	5	8	..	..
7	8	J	J	K	4	5	8	..	..
7	8	J	Q	Q	4	5	8	..	..
7	8	J	Q	K	5	6	9	10	11
7	8	J	K	K	4	5	8	..	..
7	8	Q	Q	Q	8	..	..	8	..
7	8	Q	Q	K	4	..	8	..	..
7	8	Q	K	K	4	..	8	..	..
7	8	K	K	K	8	..	..	8	..
7	9	9	9	9	12	..	..	..	..
7	9	9	9	10	6	..	..	..	..
7	9	9	9	J	6	7	..	..	..
7	9	9	9	Q	6	..	..	..	..
7	9	9	9	K	6	..	..	..	..
7	9	9	10	10	4	..	..	..	..
7	9	9	10	J	8	9	12	..	..
7	9	9	10	Q	2	..	6	..	..
7	9	9	10	K	2	..	6	..	..
7	9	9	J	J	4	5	..	..	..
7	9	9	J	Q	2	3	6	..	..
7	9	9	J	K	2	3	6	..	..
7	9	9	Q	Q	4	..	..	..	..
7	9	9	Q	K	2	..	6	..	..
7	9	9	K	K	4	..	..	..	..
7	9	10	10	10	6	..	..	..	..
7	9	10	10	J	8	9	12	..	..
7	9	10	10	Q	2	..	6	..	..
7	9	10	10	K	2	..	6	..	..
7	9	10	J	J	8	9	12	..	..
7	9	10	J	Q	4	5	8	9	10
7	9	10	J	K	3	4	7	8	9
7	9	10	Q	Q	2	..	6	..	..
7	9	10	Q	K	0	..	4	5	..
7	9	10	K	K	2	..	6	..	..
7	9	J	J	J	6	7	..	..	..
7	9	J	J	Q	6	7	..	..	..
7	9	J	J	K	2	3	6	..	..
7	9	J	Q	Q	2	3	6	..	..
7	9	J	Q	K	3	4	7	8	9
7	9	J	K	K	2	3	6	..	..
7	9	Q	Q	Q	6	..	..	6	..
7	9	Q	Q	K	2	..	6	..	..
7	9	Q	K	K	2	..	6	..	..
7	9	K	K	K	6	..	..	..	..
7	10	10	10	10	12	..	..	..	..
7	10	10	10	J	6	7	..	..	..
7	10	10	10	Q	6	..	..	..	..
7	10	10	10	K	6	..	..	..	..
7	10	10	J	J	4	5	..	..	..
7	10	10	J	Q	8	9	12	..	..
7	10	10	J	K	2	3	6	..	..
7	10	10	Q	Q	4	..	..	..	..
7	10	10	Q	K	2	..	6	..	..
7	10	10	K	K	4	..	..	..	..
7	10	J	J	J	6	7	..	..	..
7	10	J	J	Q	8	9	12	..	..
7	10	J	J	K	2	3	6	..	..
7	10	J	Q	Q	8	9	12	..	..
7	10	J	Q	K	4	5	8	9	10
7	10	J	K	K	2	3	6	..	..
7	10	Q	Q	Q	6	..	..	6	..
7	10	Q	Q	K	2	..	6	..	..
7	10	Q	K	K	2	..	6	..	..
7	10	K	K	K	6	..	..	..	..
7	J	J	J	J	12	13	..	..	..
7	J	J	J	Q	6	7	..	..	..
7	J	J	J	K	6	7	..	..	..
7	J	J	Q	Q	4	5	..	..	..
7	J	J	Q	K	8	9	12	..	..
7	J	J	K	K	4	5	..	..	..
7	J	Q	Q	Q	6	7	..	..	..
7	J	Q	Q	K	8	9	12	..	..
7	J	Q	K	K	8	9	12	..	..
7	J	K	K	K	6	7	..	..	..
7	Q	Q	Q	Q	12	..	..	..	..
7	Q	Q	Q	K	6	..	..	..	..
7	Q	Q	K	K	4	..	..	..	..
7	Q	K	K	K	6	..	..	..	..

KEY TO CRIBBAGE.

Cards	Fifteens, Pairs & Seq.	With Jack of Turn-up	If Flush in Hand	If Flush with Turn-up	If Fl& Jack of Turn up
7 K K K K	12				
8 8 8 8 9	12				
8 8 8 8 10	12				
8 8 8 8 J	12	13			
8 8 8 8 Q	12				
8 8 8 8 K	12				
8 8 8 9 9	8				
8 8 8 9 10	16				
8 8 8 9 J	6		7		
8 8 8 9 Q	6				
8 8 8 9 K	6				
8 8 8 10 10	8				
8 8 8 10 J	6		7		
8 8 8 10 Q	6				
8 8 8 10 K	6				
8 8 8 J J	8		9		
8 8 8 J Q	6	9	7		
8 8 8 J K	6		7		
8 8 8 Q Q	8				
8 8 8 Q K	6				
8 8 8 K K	8				
8 8 9 9 9	8				
8 8 9 9 10	16				
8 8 9 9 J	4	5			
8 8 9 9 Q	4				
8 8 9 9 K	4				
8 8 9 10 10	16				
8 8 9 10 J	10	11	14		
8 8 9 10 Q	8		12		
8 8 9 10 K	8		12		
8 8 9 J J	4	5			
8 8 9 J Q	2	3	6		
8 8 9 J K	2	3	6		
8 8 9 Q Q	4				
8 8 9 Q K	2		6		
8 8 9 K K	4				
8 8 10 10 10	8				
8 8 10 10 J	4	5			
8 8 10 10 Q	4				

Cards	Fifteens, Pairs & Seq.	With Jack of Turn-up	If Flush in Hand	If Flush with Turn-up	If Fl&Jack of Turn-up
8 8 10 10 K	4				
8 8 10 J J	4	5		9	
8 8 10 J Q	5	6	3	9	6
8 8 10 J K	2	3		6	
8 8 10 Q Q	4				
8 8 10 Q K	2			0	
8 8 10 K K	4				
8 8 J J J	8		9		
8 8 J J Q	4		5		
8 8 J J K	4		5		
8 8 J Q Q	4		5		
8 8 J Q K	5		6	9	
8 8 J K K	4		8		
8 8 Q Q Q	8				
8 8 Q Q K	4				
8 8 Q K K	4				
8 8 K K K	8				
8 9 9 9 9	12				
8 9 9 9 10	15				
8 9 9 9 J	6		7		
8 9 9 9 Q	6				
8 9 9 9 K	6				
8 9 9 10 10	10				
8 9 9 10 J	10	11	14		
8 9 9 10 Q	8		12		
8 9 9 10 K	8		12		
8 9 9 J J	4	5			
8 9 9 J Q	2	3	6		
8 9 9 J K	2	3	6		
8 9 9 Q Q	4				
8 9 9 Q K	2		6		
8 9 9 K K	4				
8 9 10 10 10	15				
8 9 10 10 J	10	11	14		
8 9 10 10 Q	8		12		
8 9 10 10 K	8		12		
8 9 10 J J	10	11	14		
8 9 10 J Q	5	6	9	10	11
8 9 10 J K	4	5	8	9	10

KEY TO CRIBBAGE.

Cards					Fifteens, Pairs & Seq..	With Jack of Turn-up.	If Flush in Hand......	If Flush with Turn-up.	If Fl & Jack of Turn-up
8	9	10	Q	Q	5		9		
8	9	10	Q	K	3		7	8	9
8	9	10	K	K	5		9		
8	9	J	J	J	6	7			
8	9	J	J	Q	2	3	6		
8	9	J	J	K	2	3	6		
8	9	J	Q	Q	2	3	6		
8	9	J	Q	K	3	4	7	8	9
8	9	J	K	K	2	3	6		
8	9	Q	Q	Q	6				
8	9	Q	Q	K	2		6		
8	9	Q	K	K	2		6		
8	9	K	K	K	6				
8	10	10	10	10	12				
8	10	10	10	J	6	7			
8	10	10	10	Q	6				
8	10	10	10	K	6				
8	10	10	J	J	4	5			
8	10	10	J	Q	8	9	12		
8	10	10	J	K	2	3	6		
8	10	10	Q	Q	4				
8	10	10	Q	K	2		6		
8	10	10	K	K	4				
8	10	J	J	J	6	7			
8	10	J	J	Q	8	9	12		
8	10	J	J	K	2	3	6		
8	10	J	Q	Q	8	9	12		
8	10	J	Q	K	4	5	8	9	10
8	10	J	K	K	2	3	6		
8	10	Q	Q	Q	6				
8	10	Q	Q	K	2		6		
8	10	Q	K	K	2		6		
8	10	K	K	K	6				
8	J	J	J	J	12	13			
8	J	J	J	Q	6	7			
8	J	J	J	K	6	7			
8	J	J	Q	Q	4	5			
8	J	J	Q	K	8	9	12		
8	J	J	K	K	4	5			

Cards					Fifteens, Pairs & Seq..	With Jack of Turn-up.	If Flush in Hand......	If Flush with Turn-up.	If Fl & Jack of Turn-up
8	J	Q	Q	Q	6	7			
8	J	Q	Q	K	8	9	12		
8	J	Q	K	K	8	9	12		
8	J	K	K	K	6	7			
8	Q	Q	Q	Q	12				
8	Q	Q	Q	K	6				
8	Q	Q	K	K	4				
8	Q	K	K	K	6				
8	K	K	K	K	12				
9	9	9	9	10	12				
9	9	9	9	J	12	13			
9	9	9	9	Q	12				
9	9	9	9	K	12				
9	9	9	10	10	8				
9	9	9	10	J	15	16			
9	9	9	10	Q	6				
9	9	9	10	K	6				
9	9	9	J	J	8	9			
9	9	9	J	Q	6	7			
9	9	9	J	K	6	7			
9	9	9	Q	Q	8				
9	9	9	Q	K	6				
9	9	9	K	K	8				
9	9	10	10	10	16	17			
9	9	10	10	J	4				
9	9	10	10	Q	4				
9	9	10	J	J	16	17			
9	9	10	J	Q	10	11	14		
9	9	10	J	K	8	9	12		
9	9	10	Q	Q	4				
9	9	10	Q	K	2		6		
9	9	10	K	K	4				
9	9	J	J	J	8	9			
9	9	J	J	Q	4	5			
9	9	J	J	K	4	5			
9	9	J	Q	Q	4	5			
9	9	J	Q	K	4	5	6		9
9	9	J	K	K	4	5			

KEY TO CRIBBAGE.

Cards					Fifteens, Pairs & Seq.	With Jack of Turn-up.	If Flush in Hand.	If Flush with Turn-up.	If Fl & Jack of Turn-up.
9	9	Q	Q	Q	8				
9	9	Q	Q	K	4				
9	9	Q	K	K	4				
9	9	K	K	K	8				
9	10	10	10	10	12				
9	10	10	10	J	15	16			
9	10	10	10	Q	6				
9	10	10	10	K	6				
9	10	10	J	J	16	17			
9	10	10	J	Q	10	11	14		
9	10	10	J	K	8	9	12		
9	10	10	Q	Q	4				
9	10	10	Q	K	2		6		
9	10	10	K	K	4				
9	10	J	J	J	15	16			
9	10	J	J	Q	10	11	14		
9	10	J	J	K	8	9	12		
9	10	J	Q	Q	10	11	14		
9	10	J	Q	K	5	6	9	10	11
9	10	J	K	K	5	6	9		
9	10	Q	Q	Q	6				
9	10	Q	Q	K	2		6		
9	10	Q	K	K	2		6		
9	10	K	K	K	6				
9	J	J	J	J	12	13			
9	J	J	J	Q	6	7			
9	J	J	J	K	6	7			
9	J	J	Q	Q	4	5			
9	J	J	Q	K	8	9	12		
9	J	J	K	K	4	5			
9	J	Q	Q	Q	6	7			
9	J	Q	Q	K	8	9	12		
9	J	Q	K	K	8	9	12		
9	J	K	K	K	6	7			
9	Q	Q	Q	Q	12				
9	Q	Q	Q	K	6				
9	Q	Q	K	K	4				
9	Q	K	K	K	6				
9	K	K	K	K	12				
10	10	10	10	J	12	13			
10	10	10	10	Q	12				
10	10	10	10	K	12				
10	10	10	J	J	8	9			
10	10	10	J	Q	15	16			
10	10	10	J	K	6	7			
10	10	10	Q	Q	8				
10	10	10	Q	K	6				
10	10	10	K	K	8				
10	10	J	J	J	8	9			
10	10	J	J	Q	16	17			
10	10	J	J	K	4	5			
10	10	J	Q	Q	16	17			
10	10	J	Q	K	10	11	14		
10	10	J	K	K	4	5			
10	10	Q	Q	Q	8				
10	10	Q	Q	K	4				
10	10	Q	K	K	4				
10	10	K	K	K	8				
10	J	J	J	J	12	13			
10	J	J	J	Q	15	16			
10	J	J	J	K	6	7			
10	J	J	Q	Q	16	17			
10	J	J	Q	K	10	11	14		
10	J	J	K	K	4	5			
10	J	Q	Q	Q	15	16			
10	J	Q	Q	K	10	11	14		
10	J	Q	K	K	10	11	14		
10	J	K	K	K	6	7			
10	Q	Q	Q	Q	12				
10	Q	Q	Q	K	6				
10	Q	Q	K	K	4				
10	Q	K	K	K	6				
10	K	K	K	K	12				
J	J	J	J	Q	12	13			
J	J	J	J	K	12	13			
J	J	J	Q	Q	8	9			
J	J	J	Q	K	15	16			
J	J	J	K	K	8				

KEY TO CRIBBAGE.

CARDS.	Fifteens, Pairs & Seq..	With Jack of Turn up.	If Flush in Hand......	If Flush with Turn-up.	If Fl& Jack of Turn-up		CARDS.	Fifteens, Pairs & Seq..	With Jack of Turn-up.	If Flush in Hand......	If Flush with Turn-up.	If Fl& Jack of Turn-up
J J Q Q Q	8	9	....	....	..		J Q K K K	15	16	....	....	..
J J Q Q K	16	17	....	....	..		J K K Q K	14	13	....	....	..
J J Q K K	16	17	....	....	..		Q Q Q Q K	12		....	....	..
J J K K K	8	9	....	....	..		Q Q Q K K	8		....	....	..
J Q Q Q Q	12	13	....	....	..		Q K K K K	12		....	....	..
J Q Q K K	15	16	....	....	..							
J Q Q K K	16	17	....	....	..							

Recapitulation

The following table shows the number of hands which count each score:

Score.	Fifteens, Pairs & Seq	With Jack of Turn-up	If Flush in hand	If Fl. with Turn-up.	If Fl. and J of Turn-up	TOTAL.
0	220	....	....	....	....	220
1	....	99	....	....	....	99
2	1199	....	....	....	....	1199
3	65	433	....	....	....	498
4	1295	54	220	....	....	1569
5	123	369	....	220	....	712
6	1250	49	1199	....	99	2597
7	146	310	65	242	....	763
8	841	38	815	65	74	1833
9	77	228	123	348	54	830
10	200	32	716	94	132	1174
11	8	66	146	90	29	339
12	499	1	436	128	30	1094
13	2	79	77	49	35	242
14	97	1	185	46	13	342
15	18	20	8	4	27	77
16	54	9	96	....	1	160
17	9	22	2	1	....	34
18	4	2	37	....	1	44
20	43	....	20	....	....	63
21	7	5	2	....	....	14
22	4	.	....	....	....	4
23	1	1	....	....	....	2
24	9	....	....	....	....	9
28	4	....	....	....	....	4
29	....	1	....	....	....	1
TOTAL	6175	1819	4147	1287	495	13923

It is impossible to score 19, 25, 26, and 27.

X

Rules

The mechanics of Cribbage as described in the foregoing pages are an integral part of the rules.

RULE 1. SHUFFLING

§1.a. Two decks, a red and a blue pack, should be available for play. The dealer has the privilege of selecting the deck he desires.

b. In the semifinals and finals of major tournaments, it is mandatory that two decks be available.

§2. Each player has the right to shuffle the cards.

§3. The dealer has the right to make the last shuffle.
(In order to mix the cards thoroughly, it is recommended that the Las Vegas shuffle or riffling be used.)

RULE 2. CUTTING THE PACK

§1. The pack must be cut once taking off at least four cards and leaving at least four cards in the bottom packet.

§2. Cutting for the deal:

a. The person cutting the lower Cribbage card makes the first deal of the game. The ace is the lowest card, as the cards rank from the king down to the ace.

b. In case of a tie, cut again.

c. The cut for deal holds good even though the deck contains an incorrect number of cards.

d. If a player exposes more than one card in cutting for the deal, his adversary may name his choice as the one cut.

e. If there is any other confusion in the cutting for deal, there must be a new cut.

RULE 3. DEALING—THE DISTRIBUTION AND IRREGULARITIES

§1. The loser of the previous game deals the first hand of the next game.

§2.   The cards must be distributed one at a time, clockwise fashion, beginning with the opponent, giving each player six cards.

§3.   In order to help eliminate irregularities, the nondealer has a responsibility when his opponent deals:

    a. He must observe the accuracy of the dealing process and call attention immediately to any irregularity.

    b. He should NOT reach for or touch his cards until the deal is completed.

§4.a. If dealer gives two cards together, he must correct the error provided that he moves only one card, thus keeping the cards in regular order. Otherwise, there must be a new deal.

    b. In the event a seventh card is inadvertently dealt to either or both contestants and this irregularity is noticed before the cards are picked up, the seventh card or cards should be placed on top of the pack and the game should proceed.

    (The purpose of this subsection is to save time redealing, thus making a simple correction of a situation that occurs frequently.)

§5.a. If the dealer exposes a card or cards in the distribution process, the cards must be redealt.

    b. If a card is found face up in the pack or if the pack is imperfect, the cards must be redealt.

    c. If either or both hands are dealt more than seven cards, redeal. (See §4.b.)

§6.a. If the dealer gives both himself and the opponent five cards and lays the pack on the table, upon discovery, the sixth cards must be dealt out.

    b. If the dealer gives himself or adversary (not both) fewer than the required number of cards, there must be a new deal.

§7.   Upon the completion of the deal and after picking up the cards, if either contestant discovers a wrong number of cards in the hand of his adversary, a new deal is in order. The penalty is 2 holes.

§8.a. Dealing out of turn: If a contestant deals out of turn and the error is discovered before the starter card is turned, the deal is void and the right person makes a new deal.

    b. After the starting card is turned up, the play continues, as it is too late to rectify the error.

§9.   A player shall not touch the pack after the deal is completed and before the time to cut the starter card. Penalty is 2 holes.

§10.   After the completion of a hand, the deal passes to the left.

RULE 4. THE CRIB

§1.a. The crib is the property of the dealer and it may not be examined or exposed until the play has terminated. Penalty for violation is 2 holes.

   b. The dealer turns the crib over.

§2.   If either player discards when he has too many cards, the adversary receives 2 penalty holes, and has a choice:

   a. Request a new deal.

   b. Accept the deal and then draw the surplus card or cards out of the offender's hand. He also has the privilege of looking at the drawn cards. The drawn card or cards must be returned to the pack.

§3.   If either player discards with too few cards in his hand, he must play out the hand with this handicap.

§4.   Pone is required to make the first discard to the crib and then the dealer follows with his layaway.

§5.   Cards placed in the crib may not be taken up again. The penalty is 2 holes.

§6.   If either player confuses his cards with those of the crib, the adversary is awarded 3 penalty holes and may call for a new deal.

§7.   When the crib is found to be short a card and both players have the right number of cards, pone is awarded 2 points and the deal is corrected by dealing from the pack to fill the deficiency.

RULE 5. THE STARTER CARD

§1.a.   Nondealer must cut the pack once and must take off at least four cards for the upper packet or he must leave four or more cards in the bottom packet.

   b. The dealer then turns the top card of the lower packet for the starter and places it on top of the pack, face up.

   c. The person cutting must not look at the bottom card of the packet which was cut for the starter card. The penalty is 2 points.

§2.   If the dealer exposes more than one card in turning the starter, pone may choose which exposed card will be the starter.

§3.a.   If a jack is turned up and the dealer plays his first card without scoring his heels, he forfeits the 2 holes which are allotted him for his heels.

   b. The dealer, if standing on 119 or 120 points, pegs out by turning a jack.

RULE 6. THE PLAY

§1.   Play officially begins with the turn of the starter card.

§2.   If a contestant plays with too many cards in his hand, the adversary marks 2 penalty holes and has the option of a fresh deal. If he elects to let the deal stand, he has the right of drawing surplus cards from the offender's hand, looking at them, and returning them to the pack. Also, he has the option of playing the hand from the start.

§3.   If a person plays with too few cards, there is no penalty.

§4.   Each contestant must name the running total as he plays a card.

§5.a.   If a card that will come in 31 or under is played, it cannot be taken up again.

   b.   There is no penalty for showing or playing a card that cannot be played legally because of going over the count of 31. The player in error must reclaim this card.

§6.   If two cards are played together, the card counted is deemed to be the card played, and the other card must be taken back into the player's hand.

§7.   If a person neglects to play when he has a card that will come in 31 or under, his opponent may require it to be played, or may score 2 penalty holes and the card becomes a dead card, and is eliminated from the pegging process.

   a.   There is no penalty for announcing an incorrect count, but the error must be corrected on demand.

   b.   If the wrong count is announced and the error is not noticed until the next card is played, the count stands as announced.

RULE 7. PEGGING

§1.   If a peg is placed short of the correct mark, the player may not correct this error after the next card is played or after the cut in the next deal. There is no penalty.

§2.   If a contestant pegs more than he is entitled to, upon discovery by the opponent, the peg must be moved back to the proper hole and the opponent scores the amount of the error. If the error is not noticed until after another card has been played or dealt, it stands as pegged.

RULE 8. SHOWING AND SCORING

§1.   When reckoning a hand or crib, the cards must be plainly visible, and must remain exposed until the opponent is satisfied about the nature of the claim.

§2.   If a player mixes his hand with the crib or with the pack before his claim is properly made, he forfeits any score the hand or crib may contain.

§3.   Each player should announce the value of his holding after counting it. The opponent is not required to compute a player's hand.

§4.   If a player touches his opponent's pegs except to correct an error, or if he touches his own pegs except when he has a score to mark, his opponent is awarded 2 penalty holes.

§5.a.   If a player inadvertently displaces his foremost peg, it must be placed back in the hole from which it was displaced. If there is uncertainty about the correct hole, the peg is inserted in a hole agreed upon by both players. If there is disagreement, the tournament judge must be called and his ruling is final.

b. If a person displaces both his pegs, his adversary is entitled to place the foremost peg where he believes it to have been, and the other peg must then be placed behind it.

RULE 9. MUGGINS (OPTIONAL)

§1.   This rule is NOT in effect unless both players previously agree to it or the officials make it a part of a tournament.

§2.   Muggins is the scoring of points that one's opponent fails to record:

a. The starter card (his heels): Before dealer plays his first card.

b. The play: Sequences, 15/2 combinations, pairs, triplets, quadruplets, and the go.

c. Showing and counting: The hand or crib and recording the full value.

§3.   Calling muggins:

a. A reasonable amount of time must elapse before muggins may be called.

b. Guides for determining a reasonable amount of time:

1. If a player has moved his peg and is still checking it, a reasonable amount of time has *not* elapsed.

2. If a dealer has counted his hand and recorded it incorrectly, reasonable time has elapsed when he turns the crib over.

3. In the play, reasonable time has elapsed when the next card is played in a normal manner.

§4.   Muggins does not apply to failure to record a penalty.

RULE 10. SITUATIONS NOT COVERED BY THE ABOVE RULES

§1.   In the event of a dispute not covered by the official rules, the tournament judge must be called for his decision, which is final.

§2.   Situations that come up in normal play or the decision of a tournament judge may be appealed to the National Cribbage Rules Committee for interpretation.

Summary of Penalties for Rule Violations (excluding Muggins)

The following are 2-point penalties:

1. Rule 3 §7: Wrong number of cards in the opponent's hand.

2. Rule 3 §9: Touching the pack after deal is completed and before cutting starter card.

3. Rule 4 §1: Examining the crib before play has terminated.

4. Rule 4 §2: Discarding to crib when holding too many cards.

5. Rule 4 §5: Taking up crib cards after discarding.

6. Rule 4 §7: Crib is short a card but players have correct number of cards.

7. Rule 5 §1.c: Looking at bottom card of packet when cutting.

8. Rule 6 §2: Playing with too many cards.

9. Rule 6 §7: Failing to play a card that comes in 31 or under.

10. Rule 8 §4: Illegally touching the pegs.

There is also one 3-point penalty:

11. Rule 4 §6: Confusing one's cards with those of crib.

And there is one penalty that varies:

12. Rule 7 §2: Pegging more points than one is entitled to.

XI

Bibliography and Some Cribbological Notes

1674	*The Complete Gamester*, by Charles Cotton
(?)	*Card Games Up-to-Date*, by Charles Roberts (London)
(?)	*Hoyle's Games*, by Charles Jones (London)
1882	*Cribbage*, by William H. Green (reprinted by Gamblers Book Club of Las Vegas, Nev., 1975)
1882, 1888 1910, 1974	*Encyclopaedia Britannica*
1886	*Hoyle's Games*, by Dick and Fitzgerald
1901	*Cribbage*, by Berkeley (London)
1903	*The Standard Hoyle* (Excelsior Publishing)
1910	*American Encyclopedia* (Frank K. Perkins)
(?)	*Popular Card Games* (London: Foulsham & Co.)
1925	*The Complete Gamester*, by Cavendish
1937	*Games for Two*, by Gloria Goddard and Clement Wood
1943	*Official Rules of Card Games* (U.S. Playing Card Co.)
1945	*The Complete Card Player*, by Albert Ostrow
1948	*Cribbage as I Think It Should Be Played*, by Allen J. Jarvis (Branden Press)
1956	*The New Complete Hoyle*, by Albert H. Morehead, Richard L. Frey, and Geoffrey Mott-Smith
1971	*All About Cribbage*, by Douglas Anderson
1974	*Cribbage Is the Name of the Game*, by Richard E. Lowder
1975	*The Skillful Play of Cribbage*, by Heines House
1977	*Games & Puzzles* magazine, "Jack in the Box" (May) and "Cribbological Postscripts" (July), articles by David Parlett
1977	*Encyclopedia of Games*, by John Scarne
1977	*The New Cribbage Games*, by Leo A. Blom

An educated Cribbage player seems to
be "luckier than most other players."

* * *

Be sure to read this book before your opponent does. Your honor and money will be saved!

*   *   *

Cribbage is an ideal soothing and relaxing activity for late evening, since it is very helpful in forgetting the trials and tribulations of the day. Try it!

*   *   *

They always say: "Closeness only counts in Horseshoes." Apparently gamesters have overlooked the fact that closeness counts in Cribbage, since getting close to a 31 count scores 1 hole for a go.
Let's say: "Closeness only counts in Horseshoes and Cribbage."

*   *   *

The appeal of Cribbage is evident from two facts:
1. There have been relatively few changes made in the original game.
2. It remains after more than three centuries as one of the most popular card games.

*   *   *

All evens do not a 15/2 make!

*   *   *

Postmortems are the curse of all card games.

*   *   *

Cribbage is a favorite game in all English-speaking countries.

*   *   *

Webster's says: "Card game for two, three, or four players in which the object is to form various combinations that count for points; the score is kept on a small pegboard."

*   *   *

Reference by Gayton to "Noddy boards" in 1654 implies that a board was used for scoring.

*   *   *

The jack or knave was originally called noddy; now it can be called his heels, his nobs, or his nibs.

*   *   *

An unusual procedure in this game is that the person to the dealer's left cuts the pack to determine the starter card.

*   *   *

Cotton's 1674 chapter on "Cribbidge" says that the five-card game played up to 61 points.

* * *

Cribbage is fun because:
1. It relieves tension.
2. It does not require "card sense."
3. It requires only a knowledge of simple arithmetic.
4. It affords the opportunity of applying simple logic.

* * *

Have you ever met "the goose," the person who is always stretching his neck to get a peek at your hand? Hold your cards close to your chest, since "one peek is worth two finesses."

* * *

"Luck is all," exclaims the novice, who guesses. The adept mutters, "Knowledge is power," and counts.

—A. D. Granger (1907)

* * *

The average number of holes to be made by the play on each deal is 4 to 5. The dealer has the advantage because he plays the last card, which guarantees him 1 hole.

* * *

Berkeley, describing six-card Cribbage in his 1901 monograph, referred to the skill and scientific arrangement of this English game.

* * *

In the United States, Cribbage is played by over 10 million people, principally across the northern states from New England to the shores of the Pacific. It is a favorite in Canada too.

* * *

Do not play a six on a four or vice versa, because opponent's five-spotter totals 15, scoring 5 holes.

* * *

The most important guide to playing is the score!

* * *

"At home" means having a normal position on the board in relation to the opponent and to the game hole.

When at home, it is best to play off; when the adversary is safe at home, it is best to play on.

* * *

David Parlett draws attention to the rhythmic jingles that are a part of Cribbage: "Anyone unfortunate enough to bring the count to twenty-one cannot but cringe in anticipation of his opponent's rhyming cry, when he slaps down a ten, 'and now you're done.'"

> 22—and nine will do
> 23—and eight's a spree
> 24—and seven's a score
> 25—and six alive
> 26—and five's a fix
> 27—and four's Tw'eleven
> 28—and three's just great
> 29—and two's just fine
> 31—and now you're done.

Parlett continues by asking: "What has become of the language that has given us his nobs, his nibs, his heels, muggins, pegging out, in the lurch, how's that for starters, what a turn-up, and any old irons?"

* * *

Another old Cribbage saying is "Here's a piece of cheese" (as a sly lead is made).

* * *

Do today's playing today!

* * *

When in doubt, lead a four-spotter.

* * *

The largest room in the world is the room for improvement.

—Maggie Dukes

* * *

Keep your temper. No one else wants it!

* * *

And, finally, keep this one thing in mind . . . when the day comes for you to appear before the GREAT SCOREKEEPER and all your records receive their final audit, it behooves you to have kept good and honest records for your fellowmen.

* * *

Index

Appeals, rule 10, sec. 2, 213
Attitudes, mental, 78
Averages: play selection, 71; study, 80, 81; life based on, 97; crib, hand, 98; test by marines, 100

Balking: effect of board position, 50; good throwaways, 52, 53; strategy in five-handed, 86; pone's discards, 87
Baiting, 48
Brackets, tournament 114, 117–120
Board: description, 5; playing the board, 45; bowling pin, folding, noddy, three-track, zigzag, 65–67
Boomerang, 59
Box 3, 6
Bull's eye, 61

Cards: rank, used, 6
Combinations, possible, 124
Committees: drawing 112; awards, publicity, 113
Common sense, 75
Consolation series, 116
Conversation, 77
Count of fifteen-two: definition, 3; scoring of, 13; symbol of $^{15}/_2$, 23; computations, symbols $^{15}/_4$, $^{15}/_6$, $^{15}/_8$, 24
Cradle, 7
Crib: description, 3; discarding to, 6; exposing, 21; balking, 46; baiting, 48; strategy, 45–49; favoring, 73; average score, 85; rules, 210–211
Cribbage board. See Board
Cut: by nondealer, 6; rules, 209; procedure, 218

Dealer: choosing, shuffling, 6; winning odds in six-handed, 81; winning odds in five-handed, 87
Dealing: distribution, irregularities, 209–210
Decks: standard, 3, 6; hot and cold, change, 74, 75; tournament rule 1, sec. 1, a, 209
Deuce, 3
Defensive strategy, 55–59
Discarding: two cards, 6; basics, 45–49; balking throwaway, 52; with the masters, 73; sharpies, 77; in five-card, 87; rule 4, sec. 2–5, 211
Distribution of cards, 6
Double pair royal, 14
Double run: definition, 7; doubling up, 26; triple, 27; not always best, 53

Eight ball, 58
Eleven cards: variant 101; partnership, 102
Elimination: brackets, 109; double, 113; eight and sixteen players, 114
Equalizer: delay decision, 58; auction for crib, 100
Expectancy table, 50–53

Favorable cards: expectancy table, 51; logic in discarding, 55
Five-card game: board design, 4; original game, 83–89
Fifteen–two ($^{15}/_2$). See Count of fifteen-two
First street, 45
Flush: definition, scoring, 22; examples, 30, 31; fear five-card, 46

Four-card straight, 15
Four-handed: partnership, 6; regulations, 94–99
Four of a kind, 22–25
Fourth street, stage of game, 45

Game: definition, hole, 4–5; plan, 73; original, 85
Geometry, 26
Go: definition, 4; scoring, 11–12; with sequence, 15–17; scoring order, 21; important in five-card, 85

High scoring hands, 31–36
His heels: definition, 4; scoring position, 21; starter card, 22–23; forfeit score, 211
His nibs, 218
His nobs: definition, 4; scoring, 22
Home, at, 219

Impossible scores, 32

Jack: starter card, 7; rule 5, sec. 3, a and b, 211
Jackpot, 63

Knave: definition, 4; starter 7

Las Vagas shuffle, 6
Last card, 12
Last hole, 71
Leads: offensive and defensive strategy, 56–64; with masters, 71; why open with a four-spotter, 73
League play: how to conduct, round robin series, 109; Forest Products Lab, 110
Logic, 51
Lurch, 55. See skunk.

Marine madness, 100
Matches, 13–17
Match-point system, 110, 111, 115, 116
Masters: cribbing with, 71–79

Mechanics, 7
Memory bank, 28, 29
Mental attitudes, 78
Muggins: description, optional, 82; rule 9, reasonable time, guides, 213

Nobs. See His nobs
Noddy: forerunner, 5; board, 65

Object, 5
Odds: understanding of, 49; expectancy table, 51
Old irons, 79
Ounce of prevention, 61

Pair: definition, 7; scoring 13; ends with go, 17; showing, 22; basis of scoring, 25; beware of, 56
Pair royal: definition, 7; double, 14
Partnership, tournament, 116
Patterns: artificial, freak, 74
Peg: definition, 4; go, 11; last card, 12; out, rule 5 sec. 3b, 211
Pegboard, 218
Pegging: announcing, 24; personal high, 40; set sights, 49; points, strategy, 60–64; series, 71; situations, 99; rule 7, 212
Penalties: dealing, crib, play, starter card, summary, 210–214
Percentages, 49, 51, 52
Perfect hand, 32, 66
Personal high, 40
Physical condition, 79
Picture cards, 62
Play: position, 73; unorthodox, 76; partnership, 94–99; rule 6, 211; cards together, improper number cards, wrong count, 212
Playing: non-dealer, 7; begin, 11; showing count, 21; off, 55, 56; equalizer, 58; dangerous leads, 59; on, 64; lead a four, 73; odds in five-card, 88, 89; reverse, 99
Point count, 6, 22
Point spread, 40, 110, 111, 116
Pone, non-dealer, cuts pack, 7
Position: board, 50, 51; play, 73
Positive thinking, 78

Predicting winner, 98
Psychology, 75, 77

Quadrupled, straight, 28
Quadruplet: scoring, 13, 25; pegging with, 17; unusual hand, 41; setting trap for, 76
Qualifying, 115, 116

Rank of cards, 6
Rating an opponent, 76, 116
Record hand, 39
Rectangle, 24
Regulations, special, 86
Rhythmic jingles, 220
Risky business, 63
Round robin series, 109
Rules: official, 209–213; national committee, 213
Runs (sequences and straights): definition, double, 7; scoring, 13, 14; juggled order, 14; ends with 31-count, 15; Seven-card, 16; examples, 26–28

Sacrifice, 54
Sequences. See Runs
Seven-card, 100
Score, watching, 86
Scores: procedure, 21; impossible, 32; rule 8, 212–213
Sharpies, 77
Showing: definition, 7; two-step procedure, 21; how to count, 21–28; rule 8, 212
Shuffling: procedure, Las Vagas, 6; rule 1, 209
Six-card game, 4, 5
Skunk (lurch): definition, 55; on record forms, 111; counts extra game, 115; tournament, equivalent one-half game, 116
Solitaire: double, 104; vertical, 104–105
Spot, on the, 64
Starter card: definition, 4; turning of, 7; placing in scoring procedure, 21; suit determines his nobs, 22; used in showing, 23; examples, 31; remarks about, 77; included in key, 123–205; rule 5, pegging out, 211

Straights. See Runs.
Strategy, 44, 73, 93, 96, 97
Streets: first second, third, fourth, 55
Study, averages, 80–81
Sucker play, 60
Symbols: $^{15}/_2$, 23, 46, 48, 53, 71; X (tenth cards) 35, 55

Tenth cards, definition, 7
Thirteen-card, 102
Three–card runs (sequence), 7, 27, 28
Three-handed, 6, 93
Toilet seat board, 65
Tournament: elimination, 111–119; brackets, 114, 117–120
Trap, setting, 64
Trey, definition, 4
Triple run, 27
Triplet: scoring of, 13, 22, 25; ends with a go, 17; avoiding, 57; rating opponent, 76

Unfavorable cards, 51, 55
U.S. Forest Products League, 110
Unusual hands, 36–40

Variants: five-card, 89; reverse, 99; auction, marine madness, 100; eleven cards, 101; thirteen cards, solitary, 102; vertical, 104, 105
Vocabulary, 3, 4, 7, 55

Webster's Dictionary, 75, 218
Wide cards, 55
Winner, predicted, 98, 99
Winning odds: dealer, 81, 88; five-card game, 88
Wisconsin Cribbage Assn., 116
World's worst lead, 58

X, 35

Zigzag board, 67